THE INFORMED VISION
Essays on Learning and Human Nature

THE INFORMED VISION
Essays on Learning and Human Nature

DAVID HAWKINS

AGATHON PRESS, NEW YORK

Distributed to the trade by
SCHOCKEN BOOKS, NEW YORK

Published by
AGATHON PRESS, INC.
150 Fifth Avenue
New York, N.Y. 10011

Distributed to the trade by
SCHOCKEN BOOKS INC.
200 Madison Avenue
New York, N.Y. 10016

Library of Congress Cataloging in Publication Data

Hawkins, David, 1913 –
   The informed vision.

   Includes bibliographical references.
   CONTENTS: The informed vision; an essay on
science education. — Mind and mechanism in education. — Childhood and the education of intellectuals. [etc.]
   1. Education — Addresses, essays, lectures.
2. Science — Study and teaching — Addresses, essays,
lectures. I. Title.

LB41.H34   370   74 – 81796
ISBN 0 – 87586 — 041 – 9

Printed in the United States

ACKNOWLEDGMENTS: "The Informed Vision: An Essay on Science Education"
first appeared in *Daedalus*, Journal of the Academy of Arts and Sciences, Boston,
Massachusetts (Vol. 94, No. 3; Summer 1965, *Creativity and Learning*), and is reprinted by permission. "Childhood and the Education of Intellectuals" first appeared
in *Harvard Educational Review* (Vol. 36, No. 4) © 1966 by President and Fellows of
Harvard College, and is reprinted by permission. "Nature, Man and Mathematics" is
reprinted from *Developments in Mathematical Education*, edited by A. G. Howson, by
permission of Cambridge University Press, © 1972 by Cambridge University Press.
"Development as Education" is reprinted from *Science and Technology in Developing
Countries*, edited by C. Nader & A. B. Zahlan, by permission of Cambridge University
Press, © 1968 by Cambridge University Press. "John Dewey Revisited" first appeared
in *Dialogue* (Vol. 5, No. 4, 1972) and is a revised version of an earlier essay reprinted
with permission from *The New York Review of Books*, © 1968 Nyrev, Inc. "Human
Nature and the Scope of Education" first appeared in *Philosophical Redirection of
Educational Research*, the Seventy-first Yearbook of the National Society for the Study
of Education, © 1972 by the National Society for the Study of Education, and is
reprinted by permission. "On Understanding the Understanding of Children" first
appeared in the *American Journal of Diseases of Children* (Vol. 114, November 1967, pp.
513 – 19) © 1967 by the American Medical Association, and is reprinted by permission.
   The author is also grateful to *The Colorado Quarterly* for permission to reprint "Mind
and Mechanism in Education" and "On Living in Trees"; to *Mathematics Teaching*, in
which "I, Thou, and It" and "Mathematics — Practical and Impractical" first appeared; to *Science and Children*, for permission to reprint "Messing About in Science."

Contents

Preface

The essays collected in this volume have been written over the last ten years, for various occasions and audiences. In bringing them together for publication I have had the opportunity to reread and rethink them, and to provide some guiding threads. In looking for those threads I can see a good deal that I would now modify: some to expand, some to contract and some to qualify. My thinking has, I hope, developed in the years, and the evidence is here. Readers of individual essays have given me good criticisms. Rather than trying to meet or rebut these criticisms by revision or by a long introduction, I have preferred to write a running commentary. This enables me to suggest some connections and also to qualify or explain.

The essays are, on the whole, rather polemical. Education is not a field in which we have all settled down to collaboration within an agreed professional and theoretical pattern which is somehow the right one. Ends are at stake and not means only: ends of theory and investigation, ends of education itself. Where that is so, controversy is often the best and sometimes the only fruitful means of collaboration.

I wish to give credit and thanks to a number of people who have strongly influenced my learning and writing. Philip Morrison and Jerrold Zacharias twelve years ago lured me into practical elementary school work with the suggestion that a scientific amateur and philosopher of science might help in the recasting of subject-matter for young learners, and indeed might learn a good deal himself in the process. Much of the background of these essays, as a result, began to take form during the two years when I was with the Elementary Science Study, a branch of Educational Services (later Education Development Center) of Watertown and Newton, Massachusetts. That background comes from endless staff discussion and from practical work in schools. Two others to whom I owe much are Anthony Kallet and Ronald Colton, again through much working association, discussion and amplifying criticism.

The most important person in all of this is Frances Pockman Hawkins, a teacher who is my wife. Through her lifelong work, her writing and our ongoing discussion, her influence puts me on that long list of persons—children and adults—whom she has profoundly taught.

In giving credit and thanks to these persons (and others whom I have not named) there is an awkwardness which verges on self-contradiction. Truth and gratitude require such acknowledgment to one's mentors; nevertheless, the thanks have a way of sounding boastful, a sharing of celestial credit. To avoid this a writer must fully acknowledge the imperfection of his work and absolve his benefactors. I do both, cheerfully.

Boulder, Colorado   D.H.
October, 1973

To
FPH

The Informed Vision
An Essay on Science Education

In the title essay of this volume, I have tried to capture or at least suggest an aspect of the spirit of science which seems to me to be of the utmost importance for contemporary education for all ages, though it is one which can all too easily be missed along the highways of formal schooling. Science has enriched a dimension of experience which I would call esthetic or, in an unpretentious sense, religious. But I would not use either term except, as I hope the essay clearly says, as a way of suggesting qualities of the good life which, though they have always been important, our age cries out for. The essay concerns ends, with only a hint about means and obstacles—a hint which is developed much farther in other essays.

No American philosopher can write well about education today who has not come to terms with the writings of John Dewey—or so I believe. Though my own education was not strongly influenced by Dewey in any direct way, there were strong indirect influences. His teachers were my teachers' teachers and for that reason I have always found him easy to read, in spite of his notorious style. According to one of my teachers this style was a product of Dewey's devotion to women's liberation, via several writing boards stationed in laundry and kitchen.

In the process of coming to terms with Dewey I reach many strong and admiring agreements but never am quite rid of residual dissatisfaction. I am pleased that both these reactions are visible in the first essay, though more fully developed later. This essay could not have been written without Dewey's Art as Experience, *but also not without some critical reactions against his half-truth that the method of science is somehow more important than its content. Dewey would not have relished the bowdlerized versions in which this half-truth has frequently appeared, but I think nevertheless he can share some responsibility for them.*

What I find most admirable (and comforting) in Dewey is that he, almost uniquely among philosophers since Plato, sees education as a topic so large—larger even than politics or than religion—and so pervasive, as to be a

1

kind of final challenge and focus for all philosophy. By any such standard all of these essays are groping and fragmentary. I hope they serve at least to suggest the validity of that claim.

The Informed Vision: An Essay on Science Education
(1965)

In spite of the world-transforming consequences of science, we treat it mostly as a kind of external entity or power. Corporations invest in it and governments subsidize it, but not for its inherent quality as a human interest or engrossment, not for the way it can inform the human vision. Some learned and sensitive persons, poets or metaphysicians or moralists, view it with alarm as though it were a kind of epidemic. Some, like Donne or Pascal, confess the illness in themselves as they decry it; others manage to be model outsiders. Today, it seems to me, the question of the place of science in education has a special significance. To illustrate this, let me begin by stating a sort of anthropological thesis about the mutations of culture.

The thesis is that human societies have always specialized themselves. "Specialized" is used here in the most literal sense, what biologists call speciation. Societies have been like different biological species, each of its own kind. Part of this specialization is adaptation to geography and livelihood, but that part by itself is never unique. Part of the specialization is creation rather than adaptation, the elaboration of a way of life beyond evident necessity, including much that is expressive and ornamental. A well-ordered society manages, in one or another of many ways, to hold up before itself and to dramatize, to celebrate, the means and manners of its own life. We have many expressions of this sense of involvement and commitment, this condition of happiness. One is to speak of being at home in the world. This means, of course, that we very well understand the opposite condition of non-involvement, the many moods of alienation. But even this understanding is elaborated in myths and metaphysics. Part of coming to terms, of being at home, is in the sheer familiarity of the environment and in the sureness with which one lives and walks there. In his moving account of the lives of forest Pygmies,[1] Colin Turnbull recreates the sense of the forest as home—which is so essential to Pygmy culture—and the Pygmies' veritable passion for this domesticity, reaching a high religious expression in their great forest songs. Turnbull obviously fell in love with Pygmy life, and I suppose some of the sterner sect of anthropologists accuse him of lack of objectivity. But some things are best known by falling in love with them.

It is against such a background of comparison that I wish to discuss science in our own education. The world we live in, the world we must accept as home, is a strange world, indeed, by the measures of Pygmy life or by the measures which most men of any other time and culture could supply. We have transformed the surface of nature; in a figurative as well as literal sense we have cut down the forest. But even if we do not like some aspects of our cities and their circulatory systems, we built them ourselves, and they, too, reflect a good deal of domesticity. The important kind of estrangement in our existence, or so it seems to me, is not at this level. It derives from the fact that this extraordinary technological and material evolution of the last century or two—which should be visible even from Mars!—expresses a way of life and thought that has been genuinely available only to a minority among us. To the rest it is, in essence, an alien affair. Each innovation it has produced tends to pass, therefore, from admiration to boredom, without any intervening stage of comprehension and without the enjoyment which only comprehension can release.

Examples of this can be easily found. The actual air is, in fact, a rich example. To "go by air," as so many of us increasingly do, is just that kind of deprivation if we suffer it without a certain background of experience and involvement—and we go from excitement to boredom very quickly. What is the missing ingredient? There are many, from the intuition of the symmetries of thrust and lift formulated in such beautiful simplicity in the language of mechanics, to the complex interactions of wing and atmosphere. But more rudimentary than the dynamics of flight, there is a missing intuition about the air itself, and about its fluid reality. We know from work with children (and adults) that primitive man's indecision about air is still very much with us. Is air a kind of fullness, or a kind of emptiness? Some casual experience fits the one answer, some the other. Have you ever weighed a batch of air, or played with a plastic clothing bag half full—or half empty—of the stuff? From the dearth of such experience the intuitions of air's weight or inertia are very feeble in most of us. And what of that glorious amazement that burst upon the world of the learned when Torricelli confirmed Galileo's induction of the possibility of the vacuum with his barometer, and came to the realization that we swim in an ocean of air surrounding the globe? At some upper levels we "teach meteorology" with learned words about lapse rates and dew points and the taxonomy of clouds—to people still mostly lacking any acquaintance with the rudiments. I have not meant to exhaust the esthetics of flight and atmosphere. That takes more than a note, more even than St. Exupéry. But all of it is permeated with the affections of science—cloudscape, the color gradients of the earth and atmosphere, vapor trails, the rainbowed shadow of the plane, the sight of the great solid planet revolving below, and, above all, the human involvement in a biologically alien medium, in organization, detail, decision.

Nor does the relevance of science fail when we go beyond the esthetics of flight—as we of all people must—to St. Exupéry's preoccupation with this very science as armorer of mass destruction. He loved the creativity of science but not its vision of the world. He shared, I think, the alienation that I speak of[2]—of a world that will accept science to arm its military enterprises, but not yet to inform its vision.

Another example is light—the essential element of astronomy and, in the end, of so much of physics. It has been an amazing discovery, to me at least, that many adults have no firm intuitions of even the geometry of light and shadow. Like most young children, they cannot predict a shadow before the light is turned on. Mirrors are common in our lives, yet the symmetries of reflection are but little known. And how many people have ever played with pinhole images, watched the colors in the bevel of a mirror, or seen the daytime shadows moving? How many see the moon as an illuminated sphere, and sense from it the direction of the sun? In spite of all the discussion of the marvels of space, very few of us have any instinctive orientation on the earth, let alone in the solar system. Knowing that vehicles are on their way to begin photographing Mars, how many among us can find that planet in the evening sky, and spare its mysteries a thought?

Then there is the matter of scale. Astronomical intuition demands at least a sense for that hundred million miles which approximates our distance from the sun. The stretching of the intuitions of scale is one of the characteristic accomplishments of science, both toward the large and toward the small. Yet as a firm possession this sort of simple intuition is rare except among the learned. Time as well as space demands it. Suppose we were to list the sorts of happenings we knew, that required times of the order of a thousand years, a hundred thousand, ten million, a billion. They are all around us, but the book is closed to most except to loving geologic eyes. The world of the solar system, which we now are committing ourselves to explore, and thus one day to feel at home in, *demands* the intuition of such a time scale. For we and the other planets have existed together in the same sunlight for a few billions of years, but otherwise completely isolated from each other. Such is the characteristic time of our own biological development; it is an evolutionary measure, correspondingly, of our separation from the other planets. Yet we talk and act, sometimes, as though we might just move in!

The Greek dramatists defined the sin of *hubris*, the sin of men who dared to be more than men, to go beyond man's place in the fixed order of things. "Being at home" for them was not only a state of assurance and familiarity, but of residence at a literal cosmographic and moral address. By their standards we do, I suppose, commit the ancient sin. But there is another sin we are in danger of—I think it is the same one, with definition purified—which is that of Moral Tourism, going to new places with the firm expectation of proper accommodations and a readiness to blame the natives if it turns out not so. I mean this in relation not only to the moon or Mars, but to all those extraordinary novelties we are gaining the power to encounter in our exploration of nature: of fissions and fusions, of the ecological turmoil that follows in the wake of our economic development, of our power to modify the genetic substrata of life. Even the planetary explorations are likely to have, for all our future, the most extraordinary consequences. Yet we began them in a competitive frenzy and continue them in budgetary tranquility, without appreciable excitement or debate. Because of the lack of any intervening comprehension, the idea of the space vehicle, like that of the airplane, will, I am afraid, pass too quickly from the stage of romance to that of ennui or alienation. And in this state we are, as St. Exupéry said, dangerous.

Some will object, perhaps, that this is all a gross exaggeration. By now there are many among us, a few per cent at least, who fully grasp and prize the way of science. The rest of us can trust them for advice and education. They are "experts." The word used to be a term of state, the state of being taught by experience—as a qualified technical witness, for example, in the courts. Now it has become a term of status. The scientific expert is still described as a person of purely technical competence, a knower of means rather than an adjudicator of ends. But increasingly and inevitably he is thrust into the latter position. Sometimes from vanity, I suppose, but certainly often from a heavy sense of social responsibility, he becomes a definer and a proponent of new social goals that science itself has made possible. Yet everything we know of history suggests that if this division in our society continues the scientific community will be subject to all the corruptions of caste and status. A world so deeply committed to science cannot survive with a vast majority of its population intellectually and esthetically alienated from science.

In my examples I have tried to imply a style of education that would permit correction, in our culture, of this basic defect. It has nothing in common with the need, so often put forward, to "produce more scientific experts." It has much more in common with the way of education described by Colin Turnbull in his account of Pygmy life. It is an education which begins in play suffused with enjoyment and evolves into an apprenticeship premised on commitment. Our needs are vastly different, I acknowledge, though it would be dangerous to assert that the Pygmy youth has learned much less. He has learned a great deal indeed, of the edible and inedible flora and the habits of antelope or leopard, to walk in total silence, and to sing great songs. He could not survive, in that world, without a complex and subtle education. But what we must learn is in part more remote from the immediate environment, more abstracted and dependent on symbolic skills. And that is the challenge to our education: to recover for our world the ways of learning that are concretely involving and esthetically rewarding, that move from play toward apprenticeship in work.

To see what all of this means for us and our education I must turn to the discussion of science and what the philosophers have to say about it. I myself have spent a good many years in this occupation, which has recently developed a label for itself, the philosophy of science. But I have also been distracted from this pursuit by others. Jorge Luis Borges[3] quotes a marvelous sentence from W. H. Hudson, who said that while in his youth he often undertook the study of metaphysics, happiness always interrupted him. One of my own interruptions has been science, science unphilosophically itself; another has been science teaching and, most recently, curriculum development for elementary schools.

Attempts to characterize science, as is true of all new things, have come mainly by analogy with other occupations and their products. Exploration, food-gathering, architecture, weaving, playing games, map-making, book-keeping, composing, all have played their part as analogies in the attempt to describe the process of science or define its product. The one I want to single out here is the analogy of art, of art taken rather generally and therefore with a good deal of internal variety. Like all other analogies, it will break down at various places, but I have selected it because I think it does not break down in one very important place—school.

A natural association with the word "art" is the sense of an implied spontaneity in a work of art or the enjoyment of it. In one of his most important writings on education (which, incidentally, does not contain the word in its index), John Dewey says this about spontaneity of artistic expression:

Works of art often present to us an air of spontaneity, a lyric quality, as though they were the unpremeditated song of a bird. But man, whether fortunately or unfortunately, is not a bird. His most spontaneous outbursts, if expressive, are not overflows of momentary internal pressures. The spontaneous in art is complete absorption in subject matter that is fresh, the freshness of which holds and sustains emotion. Staleness of matter and obtrusion of calculation are the two enemies of spontaneity of expression.[4]

If one were to try to formulate the quality of any achievement of learning, at its best, one could hardly find a better formulation than "complete absorption in subject matter that is fresh, the freshness of which holds and sustains emotion"—or of the opposite quality, in "staleness of matter and obtrusion of calculation."

But is it really permissible to talk about spontaneous expression in science? To be sure, the approved style of scientific communication could hardly be called lyrical. But we should not forget that *human* expression, for Dewey, is no mere display or outburst; it is a synthesized achievement compatible, as Dewey goes on to say, "with any amount of labor provided the results of that labor emerge in complete fusion with an emotion that is fresh." Emotion, then: surely science is concerned with knowing, not with feeling; with expression of fact, perhaps, but not with personal expression. Science is concerned with prosaic truth, objectively defined, publicly testable and emotionally neutral. Surely I have misled myself in thinking of science as a form of art, carried away by some wild philosophical conceit.

I know the reason for my error; it is a group of recollections and anecdotes of times in school when it did seem that children, after rather complete absorption in scientific subject matter that was fresh, emerged with some unifying and spontaneous expression of insight—and surely not without emotion. I vividly recall one child, for example, who seemed to acknowledge the reality of the great sphere of the earth as though for the first time—not from a transatlantic jet, but in the schoolroom. After long absorption in the behavior of a string-and-steel-ball pendulum, he suddenly saw it as doing *something* when it was just hanging, its motion spent. "Pointing toward the center!" The little sphere and the great sphere were joined in one act of knowing, fresh and emotion-sustaining. The only comparable experience of my own I can remember now was a recent one, when in the path of eclipse totality I became emotionally very much involved with the onrushing shadow, and quite literally felt the presence and opacity of the great occulting sphere, the moon. Surely I felt this only because, as an amateur, I have spent many hours absorbed in subject matter, exploring the moon visually and learning to picture it on the scale of earth and sun. In my case the experience came late, and I prize it; in Jeff's it came at age ten and released a flood of remarkable questions and investigations that, when we last met, was carrying him straight toward the world of Isaac Newton.

Perhaps my analogy is not lost, after all. Perhaps it is just that our usual account of science is a sort of timid and official one, correct as far as it goes, but leaving out the personal act in favor of the public process, the privately consummated experience in favor of the social achievement. And perhaps those who immerse themselves deeply in scientific pursuits do so because of their initial attraction to science and then *learn* to prize the dry, austere, and impersonal mode of expression, as one which they think best keeps a sort of subject matter fresh, and best holds and sustains the emotions appropriate to that subject matter. From this point of view there is much about the style of scientific thought, expression, and teaching that we need to reexamine. Later in *Art as Experience* Dewey refers to the fact I have already discussed above, that science

. . . as now practiced is too new to be naturalized in experience. It will be a long time before it so sinks into the subsoil of mind as to become an integral part of corporate belief and attitude. Till this happens both method and conclusions will remain the possession of specialized experts, and will exercise their general influence only by way of external and more or less disintegrating impact upon beliefs, and by equally external practical application.[5]

Is it possible that the style of scientific expression and communication depends more upon its cultural *newness* than upon the inherent necessities of the case? If we imagine a society in which what we call science has sunk deeply "into the subsoil of mind," what would be its style of expression? Would science any longer even be *called* science? The above passage occurs in the context of a discussion of the isolation of fine art from the vital centers of community life, which Dewey, like many other critics, attributes partly to the "external and more or less disintegrating impact" of science and technology upon older beliefs and ways of life. More than any other recent philosopher—except possibly A. N. Whitehead—John Dewey spent his life attempting to naturalize and humanize the scientific way of life and thought. In his educational philosophy he saw deep affinity between the style of research in science and the natural probings and explorings of children. In his strong desire to reinforce the latter as the basis of all true education, Dewey likewise was moved by the belief that in this way the external and disintegrating influence of science would be transformed into an internal and creative one, penetrating into the subsoil of mind. Long before the recent "two cultures" debate, John Dewey had formulated the dichotomy for a generation of American thinkers and school reformers and had set forth a program to heal the split. This program was to look beneath the surface of achieved scientific knowledge as dogmatically formulated in textbooks (and popularizations) to the underlying life of scientific inquiry, to the scientific method.

In good part because of the influence of Dewey, a generation of American teachers was brought up with the slogans and shibboleths of the scientific method, and in not a few centers schools were started which undertook to demonstrate the feasibility of an education centered around practical involvement of children in enquiry and creative expression. For a time, some of the public schools became more or less involved, and "progressive education" was *the* term of praise.[6]

Judged by the aspirations of the originators of the movement, very little is left today—little of the slogans, and even less of the practice. The most recent wave of educational reform has been motivated in part by a stern emphasis upon "the return to subject matter," both in the classroom and in the training of teachers. Are we to conclude, then, that the Deweyan program of education has been tried and failed? I do not believe it has really been tried; but I also do not want to declare the experiment irrelevant. At their best, the progressive schools were excellent; but the best was rare. At their worst, they may have justified the abuse heaped upon them by scornful critics. There are, I believe, two conclusions which can be extracted from the history of this institutional movement. One is a conclusion of theory, one of practice.

The theoretical conclusion I would urge is that the key conception of scientific method, of what Dewey called "the supremacy of method," is subtly wrong. Those who have read Dewey's more philosophical and less propagandistic writings will know that he is not always guilty of any real separation of "method" from "content."

But there are some truths that require at least *two* sentences for their utterance, and slogans are generally expressed in one. The first truth may well be that the art of scientific inquiry is educationally more fundamental than the facts and principles established by that practice. But the second truth, no less important, is that the art cannot grow except by what it feeds on; and what method feeds on, the whole source of its power and authority, is the very order and organization of the world it investigates. The mind equipped with method and no content is not more than the grin of a Cheshire Cat, an absurdity of misplaced abstractions. Dewey knew this, but he did not relish and emphasize it. So now we are in danger of new slogans, which in the re-emphasis on content will assume that method grows spontaneously out of improved "subject matter."

Try as I may, I cannot put it all in one simple sentence. "Method is the *use* of knowledge to *extend* knowledge." But then I must add, with the John Dewey of *Art as Experience,* ". . . through complete absorption in subject matter that is fresh." And this leads me to my practical conclusion from the failure of progressive education to win its way into a permanent place. Where that movement succeeded, it did so because the world of children's exploration was amply provisioned with subject matter they could explore well, could penetrate deeply. Where it failed, it did so because the freedom for active involvement was inadequately provisioned. This inadequacy was often concealed by a preoccupation, illegitimate in the *absence* of provisioning, with the maturation of the child personality. "Freedom of expression" was often seen as a good in itself, unmindful of the fact "that man, fortunately or unfortunately, is not a bird." Faced with the all-too-real maladies of psychic development in our children, and influenced by popular Freudian beliefs about the curative effects of "permissive" adult behavior, some few schools no doubt earned that indignant reflex utterance that "freedom is not license!"

It is my impression that the success of the progressive education movement was greatest for the earliest years, where its ideas and programs merged with the already solidly-based practical tradition of the kindergarten, imported to these shores a half-century before, with philosophic roots, many of them, common to Dewey's own background. Here there was not only a style of teaching that involved children deeply in subject matter, but the subject matter grew with the style—water, sand, clay, paint, good infant literature, the cultivation of story and song, carpentry, lenses, prisms, magnets, blocks, the house of packing boxes and orange crates, soil and seeds, animals, the dance, and all the rest. I do not believe that this tradition failed at all; its influence has been reduced by erosion (sometimes to the vanishing point), by pressures for thin mechanical programs of "reading readiness," "number experience," and the like, most of which tend to reduce the very readiness they seek to cultivate.

The moral, then, is that absorption in subject matter requires a major effort of provisioning for that subject matter. If children are going to emerge from our schools secure in the practice and enjoyment of the arts of inquiry, it will be only because they have long practiced those arts, in engagement with the world around. In relation to science, this means that their involvement with it will have been of a kind such that we can truly say it has penetrated the subsoil of their minds and earned their loyalty because it has liberated them from the boredom and sophistication that come with living in an unexamined world, because it preserves the freshness of subject matter and sustains emotion.

In my own way, then, I agree with the present emphasis on a "return to subject matter." In the newer science curriculum developments, there has often been an emphasis on individual work, by children, that is laboratory-like in its style. This seems to me to be of great importance. It constitutes a delayed recognition that the subject matter of science is not, except in a derivative sense, to be found in books. The subject matter of "the liquid state of matter" is the liquid state of matter, and we had better sometimes have some of it in the classroom. Along with aprons and mops as needed! The subject matter of sea animals may make more sense for coastal schools than inland, but if it makes sense inland it will be because the provisioning of salt-water aquaria has been reduced to a simple routine that schools can and will maintain. The subject matter of atoms is a puzzle. There are plenty of them, of course, in every classroom, but there must be a long course of evolution, and much penetration of experience into the subsoil of the mind, before the world of atoms will prove to be fresh and absorbing subject matter.

The beginnings are there in the kindergarten, in sand and sawdust worked with, and then seen with magnifiers. They are there in the drops of food-coloring billowing out into the water. Do the dye and the water really *mix*, or is it like a tangle of colored threads that just get thinner and more numerous until you can't see them any more? An honest answer is not yet available from nature, at the elementary laboratory level of investigation. But what a question! Later there is more, in the disciplined use of serial dilution, of saccharin and quinine and vinegar, of dyes and yeast suspensions, or Chlorella. Still later come the beginnings of simple quantitative chemistry, after the uses of quantity have been elaborated in other and more urgent contexts, and after the hand-lens and microscope have led to Lilliput and even smaller worlds. The direct evidence of chemical atomicity is not to be found in the elementary-school laboratory. Radioactive scintillations from a watch-dial? Perhaps, but what absorption in previous subject matter is implied, to see these as atomic events! The philosopher and physicist Ernst Mach disbelieved in atoms through all the evidence of nineteenth-century chemistry. What convinced him, in his old age, were the phenomena of radioactivity. I would not demand this much for children. Mach was stubborn. The important thing is not to *prove* the reality of atoms, but to bring them alive in the imagination and intellect. Otherwise, why push? To please parents with the appearance of understanding? Or is this high-school-chemistry-readiness?

I have tried to suggest what laboratory style might mean in elementary-school contexts. Peter the Great said he would open a window onto the West, and the elementary-school laboratory might do as much, onto the world. But nowadays the pressures are toward the windowless school, and I have very honest doubts. The laboratory traditions, in college and high school, are in many ways not encouraging. Nor do I wish to underestimate the difficulties in avoiding a style of laboratory work limited, as in fact our laboratory traditions mainly are, to the attempt to certify the truth of previously announced propositions, not yet *understood* by the majority of students who, recipe book in hand, dutifully perform.

I know the difficulties are real because I have perpetrated the crime myself as a college science teacher, and I have done it often rather than seldom. It is certainly possible to program work, in some kinds of laboratory science, so as to rob it of almost all romance and reduce it, nearly, to the status of rote—perhaps not quite, if only because a student very soon discovers that the experiment seldom works the way he has been told it will, that the "best" answers still come from the book rather than from his data. In some secret way, perhaps, he learns to mistrust the book. Or does he draw the opposite conclusion, that, in this great world he is being educated into, nature is to be taken with a grain of salt?

A partial explanation of these difficulties can be found, I think, in the psychology of us who teach science. In some measure, by some accidental pathways not commonly followed in our age, the culture of science has penetrated at least a little into the subsoil of our minds; we have pursued it much beyond the average. But from this there are two results, contradictory to each other. One is that we have some art in scientific inquiry; we have been absorbed in scientific subject matter and we know the fruits in our enjoyment of them. The other is that we have proven or declared ourselves, and are certified to teach. The consequence is social caste. We are the knowers, the explainers. Nothing moves us to such generous efforts as to be asked for explanations. Shrewd children, even shrewd adults, learn to ask these flattering questions, though their interest is slight and passing. For the deeper the perplexity, the more burning the curiosity, the less children or adults seek prompt explanation. When you have exhausted your own resources and still fail, *then* you will go for help. If you go too soon to an explainer, he does best to turn you back on your own resources, or to direct you toward acquisition of new ones.

What is true of the initiates is true, also, of those whose misfortune it is to teach science without any conviction of inner illumination. Here is the book, they are told, or the syllabus, or the teachers' guide. Now teach! The style is set for them; they know they are supposed to teach, to give explanations. And we, alas, the devotees, the mystics, have set that style.

I mean no offense to men, only to methods. There is of course a place for explanations, for didacticism in all its plumage. In the last part of the curriculum, in the homestretch toward professional degrees, we may even glory in it. The apprentice has made his decision, and we must make a tough professional of him and try him by ordeal. But our motives are still suspect, and even here, I think, there can be radical improvement. What distinguishes science from the personalized arts—as poetry, or painting—is the essentially social nature of its product. The cathedral that took a century to build is more nearly the model. No single architect planned it, though the mark of individuality is everywhere, of craftsmen absorbed in a common subject matter, whose expression sustains collective emotion. But here none of the analogies is really good. The art that is science is a distinct genre. Its constructions are not buildings, not machines, not instruments, though these may be among its modes of expression—as may be the textbook and the syllabus. The essential construction of science is a personal way of being related to the universe. This way has many expressions and can have many more, in conduct, artifact, or text; but it is primarily a way of knowing, and the knower is always the artisan of his personal knowledge. The social character of science is misrepresented when we forget this artist, pretending that the depersonalized social expression is the essence. Every art has its constraints and disciplines, and one of the disciplines of science is the demand for logically coherent formulation and noise-free communication. Hence the syllabus and text, hence the refinement of terminology. Yet, ironically and sadly, it is this very discipline which raises the barriers to communication in our schools. The letter of the discipline has too often been taken to be its substance. Here as always the letter kills, especially in the early and crucial years. The tight formulation and logical sequencing must be learned, but they cannot be learned first. They will be learned only when a knower comes to prize them for their power of liberation and guidance. What comes first is absorption in subject matter. No one learns by being led blind along a path he cannot begin very soon to see for himself.

And here I come to what seems to me to be the crucial and largely unsolved problem of science education (or of any education). Method consists in using knowledge to gain further knowledge. Yet what each individual knows that he can use in this way is, at any moment, a highly individual affair. In reducing our experience to order, the distance we must travel to achieve any component of this order is not a well-defined quantity; for there are many paths to a goal of understanding, and along any path there are *many* available important goals. Logically considered, the relations among the ideas which bring order to our experience constitute a complex network;

ideas are not stations along a single road. In this psychological world, what we mean by distance along a given path can be measured by the number of probings and testings, of discriminations, we must make to traverse it. Paths already well-trodden are short *because* they are well-trodden. For this reason the patterns of optimal learning are highly individual. In the early and deep learning that goes with play, some of the conditions for approximating these individual optima are present. Since there are so many important things to be learned, the direction of exploration is not critical. What is learned will add to the power of later learning. What is important is the confrontation with materials which play can exploit and incorporate—absorption in fresh subject matter! From what we now know of informational processes, even machines designed for pattern recognition and classification will function most efficiently—when dealing with a very complex system of data—if they are deliberately programed for such "nondirective," in some respects even random, "Monte Carlo" exploratory behavior. In spite of the anxieties about machines in our culture, it may be that the machine designers are closer to an appreciation of what is involved in human learning than are those circumscribed by the simplistic traditions of behavioristic psychology and "programed learning."

But there comes a time for harvesting, gathering, organizing, even programing, and here individual learners must be drawn together under a common discipline. In our schools, this time comes much too early. Or better, it is too little preceded and followed by periods—long periods—of individualized and diversified work of a more exploratory and self-directed kind. In being so critical of the prevailing style, however, I do not want to make an opposite error, of forgetting that apprenticeship phase of their education when the young Pygmies go out on their first hunts or build their first houses under adult direction. It seems to me that in our context the great teaching art must prove to be the art of combination. We must learn better to instruct children, when, after absorption in subject matter, they communicate by their behavior those directions which they are prepared to find meaningful because they themselves have begun to define and seek them. And then there is the opposite transition, when formal instruction has brought children to new levels of understanding and interpretation: to open again the door to less directed probing and testing at these new levels—and thus to consolidate what has been learned, to use it for further learning.

There are certainly some superbly resourceful teachers among us who practice and understand this art, although perhaps they are not articulate about it in the context of educational discourse. Can we identify them, we who want to know the art better? And can we go and watch, and thus learn? And can we, after watching, begin to help them with the provisioning, with plants and animals and laboratory equipment—and ideas! Can we then find ways to resonate, to amplify, to strengthen the apprenticeship of other teachers? The job is not easy on any scale. On the scale I have tried to suggest, that of a whole society in which the esthetic meaning of our commitment to science will have penetrated the subsoil of the human mind, it is difficult indeed. But on this scale the motivation should also be strong to find meeting places where these present realities of our future, children and science, may be brought more happily together.

REFERENCES

1. Colin M. Turnbull, *The Forest People* (New York: Simon & Schuster, 1961).
2. In some disagreement with Harcourt Brown's careful discussion in "Tensions and Anxieties," *Science and the Creative Spirit* (Toronto: University of Toronto Press, 1958).
3. Jorge L. Borges, *Other Inquisitions,* tr. by Ruth L. C. Simms (Austin: University of Texas Press, 1964), p. 144.
4. John Dewey, *Art as Experience* (New York: Putnam, 1934), p. 70.
5. *Ibid.,* p. 338.
6. Lawrence A. Cremin, *The Transformation of the School, Progressivism in American Education* (New York: Knopf, 1961).

Mind and Mechanism in Education

The view of learning and teaching suggested in the first essay is more fully developed in "Mind and Mechanism." To outline the scope of this development I have chosen to start with an image developed by a wise and able engineer and writer, Hans Otto Storm. I do not know whether he would have approved of the use I have made of his essay "Eolithism and Design"; I hope so. (By an act of self-plagiarism I won't try to explain I have used it again in another essay not in this volume.) Here at any rate the intent is to define the dimensions of educationally significant learning. To be at home in the world—our world—is, among other things, to possess and enjoy a kind of generalized competence. This competence is acquired through practice, and practice itself is the measure of it. Such competence has not a few dimensions, it involves the whole dynamics of ends and means, of goal seeking and goal setting, of learning and enjoying.

A part of the argument here may seem intemperate to some. The polemic is directed against theories of learning which have some limited validity in special areas of investigation but which cannot be generalized to match the needs of education without revealing a profound conceptual incoherency. Behind the polemic is an alternative conception of learning and knowing which was first mapped out by the philosopher Immanuel Kant. Kant saw both knowledge and conduct as outcomes of an active and constructive process, a process of building and testing models of our environment and plans of our behavior. While on one level our behavior can be described by systems of responses to frequently impinging stimuli, on another level it can be described as an ongoing process of reorganizing and testing, through which new knowledge and new plans may modify our behavior. Thus the "conditioning" of our behavior does not depend simply on the stimuli of our environment, but also on internal processes of model building and planning which use the external environment as a testing-ground but are not controlled by it. It is this second level with which education, in any proper sense of the term, is concerned.

18

What Kant did not say—it was not within the range of his concerns—is that learning on this second level takes place within developmental sequences that show strong similarities across a wide range of differences in individual tempo and style. These differences begin as congenital and diverge toward individuality; they do not regress toward a common mean. Nevertheless, as each individual child builds his way into the future he works from a pool of shared materials in a common ambiance and so grows, through human association, in the possession of a common world and a common history.

Such a conception of learning and of knowledge is central to the criticism of narrow extrapolations from the psychology laboratory, but also to that of long-established school habits which severely limit the range and motivation of children's learning and deprive them of that kind of practice, in school, on which the growth of human competence depends.

These criticisms of theory and practice are radical in the sense that they imply a strong contrast between what prevails in our schools and what is possible, what can be (and has on occasion been) reduced to practice. They are also radical, I hope, in the sense of getting at some of the roots of the problems involved. Denunciation of our educational system is easy and easily supported with evidence. It is not clear, and sometimes not true, that many of the denouncers would know how to do a better job if given the opportunity. The art of teaching can evolve and be transmitted as a high art indeed, but not without long-term devotion and not without support and esteem for the devoted. So I am very far from offering panaceas. Roots ramify. Yet there are uncomplicated steps, steps which ought to be uncontroversial, which would improve education and which would make it more easy to face the harder problems. Why don't we take them?

This question leads into another area where these essays do not follow, that of a more general social criticism. Suggestions do appear in the essays, and in commenting on them I shall try to amplify. My viewpoint is not one of washing my hands of our present—and my own—society. A radical may criticize and even denounce, but he must come to terms with the fact that in this self-appointed task he takes his society to have a conscience he can stir, an intelligence he can appeal to, and some wisdom he can learn from. Otherwise his labors are only a dubious exercise in self-gratification. I take comfort for this article of faith in a quotation from that undeniable nineteenth century radical, Karl Marx:

"The materialist doctrine that men are products of circumstances and upbringing, and that, therefore, changed men are products of other circumstances and changed upbringing, forgets that it is men that change circumstances and that the educator himself needs educating." From "Thesis on Feuerbach," (*Selected Works* of Karl Marx and Friedrich Engels. New York, 1968, p. 18.)

Mind and Mechanism in Education
(1968)

In an essay published posthumously in 1952, the American engineer-novelist Hans Otto Storm undertakes to contrast two principles of human workmanship, which he calls the principle of design and the principle of eolithism. The principle of design he describes out of the engineering textbooks and out of his own experience. He is thinking, for example, about something in the way of a bridge, a building, or a machine. The designer must first know approximately what he wants and how it is to be used. The next choice is of material with which to build, which must be of known and preferably uniform properties. This certainty and uniformity are essential to the whole process: they affect not only the physical result of good designing; they also affect deeply the mental discipline which the process of designing demands. Given knowledge of the material and the final objective, the designer applies one to the other and a plan begins to emerge checked and extended by the use of well-known arithmetical rules, this process being continued until the whole becomes realistic in detail, making contact with the existing world. At this point the change is made from thought-construction to physical construction. The direction of the operation is reversed, starting at contact with the material world and extending the structure until it embodies, finally, the objective with which the whole process started.

In his essay Storm wishes to challenge an assumption which comes with the principle of design in our society: that this principle is basic and universal, an ideal by which we can measure all craftsmanship from its most primitive and blundering beginnings, a presupposition which all craftsmen are committed to even if they are not trained or intelligent enough to understand the pure ideal for which they should be striving.

To challenge this assumption Storm, a professional radio engineer himself, puts forth an alternative and wholly different principle of workmanship, one as distinctively human as, and I would say far more distinctively human than, the principle of design. This is the principle for which he borrows the term, of a slightly bastard etymology, "eolithism." To establish the human character of this method Storm first describes the basis of *animal* craftsmanship. In an amusing and accurate description of nest-building, he shows it as the accidental by-product of a number of specific tropisms, little programs of congenital behavior released by the occasion, such as picking up twigs and dropping them with what would appear to be a studied casualness and with no evidence of interest in the final product which happens, as though by a conspiracy of nature, to assemble itself in the end. With repetition this process becomes more workmanlike, but it would never strike us as work of design. Storm finds a few examples of this sort of craftsmanship among humans, for example, among the activities of the collectors of books, stamps, crockery, or automobile parts. But generally it is very rare.

Far less rare, though in our society pushed into a corner of disesteem and lowered social status, is the eolithic pattern. While most men occupy themselves with war, literature, business, or odious routine labor for wages, the eolithicists carry on for the rest.

An eolith is literally a piece of junk remaining from the stone age, often enough rescued from some ancient buried garbage heap. Storm quotes a definition: "stones, picked up and used by man, and even fashioned a little for his use." The important matter in the definition, Storm says, is that eoliths were *picked up,* already *accidentally* adapted to some end and, more importantly, *strongly suggestive* of the end.

We may imagine the person whom the anthropologists describe so formidably by the name of *man* strolling along in the stonefield, fed, contented, thinking preferably about nothing at all—for these are the conditions favorable to the art—when his eye lights perchance upon a stone just possibly suitable for a spearhead. That instant the project—the very idea—of the spear originates; the stone is picked up; the spear is in manufacture. Not only do the shaft and the thongs remain in the background, as something which will in due time no doubt be thought of, but the very need and usefulness of the spear are in a way subsidiary to that instant's finding. And if the spearhead, during the small amount of fashioning that is its lot, goes as a spearhead altogether wrong, then there remains always the quick possibility of diverting it to some other use which may suggest itself.

And now we come to the serious point of Storm's argument. To sharpen the contrast with the principle of design, he says, "Let us remember the basic principle of the designing workman—he must know what he wants, and, even before the design begins, he must decide on his material." The fashioner of eoliths, on the other hand, must have a continually open mind about materials, and he must be very adaptable in the matter of ends, of what he wants. If the eolith defies the use it first suggested, then perhaps there is another, equally interesting and worthy. The essential limitations of the principle of design lie in the givenness and fixity of goals, and in the need to eliminate variety and inhomogeneity from the means and materials, which are thereby reduced in any significance or value they may have *except* in serving those given ends.

A characteristic of eolithic craftsmanship, Storm says, is that it never goes twice the same, and therefore uniform procedures, theories of design and such are of little use. A designed building may well collapse if there are serious errors in calculation. But an eolithic building comes into existence in a way that owes nothing, for example, to Euler's theory of columns. The doorpost picked up on the beach was many times more rugged than design would require, and the structure that appeared so redundant in the bracing, which suggested itself as eolithic intuition dictated along the way, revealed that the problem of stability simply did not require advance planning. Alternative ends further weaken the requirements of design. The unruly ox, an eolith by Storm's analogy, is "readapted to usefulness in the stewpot, and the tree that fails to bear fruit becomes firewood, both by sound principles of husbandry."

Storm now turns, armed with these distinctions and illustrations, to the examination of our contemporary society, which he says has come to be so dominated by the principle of design that eolithism is all but excluded. All natural eoliths have been long since swept up from urban settings, the only source for the unsuppressible impulse lies in the availability of materials which were once designed for a specific use but are now worn out or obsolete. Thus the great symbol of the eolithic impulse, submerged but not suppressed, is the junk-man, the purveyor of odds and ends which can be put to naïve and unexpected use. Both he and his customers suffer from social dises-teem because they do not bow to the dominant principle, which sees in the broken concrete stepping stones, the made-over clothes, the car frame and wheels turned into a wagon something mean and comical.

I shall not continue here with Storm's argument, which has some further wry and Veblenesque comments about the fate of a culture committed wholly to the principle of design. I have extracted what I want for my own argument, which concerns itself not with towers of concrete and steel or the circuitry of the computer, but the creation of structure and order within the human character, and thus with the principles of craftsmanship in the domain of education. But first let me restate and generalize.

The principle of design as Storm defines it requires that we have goals well-enough defined to provide criteria of choice among alter-native means. It also requires that we have materials available to us which are sufficiently homogeneous and sufficiently understood so that we can apply well-tested rules to the selection and organization of an efficient means of reaching our goal. Only when these two conditions are satisfied can we proceed to specify ahead of time just how our structure or mechanism will be put together.

The principle of eolithism, on the other hand, thrives on the nonsatisfaction of both the above conditions. To be effective it requires that our system of resources be intrinsically varied and qualitatively rich, for that is the condition under which such a system, the world as immediately and concretely available to us, will be maximally suggestive of new goals. But such suggestions can gain a hearing only if established goals can be shaken and recast.

Clearly human life requires and exhibits an interplay of these two principles, which describe distinguishable but not separable phases of mind or of mindful activity. We seek goals and we set goals. As the seeking becomes routinized, we design mechanisms to help us. In seeking goals we encounter realities, however, which tempt and beckon, which bring us to redefine the goals we seek, and thus also to alter the directions of our seeking. The chemistry of these interactions allows a wide variety between extremes—those of monomania and disorganization. To understand this variety and to seek norms for guiding it is, I suppose, an explicit or implicit aim of philosophical ethics and, in particular, of the philosophy of education—where my concern centers.

In order to assess the significance of the contrasting principles of eolithism and design for the philosophy of education, let us start from the fact that neither of the conditions is well satisfied for *designing* an educational system in the strict sense of Storm's contrast. We can indeed set some goals for education which are relatively stable across the range and variety of social situations and social needs and we can count on a certain homogeneity in the material to be fashioned—the children, adolescents and adults whom we seek to educate: they all have eyes, and ears, and human brains. But when we look more closely at the *way* in which either condition can be said to be satisfied, we see an enormous variability.

The effective aims of education, which determine the design of schools and of instructional patterns and of curricula, are subject to constant re-examination and controversy. The still more general aims, which link education to an aspiration toward greater human competence and happiness, are as shrouded in uncertainties as the ends of life itself, immensely important, always open to the cultivation of insight and conviction, but not crisp simple little formulae which will guide the educational draftsman at his drawing board.

The raw material which educational design would think of shaping not only lacks the homogeneity of concrete and steel but is inherently parceled in unique individuate form, in the form of live human beings. The product number, of possible congenital patterns multiplied by possible early biographies of children, is of higher arithmetical order than the total number of children, past, present, or future. The probability is effectively zero that there should be two children presenting the same educational challenges and opportunities. One could of course assert the same heterogeneity of apples or blades of grass, looked at closely enough. But in education the heterogeneity of human kind is not trivial in that sense, because it affects the *aims* of the process, and is indeed required by them. It is a superordinate goal of education, and if it is not it ought to be, to help children on their way to become competent eolithic craftsmen in building their own lives. This requires from the start a recognition of individual competency and situation. Not to recognize individuality is not to educate.

Thus in our own designing for education and in the execution of such designs there is required an essential component of Storm's other principle, of the eolithic mode. If we must talk about design, as we must, then let it be design which facilitates and strengthens the capacities unique to our kind, capacities for rebuilding and reorganizing the specific commitments and pursuits, including education, that guide us and constitute our lives. To deny this component is to forget that the child becomes the adult and the pupil the educator—possibly even before the product has been duly graduated. We have excellent reminders, in our tradition, that children can be leaders as well as followers and it is even conceivable, at times, that universities could be instructed by *their* students.

I am speaking here rather ironically, but I think correctly, about the aims of education, because it seems important to explicate a certain emphasis and a pattern which are at variance with standard educational practice and also, unfortunately, with the aims and thought patterns of much of contemporary educational innovation. It is often conceded that a superordinate aim of education should be the cultivation of competence in children to fashion well their own lives. But it is *not* supposed steadily that such competence is gained through exercise of it.

It is supposed, rather, that self-organization will appear magically *after* years of schooling subordinated to a quite different principle, according to which children are *deprived* of autonomy. They are deprived in the interest of what is conceived to be an efficient imparting of information and guidance. During all this time, and in the interest of such efficiency, children are essentially deprived of any significant exercise of autonomy in choice, discrimination, and judgment. They are reduced to a state of passivity and, often enough, of boredom. They are coerced, however politely, into a frame of organization intended to promote their acceptance of information and exercise in specific curricular topics, these being justified, or once justified, on the ground that they are necessary to competent adult functioning.

This induced organization, which children in schools are helpless to combat effectively, is thought of, when it is thought of at all, as a kind of scaffolding to be torn down after the process is finished and the product certified as complete. But it is in fact a powerful molding of character, and of a kind of character antagonistic to the superordinate aim which education professes to serve. The scaffolding gets built into the structure and cannot be removed.

Some succeed under such a regime in spite of the relative irreversibility of its structural effects. They succeed because they have been given, have, and are able to invest resources which enable them to take *from* school much that they can assimilate, reorganize and use independently of school. The center of gravity of their learning exists outside of school in another—and better—world.

But children are very unequally endowed by previous condition and experience with this capacity for independent choice, which the schools do little to help them cultivate. No one can catalogue all the conditions of such relative success, but it is a conspicuous statistical fact that the successful come commonly though not universally from a background which could be called the folk culture of the already well-educated. The deeper conditions of academic success, which schools often unconsciously work against, are in fact supplied from another cultural source. But for vast numbers of children the mismatch between their own developing capacities and the experience available in school is so great that they are unable to avoid the induced pattern, with its constant accompaniment for them of failure and boredom, withdrawal, manipulation, or rebellion.

These are harsh statements and I make them with a good deal of personal consciousness of the efforts of many people inside the educational establishment to experiment along new pathways toward greater understanding and better schools. But I think these harsh statements are among those needed to dramatize the importance of all such good efforts; it is not in the interest of truth nor in the interest of policy to soften them. They are aimed at an institution which is both vast in size and crucial to the future, not against persons or groups of persons for querulous criticism. On the other hand, my harsh statements do not yet define agreed ends which those who consider themselves specialists in educational design should or could, or in most cases would, be willing to lay down as the basis for a new educational design. For ends are still at stake and none of us is wise enough, as yet, to see where the argument may lead.

For one thing, as I see it, there is a new wave of educational design inimical, or at least indifferent, to the implications of the sort of critique I have been suggesting. Here I should like to speak more personally and more concretely. For two years I was completely involved in an effort of elementary school curricular innovation. From the wide range of the natural sciences there is a vast amount of concrete material—prized by scientists because of the intriguing and esthetically captivating phenomena associated with it which are, at the same time, intimately interwoven with the deeper laws and histories of nature which science has found. To survey this vast field and take from it materials which can be put in children's hands, to entrap their interest and to stimulate their capacity for wonder and inquiry, seems an important undertaking for this age when science, so interwoven into our lives, yet remains for most an alien and forbidden territory.

During the time I was involved with the Elementary Science Study, and in the work some of us have tried to continue since, there have been many times when we were called on to do something called "stating our objectives." Now that is always a reasonable-sounding sort of request, if by someone who genuinely doesn't know what you are up to—and especially if you are asking him for financial support. But it gradually became clear to me that many people were not satisfied with the sort of answer I and my associates were prepared to give. I came to realize that it was somehow expected that we could lay down, in advance, a set of specifications as to what we hoped to accomplish, and by which our work could be *evaluated*. The truth of the matter was that we were explorers working our way through the heterogeneous world of schools, children, teachers, and phenomena of science. In short we were eolithicists being confronted, and literally "called to task," by the culture of the educational designers, being asked to show cause why we should not be classed with the junkman and his customers. Somehow one was supposed to be wise enough to define an all-encompassing set of ends *before* one had acquired the slightest bit of good sense about the nature and potentialities of the materials.

To all such questions our answers were characteristically, and I must confess for my own part deliberately, coy and evasive. We often said some general things, hoping to suggest that we knew what we were about. We said that we hoped to make it easier for teachers to induct themselves and children into a frame of mind conducive to the enjoyment and close observation of natural phenomena, and then into the practical art of scientific investigation; that so far as we knew this could only be done by getting involved in that art from the beginning. This meant designing inexpensive laboratory materials and apparatus and in best eolithic fashion surveying the resources of wood and field and stream, of back alley and junk pile. We said we did not believe it possible to transmit the intellectual and practical tools of science through a sequence of little isolated exercises, but rather that we should first involve children in observation and inquiry with the tools they already possessed, and in this way to help them create or assimilate sharper tools and more adequate knowledge. We said that we therefore thought it best to try to evolve curricular materials and strategies out of repeated attempts to *in*volve children in inquiry, *their* inquiry. We were thus committed to be very opportunistic, that is to say very empirical, in selecting for further trial just those materials and strategies which did in fact best beckon to and absorb children, of various ages and conditions. Nor did we believe that we could become final authorities on this subject. What we hoped, rather, was that in enlarging the store of materials and ideas available to teachers, we would help them in *their* proper task of helping children on the road to more competent choice and learning. That also meant giving teachers wider opportunities for choice and learning, not circumventing them with detailed curricular guidance which would substitute for their inventions and denigrate their professional role.

But often the demand for objectives was not satisfied with this kind of "vague loose talk." What was expected often, whether from sheer habit or from anxiety or extreme narrowness of vision, was that we should produce a completely organized and sequenced guide for everybody who "adopted" our program. And that was where we stuck. We said we thought we were learning some of the *means* of good science teaching, but that we were not yet nearly wise enough to present what is vulgarly known in the trade as "a complete package," with objectives spelled out, little texts, and words in teachers' mouths. We said we thought this should be left quite flexible and open to decision in the careers of particular schools, teachers, and children; open to significant choice.

And then of course came the clincher: "Ah yes, but how can you evaluate your work if you don't state carefully defined objectives?" The phrase "behavioral objectives" had not yet come upon the scene, final expression of the primate dominance order which puts "design" on top, but we took the question to mean, as it typically does, a detailed setting forth of performance criteria related to subject-matter and skill. And that, as I have said, we thought we should be more than a bit hesitant about.

As I look back on that period I think we should have been less hesitant. We should not have answered the question about detailed objectives of subject-matter and skill, but we should have explicitly *questioned* that question. Suarez said that it was the philosopher's job to question the questions and answer the answers (to provide what a well-known mathematician, Stanislaw Ulam, once called "the necessary don't-know-how"). So I, as a philosopher, especially should have been bolder. But we all need time to learn, and I hope now to begin to question those questions about objectives, and in the process to get into what might be called the higher theory of design, the theory of a design which seeks to optimize the eolithic component in education, to optimize children's capacity to conduct their own learning and to become their own teachers.

This theory starts with the same superordinate goal, that children should be helped always on the way to greater competence in organizing their own lives, lives in the here and now which project into a world that none of us can adequately foresee. The key proposition in this theory is that learning, in its most significant educational dimensions, is not something of a different kind from self-government, self-organization, choice, but is a species of that very genus. Learning in an educationally important sense is an active process of self-organization and reorganization, which takes place through the mediation of choice among significant alternatives available to the learner. If you want to put this proposition in a general context it is at the opposite pole from dominant theoretical positions associated in this country with the title "Learning Theory" and in essential agreement with the theoretical position of Jean Piaget.

Let me start with a reference to the dominant (and classical) position. It states that learning takes place through selective reinforcement or inhibition of responses set off by stimuli. In case you don't normally think in these terms, let me substitute for you the images, which you all have buried in abundance, of little tasks set for children in school, simple enough so that, in view of assumed previous learning, children have a fair chance of doing them in the "approved manner": reading a line, spelling a word, saying "Denver" in response to the stimulus "capital of Colorado," or drawing four squares in a blank space following an "=" sign following two bracketed sets of two squares each, with a "+" sign between.

Reinforcement and inhibition are implied in that phrase "approved manner"; the great contribution of Learning Theory to this traditional pattern has been to simplify tasks to the point where failure is unlikely and positive reinforcement is the order of the day, a reinforcement more reliably provided by little bits of candy or potato chip than by teacher's approbation—which particular children may not, in fact, be seeking. The comparable treatment, applied with patience and skill, works wonderfully in the training of pigeons and it can be seen to work when applied to children. "Work" here means that tasks are indeed learned; and what is particularly impressive is that they are learned even though a child is minimally attentive and totally bored. He sizes the situation up well enough to realize that his choice is to be a pigeon or to be nothing. There are no problems about objectives, because the desired objective is simply the performance for which the training routine has been designed. (Who decides these objectives, or how, is left a mystery.) If you will just tell us how you want people to behave, we will design the necessary training procedures.

I don't wish to imply that all those who accept and support Learning Theory would regard such applications as commendable. Many understand that human learning can be rather complex, but they nevertheless believe that someday it can all be described adequately in S-R terms; then we can do a proper job; in the meantime education will have to limp along as best it can. Thus only the *esprits simplistes* are left active in the field.

Let me suggest the nature of an opposing way of looking at educationally significant learning, from a lecture given by Jean Piaget in 1964:

... when you think of a stimulus-response schema you think usually that first of all there is a stimulus and then a response is set off by this stimulus. For my part, I am convinced that the response was there first, if I may express myself in that way. A stimulus is a stimulus only to the extent that it is significant and it becomes significant only to the extent that there is structure which permits its assimilation, a structure which can integrate this stimulus but which at the same time sets off the response. In other words I would propose that the stimulus-response schema be written in the circular form—in the form of a schema or of a structure which is not simply one way. I would propose that above all, between the stimulus and the response there is the organism, the organism and its structures. ... Of course we would want to understand how these structures come to be.

Earlier in the lecture, and in many other places, Piaget has talked about how the structures came to be through a process of developmental equilibration, which takes place in a context of neurophysiological maturation, of massive experience, and of social transmission of the human culture.

The structures do not come about by summation of operant conditionings; rather, the process is one of self-regulation and self-organization. It is a kind such that at a particular level of mental development the child is able to assimilate certain complex stimuli and produce a matching response. For example, at a certain stage a young child who has been playing with blocks distributed on a balance board may push weights leftward on the board when the left side is tilted up, and thus will make the left side go down. Then he will push one or more weights rightward until the right side goes down again. He may repeat this process many times with complete absorption in his self-appointed task. In Piaget's language, he is assimilating this complex experience in relation to a structure, an intellectual schema, involving weight, left-right symmetry, and displacement from a center. At a later stage his pattern may have changed, so that by such displacements he will concentrate on the intermediate state, that of balance, first moving one block to produce imbalance and then moving another to restore balance.

When we examine the operations that are being performed we

can describe what is happening, in Piaget's language, as the evolution of an operational structure within which experience is being assimilated in a highly selective way, namely to fit into that structure. The selectivity amounts to a process of abstraction, in which only *certain* features of the situation are being attended to, namely those which we would describe as more or less relevant to tilting or balancing; these features are being attended to perceptually and they are also just the features which are being actively manipulated.

The circularity of the S-R relationship which Piaget alluded to comes out clearly here: the child not only is stimulated by the tilt or balance pattern in the concrete situation, but he in turn produces an appropriate response. To say that this response is appropriate is not to say that it is one which we as teachers might desire and reward, impertinently, but rather it is one which in turn stimulates the apparatus so that it responds and produces a new stimulus to the eyes and hands of the child.

The process is not one way but circular. The structure which is being evolved is in this case one which a mathematician would describe in the language of group theory: The child is developing a group of operations such that for any operation (displacing a block) there is an inverse operation (a shift in the opposite direction), and such that the product of two operations is itself an operation in the group. This structure is logically rather complex, involving a three-valued function of the distribution of blocks—tilt left, tilt right, and balance. It involves the invariance of these states over certain subgroups of transformations, so that for example at a late stage the child will be able to demonstrate that congruent opposite displacements will preserve the property of balance.

When I say "demonstrate" here I do not mean to prove formally; I mean to evidence in his behavior. But it is interesting to notice that such operations as the child singles out are precisely the ones in terms of which, following Archimedes, we *define* the problem of the balance and proceed to construct a formal proof of the law of moments. In the process of assimilating rather massive information from his interaction with the balance, if he is totally involved, the child is taking in relevant empirical information and excluding the irrelevant, he is testing relevance by operating on the balance, and in the process there is an *accommodation* of the operational scheme he is

using to the informational pattern he is receiving, so that his behavior *changes* from one phase to another. Sometimes these changes
are gradual and fluctuating, sometimes they are dramatic and radical; in either case accommodation occurs.

I have said nothing here about social communication. Typically
such a development as I have been describing will happen, if it is
allowed to happen, in a context with other children and a teacher.
There is group talk, and the teacher may intervene to facilitate. But
the teacher *may* also intervene in such a way as to decouple the child
from interaction with the balance, and at that point assimilation and
accommodation are interrupted. If the teacher tries to "explain"
while the underlying conceptual, operational structure is still
fragile, the language being used will not couple with the operational
structure and reinforce it, but may instead disconcert and bewilder.
The accommodative learning process can be facilitated by informal
talk in context, but talk cannot be a substitute, and can destroy, as
it frequently does.

Perhaps this example will be enough to suggest relationship between self-government in life generally and self-regulation, the
assimilation of new modes and patterns of experience, involved in
cognitive learning. In a good school environment children are not
only actively absorbed in concrete subject matter and in communication about such subject matter, but they are also acquiring some
multiplicity of investigative interests, in an essentially social milieu.
They are in position to see relationships between the subject-matter
of these interests and to communicate their interests and findings.
Thus larger units of self-organized activity begin to crystallize, raising intellectual problems, problems of the allocation of resources, of
division of labor, and of personal association.

Such learning is, as Dewey often insisted against the dominant
individualistic tendency of the Progressive Education Movement,
essentially social. Schemata of interpersonal and social relations
develop through the same kind of processes as in the assimilation of
and accommodation to the natural environment. The schema of
treating others as symmetrical with oneself, for example, is the basis
of all more particular rules and relations of morality, including the
conceptual foundations relating to moral reciprocity and compensa-
tion. Such structures, as Piaget calls them, are fundamental to all of

man's rational capacities and practical social competencies, and it is only as they evolve through experience that there can occur that internalization of logical operations which permits us to distinguish at all sharply between overt and covert activity, between physical exploration on the one hand and thought on the other. It is only as structures and superstructures of this kind become evolved and stabilized that language, communication from a common social fund, becomes an essential vehicle of information. Children can give meaning to symbolically codified information, can accept and transform it to their own uses, only as they themselves have built up, through their schematizations of experience, the meanings which are exploited in discourse.

It is useful here to think of the relationship between learning a code and learning what is conveyed to us in that code. The acquisition and refinement of spoken and written language presupposes that a child can encode and decode messages to and from the meaningful terms of his own primary preverbal discourse with his environment. One may assimilate and file away vast amounts of symbolic information and transform this to significant use, but *only* as there is already available a system for storage and retrieval for such information which is richly and effectively connected with one's established modes of operation. Thus the primarily verbal style of most school instruction must presuppose such underlying structures of thought to be at a stage of momentary readiness for assimilating just that instruction. Not only is such a presupposition typically false for a majority of children in a group, with their wide diversity of individual differences, but verbal instruction does little or nothing to make them ready. The learning that does take place is stored, if at all, in an irretrievable manner. Since it is then unavailable for relevant future use we can say that there is no transfer of learning, and in effect no learning.

In the light of such a description of educationally significant learning, as an active process of selection and transformation, it becomes possible, I think, to define the essential limitations of that mechanistic way of thought which is implicit in much of our traditional pedagogy, which is explicit in the traditions of behavioristic psychology, and which reappears in the aims and claims of those who, with their neat division of labor between ends and means, would substitute a fond image of educational engineering for the richer and more complex eolithism which our nature and our situation inherently requires.

Between the stimulus and the response, says Piaget, lies the developing structure of the human being. It is this structure which not only determines response but also determines how and whether externally available information will be accepted as stimulus. As Richard Jessor once put it, the stimulus is not an independent variable for the psychologist, but must be inferred by him in context from an observed response. And I would add, we make this inference on the basis of hypotheses we construct from a *reading* of behavior, as to the present state of intellectual and purposive structures. If you watch a child working with the unequal arm balance of Archimedes, and have steeped *yourself* in the complexities and niceties of its behavior, you can then and there locate, with some reasonable probability of success, the stage and level of the child's pursuit, *and* as circumstances may suggest, you can enter the situation, for a shorter or longer spell, as one who shares with the child a well-defined and vital interest. Or you may judge the situation to be one in which even the gentlest intervention will still be disruptive, and stay away.

In any case the philosophical point of my argument is suggested: that the process of assimilation and accommodation which is crucial to education, and more generally to human conduct, is one which is so largely self-organizing, and so minimally a product of the summation of stimulus-response-reinforcement episodes, that any mechanistic program is doomed which would hope to describe human behavior by surrounding the organism by an envelope of external causal conditions. To try to explain behavior by behavioral laws patterned wishfully after the laws of physics is quite contrary to good scientific style. We can indeed try, more or less successfully, to manipulate people; we can even teach them in a manipulatory fashion, as in the mechanistic practical traditions of education and in the purportedly more refined versions that have been designed in the name of Skinnerian psychology. Such instruction works, as it does and in the way it does, not because the theory underlying it is correct but because in such situations the learner accommodates to a coercive situation and brings his considerable talents to bear in constructing a defensive framework of performance. The fact that in such a situation only so-called positive reinforcements are used (at least by the orthodox Skinnerians) should not blind us for a minute to the fact that the situation itself is coercive and is recognized as such by children.

A common criticism of such routines, made by observers who might be considered naïve and untutored, is a moral one. It does not appear right to them to push and coax children into performance by little bribes. (Humanity knows enough about this already.) And one may well agree. I have known the proponents to reject these criticisms as "unscientific." The real point, I think, is that the moral reaction is implicitly a reaction to the perception of scientific error. It is not right to treat people in that way, except where coercion is justified as coercion, because people *are not* that way. The dismissal of such criticism as "unscientific" is on a par with the old Freudian dismissal of critics on the ground that they were exhibiting something called "resistance" to the indubitable Freudian truths.

What then is the alternative or the alternatives? The essential alternative is to recognize that the developmental processes related to learning require a different framework of ideas, a different kind of descriptive metaphysics. This basis, in terms of its common sense expression, is as old as the hills but not, I think, in its scientific extensions and implications. The common-sense expression has as key terms the idea of *mind* as a capacity and the idea of a human agent who sets and seeks goals by means of that capacity. These framing ideas, within which we organize our experience of persons—including children!—do not contradict, but also do not belong in the same family with, either the behavioristic or the neurophysiological description of the human organism. Interestingly enough, however, there are many suggestions, in the findings of neurophysiology, neuroanatomy, and the infant cybernetic theory of self-organizing systems, which are far more consonant with the idea of personality and agency implicit in our practical existence than they are to the behavioristic schema.

Whatever may be the significance of present and future developments in those fields, we have here and now available to us a wide area of investigation, a rich phenomenology of developmental learning which is accessible to those who would invest their careers in it in the manner in which the ethologists, including Colorado's Professor Margaret Altmann, have revitalized the study of herring gull, ape, and elk. It would be ironic, and perhaps almost correct, to say that there is a greater investment in the observational study of other animals than in that directed to any comparable study of human beings, adult or children. But in the study of human beings outside the laboratory capsule, in what might by analogy be called the wild state, we have resources which are—so far—mostly lacking in the study of other species. In human affairs we are participants as well as observers, and the role of the classroom ethologist, remote and decoupled from its activity, can merge into the role of teacher who, by precise and perceptive diagnosis and skill can create for children a kind of atmosphere and responsiveness in their environment which serves not only the cause of advancing the educational art but also that of knowledge.

In such work as this the observer-teacher is not only the experimenter but also the principal instrument of observation, not only recording but also interpreting and planning next steps. What makes such work scientifically significant is that, while violating most of the tight and narrow canons of laboratory methodology, it can and reliably does catalyze transitions in children which, in comparison with what can be found in the social environment generally, including that of schools, we would all recognize as extremely rare and very good. In such situations there is, indeed, an external causality but it is not the causality of stimulus and reinforcement. It is the causality of the catalytic agent, the external feedback loop which enhances the resources available to children for their assimilation, invention, and thus their growth.

Such work as I speak of has been relatively rare, passed on through a craft tradition, not highly credited either in the schools or by the high academics and often dismissed as the work of eccentric genius: "So and so can do it, she (or he) is just a natural-born teacher, but it couldn't be reproduced." It is an interesting kind of disparagement to reflect upon. In fact such work can be reproduced, and there is now some hope—and danger to its critics—that it will be reproduced on an expanding scale for all to see; not so far, I am sorry to say, very conspicuously in the United States, but notably in some infant and junior schools of England.

In England there is a large and successful educational movement which represents a first—only a first—major step away from the coerciveness and stupefaction of schools traditional in all countries. A tiny minority of these schools—but still a fair number—have taken second and third steps, or at any rate know they are there to be taken and are busily working at the human and intellectual problems involved. These problems are many, but they are being attacked with a high morale based on first success.

But it is not my purpose to discuss the styles and strategies of better schools, and I leave you with an admonition. Our kind cannot live without learning, and cannot live well without constant interplay of acceptance and control, exploration and consolidation, eolithism and design. But we live in a society which, for whatever reasons, values these phases very unequally and often fails, therefore, to see the connection between them. Whether by traditional puritanism or present preoccupation and neglect, and in either case faced with far greater educational problems than our schools were originally evolved to meet, we must now look seriously to define the nature of our most radical educational deficiencies. I have been concerned to suggest a beginning for such a definition, resorting here to an image from the study of man's antique past, to a figure wandering through a stonefield, for the moment well-fed and content, uninstructed, who in a flash conceived the project of the spear—or was it in the end a hammer? The definition is not new; I could find the tradition to put it in by referring to Plato, to Locke and Rousseau, to Hegel and Froebel, to John Dewey, to Jean Piaget. But what we need goes beyond that tradition, in scope and detail, in invention and knowledge. Among all countries in the modern world we in the United States are least able to argue that we need no such reforms, or that we cannot afford them. The question is that of definition and direction. There I have tried to make my case, and now rest it.

Childhood and the Education of Intellectuals

The previous essay is intended as a rather serious criticism of the practice and the implicit philosophy of our present-day educational system, specifically in its elementary schools. But it is not the sort of criticism which singles out one institution or one profession. It rather tries to put these in a wider context, one in which responsibility must be shared. The criticism was directed against a certain sort of technocratic mentality. It is a mentality which cannot cope with the complex interactions of goal-seeking and goal-setting, which rigidifies and mechanizes because it is incapable of displaying its virtues in any other way.

Yet these technocratic habits of thought are not universal, and we have powerful traditions to oppose them, traditions of humanism and of science. But somehow these latter traditions are singularly weak and inoperative when the lot and welfare of children is at stake. The historian Phillippe Aries (Centuries of Childhood, New York, 1962) has shown great penetration in setting before us the fact that childhood is a fairly recent discovery. What has in an obvious sense been known all along in the privacy of the home has only recently and incompletely become a fact of public, of political and intellectual, concern.

Aries' thesis can be extended in other ways; by a study, for example, of the recency of any serious legal protection of children against exploitation, against violence and even infanticide. There is a curious contradiction in the fact that a society which for so long outlawed abortion as a crime against the unborn fetus continued to deal in so gingerly a way with the power of unhappy adults to abuse and batter children in the post-partum and undeniably human state.

But such matters are beyond the range of the present essays. In that which follows I have attempted to suggest that the lack of serious sustained concern about childhood represents — of course with honorable exceptions — a gap in our major intellectual traditions, and that it is this ignorance or indifference which has allowed the public management of children—schooling—to remain in low social esteem among the professions, and in the process has allowed itself to overlook matters of the greatest humanistic and scientific importance.

The aim of the essay is, I suppose, both to castigate and to entice. Both are needed. We draw increasing proportions of mothers into the wage-labor force and increasingly demand institutional day-care for their preschool children. In doing so we have shown little concern for the implications of earlier American experience and more recent experience in other parts of the world, not to mention observant and loving parental common sense; all these sources tell us rather clearly that even decent custodial care in institutional settings can be rather seriously damaging to babies and young children. The evidence also points to the general conclusion that fully adequate care in any appropriate setting ought hardly to cost less than the wages earned by full-time working mothers. If healthy non-criminal adults in our population were subject to the kind of treatment accorded young children in many day care establishments we would all be up in arms against this as a violation of human rights and we "intellectuals" would be in the vanguard. But as it is vanishingly few of us have taken on the cause of what might be called Children's Liberation. And what is true of very young children is true only in lesser degree of school-age children. The custodial function of our public schools has very often overridden their educational function. Concern about child welfare can hardly be cut off at age five or six. Wide indifference to such matters by those who would guard our moral and intellectual traditions is surely a cause for some castigation.

But the second aim is more inclusive, that of enticing the intellectuals to pay more attention to childhood—all aspects—in the interest of advancing their own education. Apparently for some this is a mildly insulting suggestion.

Childhood and the Education of Intellectuals
(1966)

A young friend of ours was just receiving her B.A., deservedly honored, from a well-known Massachusetts college east of Dedham. In some exchange over futures she told her plans, to become a teacher of young children. "But," was the response, "couldn't you at least be a *high* school teacher?" John Dewey speaks somewhere of the phobia of raw materials in the hands of children, even among those who most professed the belief that we learn by doing—specifically, Froebel and Montessori. With the image of the teacher dealing with the unformed child, who in turn is happily involved with the unformed clay or sand, we just about hit bottom on the prevailing scale of intellectual worthiness.

I speak feelingly of these invidious distinctions because I have known them in myself and in many of my intellectual friends. Having found us out, I wish to argue both the moral urgency and the intellectual rewards of major reform in our scales of value, reform which gives the nursery a far more central place in the house of intellect than most would suffer gladly.

But first let me say I am not sure of the category, "intellectuals." I think the trouble is perhaps on a wider front, and lies in the mode of life, and of aspiration, of our whole middle-class and professional society. I do not know how to marshal the evidence or state the thesis with proper qualifications, but speaking bluntly, I feel we are busy building a society in which children are not wanted. I am not talking about the birth rate but about the *estate* of childhood. Much of our present zeal for reform in education is consistent with the interpretation that we don't really like children and want to get them over being children as early as possible. I do not suppose that these symptoms are a result of individual choice, but rather of the failure to make corrective choice in the face of pressures which tend to squeeze out the child-centered institutions, family or school, as prosperous ones. This is true in the slums for one kind of reason—the widespread destruction of livelihood. It is true in suburbia for another—the pressure for increased household income.

An upper-class aspect of the destruction of childhood is the kind of coercion which a psychiatrist friend calls *Harvarditis,* and to which she traces many current adolescent woes. Higher education is the pathway, increasingly necessary and presumed sufficient, toward all good things. The good college presupposes the right secondary school, one which used to be "progressive" but now specializes in College Boards. The pressure telegraphs down even to the pre-school in some cases. The result is a species of moral futurism which is not attractive, and children of a certain independence or desperation drop out. The situation of such children is matched by the far commoner plight of the slum child who does not drop out at all, because he has never really been able to climb in. To both the signals are clear: "You are not wanted in your present estate."

To define childhood as an estate is to bring back into use a cyclical rather than unidirectional way of conceiving human affairs. The futurism I see in much present thinking accepts the child only as the future adult, and the adult only as contributing to, or anyway acquiescing in, a world of wholly adult affairs. We make what has been called, in some applied mathematics contexts, a "tearing transformation," mapping a two-way process, a cycle, into a linear pathway, thus making it easy to forget that the sustenance of childhood is also an essential function of adulthood.

One instance of this tearing transformation, widely prevalent, is the preoccupation one sees, through the domain of present educational practice, with a conception of "evaluation" that is naïvely and self-revealingly futuristic. We teach "skills" in reading or science as though the practice and enjoyment of these skills were postponable. We say that a child "reads" at the age level of 7.9 years, but we publish no estimates of how much groups of children actually do seek and enjoy reading, nor of the quality of their engagement. Are we assuming that there is no feed from use and enjoyment back into skill?

I once visited an unusual English system which has thoroughly reversed the pattern I complain of, and was successfully demonstrating the belief that reading and writing skills are mainly a product of intensive use and enjoyment of writing and reading with no "lessons." I pressed for reading scores, for evaluations. They were buried somewhere. Was I being a typical American? "But we have now no reading failures," they insisted. The headmaster finally said, in some exasperation, "You know, we think that a child should have a good day, every day. That is the main thing we are after." It even sounded Christian.

In these schools, I was bothered, for a time, by the impression that children were treated as if they were likely to remain children for a long time. They were most certainly expected to learn, even to grow up. But there was no pressure, in the learning, toward adulthood. It seemed to be assumed that adulthood would come in due course.

Children would learn but manage, in the process, to remain children. In twelve years of childhood one lives about a sixth of a human lifetime. If we weight this fraction by the endless time vistas of children's subjective experience, we are forced to admit that childhood is indeed a human estate, and not merely a transition. It is, of course, full of transitions, more profound, at least on the intellectual plane, than any to follow.

Where are the emissaries and anthropologists from the intellectual stratum to the child estate? There are great childhood themes in the arts, in painting and prose and music. That is part of what I mean, but there should be much more—not argument, like the Freudian literature, but social intercourse, a wider acquaintance. Lacking it we remain, as adult intellectuals, ethnocentric, i.e. adult-centered. Some very important things remain alien to us and our humanity is impaired.

Thus, I am of two minds about the greater involvement of intellectuals in the processes of early education. If the effect is to intensify the embargo on leisurely enrichment of childhood, to press harder for attainment, I have doubts and am troubled. If the effect is that the intellectuals should savor and enjoy more of that other estate, and should become, in the process, a little more like children, it seems to me there could be great gain, both educational and intellectual.

Lest these sentiments be read as sentimental, let me concentrate on some intellectual gains that may be available. One of the mysteries that philosophy has guarded over the centuries is that of the nature and origin in the mind of Universals, of the generic traits and categories implicit both in the perception and in the understanding of the world. Since the myths of Plato, which pegged many of the problems about universals, and with added point since the critical investigation of experience by Hume and Kant, these problems have been recognized, though inconstantly, as fundamental to the description of learning and knowing. Plato suggested, vividly and perversely, that perception is possible only as it presupposes the mind's ability to recognize and classify, only because of its *prior* acquaintance with the Forms and the ultimate reality which they constitute. Thus he casts doubt on the empirical origins of knowledge. Aristotle took a position against any such view and introduced instead the doctrine of abstraction, according to which the forms of knowledge are drawn from repeated passages of experience, not communicated by experience, it is true, but evolved *in the course of* experience. Thus the order of nature is abstracted or borrowed by the mind, and internalized as its own.

Hume and Kant, working from within the modern tradition of empiricism, demonstrated to their own satisfaction, and the satisfaction of much subsequent philosophy, that at least the most generic categories used by the human understanding are not conveyed with experience, but are somehow contributed by the nature of the human knower. Many of us today, influenced by this tradition but also by the nineteenth-century deepening of evolutionary ideas, see it as only one further step to a doctrine of abstraction more thoroughgoing than the Aristotelian, and thus back to the view that mind exists and is formed only in a rich informational commerce between itself and nature.

If this view is correct, as I believe it is, the feature of modern education which it renders most conspicious is the practice of assuming that the categorical framework of understanding is somehow already there in the young child, and that the major undertaking of the school is the fleshing out of the structure with skills and verbally transmitted knowledge. It is predominantly the kind of practice that could be justified only through a doctrine of innate ideas; a doctrine that is, in fact, no longer respectable. Or else practice altogether ignores the problem and treats the acquisition of category and concept as though this were adequately taken care of by illustrative demonstrations in the context of something like "vocabulary building."

Kant contributed a notion that will suffice to suggest, at least, some of the psychological problems. His notion is that we develop ways of filtering and reorganizing the material of sense-perception in accordance with what he called schemata. He saw that the mere possession of abstract concepts and categories did not account for our ability to deal with the concrete, the particular, and the novel in terms of such universals. Thus the concept of number must be associated with a schema of counting, or that of substance must be associated with a schema of invariance to reversal of temporal order. For Kant these schemata were activities of something eulogistically called the "human mind." Nothing is lost if we say they are activities of the human being, child or adult. Much is gained, moreover, if we place the covert activity called mental in the same dimension as the overt activities of play and exploration, and if we recognize these as the childhood source, for reflection and abstraction, of the intellectual tools which we later take *to* experience when we cope competently with the world around us.

From a modern evolutionary point of view there is no metaphysical distinction between that which is phylogenetically evolved and that which is ontogenetically learned. By the evidence of animal ethology, matured behavior is typically a complex product of inherited tendency elaborated and subtilized by extensive experience in a variable environment. It is known, at least in some cases, that this elaboration takes place during special maturational stages after which behavior becomes less plastic in its accommodation. Of the many dramatic accomplishments which crowd after one another in the lives of young children, the acquisition of speech is most suggestive of a special ability during the normal period of its acquisition. Such phases may be responsible, in part, for the belief that mental development takes place in stages of a biologically developmental kind without any essential patterning from the child's active commerce with his environment. In the intellectual sphere this takes us back to some notion of a gradual unfolding of innate ideas.

The truth is that there has been relatively little close and disciplined scientific observation of the learning behavior of young children as related to their distinctively intellectual development. It helps to work by stages, as Piaget has done, but we need to see such developments *in statu nascendi*. Nor is such observation likely to prove fruitful under short-term, transient conditions arranged for the benefit of the psychologist or psychiatrist observer. A Lorenz swims with his goslings, a Schaller lives with mountain gorillas, ethnologists live the life of the peoples they would study. To expect more from the ethological study of young children, for a lesser effort, seems naïve indeed. The time scale of such observation is very clearly not the day or the week. The transitions and transformations of intellectual development may be rapid indeed, but they are statistically rare and must be observed in context to be given significance. That takes time enough to be called devotion.

The most important area of control, for making the intellectual development of children more visible, happens to coincide with the major practical aim of educational reform: to provide both the material and social environment, and the adult guidance, under which the engagement of children with their world is most intrinsically satisfying and most conducive to the development we would study. Thus to be the best scientific observers we must be at once the best providers for and the best teachers of those whom we would study. If this seems too much to ask, we must then associate ourselves in teams which work harmoniously and with considerable overlapping of these various functions.

At this point I will be asked, inevitably, how we can *define* the good environment, and the good teacher, without first having scientifically evaluated these in terms of their contribution to children's intellectual development. The answer is very simple. Science does not go simply from methods to results, or from results to methods; it goes from one to the other, and back again, many times. And it starts always with some status quo,with what is *already* known. Later, once or several times around, the initial knowledge will be reformulated and recast. The important question is *who* knows what is already known?

The demand that nothing should be accepted in educational practice that has not first been certified through academic educational research is basically, I think, a bit of professional arrogance, harking back to the dominance order I alluded to at the beginning. For it will turn out, at least today, that the authorities in this area are persons who have made a great investment in working with the unformed child who in turn is happily involved with the unformed clay or sand. . . . "But how can I identify these good and insightful teachers—who must be rare if what you say about the schools is true!—without first using my scales of creativity, or tolerance of ambiguity, or intelligence? One must be scientific!" The answer is you can't so easily identify without knowledge. Let the successful teachers first identify each other. That means giving them time and opportunity—a little more honestly professional status. Let them tell you, and abide by their judgment until you can improve on it. Science recognizes no absolutes, and assuredly not the institutional absolute that science is only that which is certified by "scientists" or their prevailing methods. The time has not yet arrived when metallurgists can be replaced, in their area of competence, by solid-state physicists, in spite of many gains in the solid-state theory of metals.

Most of those gains would be far longer in coming without the guidance of the long tradition of metallurgical practice. Perhaps it is easier, from the outside, to identify a good metallurgist than a good teacher, but even in such a field it is not so easy that we can ignore the informed judgment of peers. Indeed, it is that condition of peer judgment which is the main defining condition of a profession as distinguished from a trade.

Thus, it is my plea to the intellectuals who would seek a greater understanding of the human mind and of its capabilities, and who would contribute to the practical improvement of education in the process, that they first seek out the best of existing practice and apprentice themselves to it. They will have much to contribute along the way, of course; but in their basic undertaking they must learn before they can teach, and the most important place for their learning is the operating milieu of children and teachers. Being naïve in such matters, I have only recently come to learn that the term "apprentice" is a bad word in many educational circles. The connotations, I suppose, are those of the trade rather than the profession. I think the word is good, and I know some teachers of young children to whom I would most happily be apprenticed. But let us speak instead of internships and residencies. And let us seek them if we mean to give fuller and deeper attention to the process of education.

I, Thou, and It

A proper and serious study of childhood would raise questions, I think, about one tendency widespread among us. Reference to it is there by implication in the previous essay with its suggestion that we send "emissaries to childhood." But of course that is only half the need; the other is to recognize that we will learn in the process only what we are prepared to observe and accept. Being repelled by the typical formality and sterility of our institutional treatment of children, many of us react by seeking and advocating patterns of association which are arranged for easy two-way communication, warm and loving. If that is half the story, it is a half which needs redefinition when the whole story is told. Long before Bettelheim, Immanuel Kant had given profound support to the proposition that, in human affairs generally, "love is not enough." The more basic gift is not love but respect, respect for others as ends in themselves, as actual and potential artisans of their own learnings and doings, of their own lives; and as thus uniquely contributing, in turn, to the learnings and doings of others.

Respect for the young is not a passive, hands-off attitude. It invites our own offering of resources, it moves us toward the furtherance of their lives and thus even, at times, toward remonstrance or intervention. Respect resembles love in its implicit aim of furtherance, but love without respect can blind and bind. Love is private and unbidden, whereas respect is implicit in all moral relations with others.

To have respect for children is more than recognizing their potentialities in the abstract, it is also to seek out and value their accomplishments—however small these may appear by the normal standards of adults. But if we follow this track of thinking one thing stands out. We must provide for children those kinds of environments which elicit their interests and talents and which deepen their engagement in practice and thought. An environment of "loving" adults who are themselves alienated from the world around them is an educational vacuum. Adults involved in the world of man and nature bring that world with them to children, bounded and made safe to be sure, but not

48

thereby losing its richness and promise of novelty. It was this emphasis which made me insist upon the third pronoun in the title, the impersonal "It" alongside the "I" and "Thou." Adults and children, like adults with each other, can associate well only in worthy interests and pursuits, only through a community of subject-matter and engagement which extends beyond *the circle of their intimacy.*

The attitude of deprecating subject-matter, and of deprecating curriculum as a guide to the providing of worthy subject-matter, reflects therefore the half-truth badly used.

Such is the background. As to the foreground of the following essay, some readers will astutely recognize in it a principled opposition to a widely popular belief in the efficacy of certain patented techniques of group association and therapy which are levered upon the art of inducing personal "confrontation," or some equivalent form of what I have called "artificial intimacy." Some of my friends disagree about Group Dynamics not so much in theory as in practice. They may agree that good human association must of course be premised upon common concerns and commitments with respect to what is "out there," something not "I" and not "Thou." But even without such commitment, they say, it works.

I think their attitude is rather like that expressed in a story about the physicist Niels Bohr. When a friend saw a horseshoe over the door of Bohr's country cabin, he said in mock astonishment, "Surely you don't believe in that old superstition!" "No," said Bohr, "but they say it works even if you don't believe in it."

I, Thou, and It
(1967)

I want to talk about children's understanding in the context of a proper education, more specifically of a good school. My topic, therefore, is the relationship between the teacher and the child and a third thing in the picture which has to be there and which completes the triangle of my title.

This is a relationship that has been much talked about, but truncated too often. People have made analogies between the teacher-child realtionship and many other sorts of relationships. For example, in olden times people said, "What this child needs is good hard work and discipline," and that sounds rather like a parent-child relationship, doesn't it? Or they said, more recently, "The child needs love." That also sounds rather like a parent-child relationship. I'm sure that neither of these statements is completely false, but it seems to me they're both very unsatisfactory and that the relationship between the teacher and the child is something quite unique that isn't exactly paralleled by any other kind of human relationship. It's interesting to explore what is involved in it.

I know one rather good teacher who says he doesn't like children. He says this, I'm sure, with a rather special meaning of the word "like." He doesn't like children to be bewildered, at loose ends, not learning, and therefore he tries to get them over this as soon as possible. I mention him because I think the attitude of love, which is the parental attitude, isn't really the appropriate one. Perhaps the word "respect" might be more appropriate. I don't want to deny a very important element of affection for children in the make-up of good teachers, but the essence of the relationship is not that. It is a personal relationship, but it's not that kind of personal relationship. I want to talk about this in the context of the kind of thing we've been investigating in recent years, in the context of a kind of schooling we are interested in exploring further, marked by the more frequent and more abundant use of concrete materials by children in schools, *and* by their greater freedom of choice within this enriched world. I'd like to talk about how the third corner of the triangle affects the relations between the other two corners, how the "It" enters into the pattern of mutual interest and exchange between the teacher and the child. Being an incurable academic philosopher, I'd like to start on a very large scale and talk about human beings—of which children are presumably rather typical examples.

There's a tradition in philosophy which always comes to my mind when I'm thinking about this kind of question and which seems to be a more significant tradition than some others. It's a tradition which is expressed by saying, in one way or another, that people don't amount to very much except in terms of their involvement in what is outside and beyond them. A human being is a localized physical body, but you can't see him as a *person* unless you see him in his working relationships with the world around him. The more you cut off these working relationships, the more you put him in a box, figuratively or literally, the more you diminish him. Finally, when you've narrowed him down to nothing more than the surface of the skin and what's inside, without allowing him any kind of relationship with the world around him, you don't have very much left.

The ancient Hindu philosophers expressed this definition of human nature by using the metaphor of the mirror. In the *Baghavad Gita*, the Hindu scripture, there is a marvelous image of the soul which is said to be "the reflection of the rose in a glass." Like most religious philosophy, this one is concerned with the problems of death and consolation. The theory of immortality in this philosophy is expressed by saying that when death occurs, you take away the mirror—but the rose is still there. This image seems to me a very powerful one. It's not the same as the Christian idea of the soul, of course, but it emphasizes the thing I want to talk about, which is that you can't dissociate the person from the world he lives and functions in and that you can somehow measure the person by the degree of his involvement in that world. The soul is not contained *within* the body but outside, in the theater of its commitments.

The most precise expression of this idea that I know of in our literature is by a famous English poet. I want to quote it because it says something rather nicely about the relationship of two human beings, and the great It, the world. This is in *Troilus and Cressida,* where *It* is a famous Hellenic enterprise. There was a time when Achilles was having some difficulties about the siege of Troy and people were trying to buck him up. At one point Ulysses comes on. It's part of the play where nothing much is going to happen for a few minutes. Sometimes in Shakespeare when nothing is going to happen, you have an exchange of bawdy jokes for the boys in the pit and sometimes you have a bit of relevant philosophizing. In the play this bit of philosophizing is relevant to Ulysses' effort to goad Achilles into action; but it has a universal relevance as well:

Ulysses   A strange fellow here
    Writes me that man—how dearly ever parted,
    How much in having, or without or in—
    Cannot make boast to have that which he hath,

Nor feels not what he owes, but by reflection;
As when his virtues shining upon others
Heat them, and they retort that heat again
To the first giver.

Achilles   This is not strange, Ulysses.
The beauty that is borne here in the face
The bearer knows not, but commends itself
To others' eyes; nor doth the eye itself—
That most pure spirit of sense—behold itself,
Not going from itself; but eye to eye opposed
Salutes each other with each other's form;
For speculation turns not to itself
Till it hath travell'd and is mirror'd there
Where it may see itself. This is not strange at all.

Ulysses I do not strain at the position—
It is familiar—but at the author's drift;
Who, in his circumstance, expressly proves
That no man is the lord of anything,—
Though in and of him there be much consisting—
Till he communicate his parts to others.
Nor doth he of himself know them for aught
Till he behold them formed in th'applause
Where th'are extended; who, like an arch, reverb'rate
The voice again or, like a gate of steel
Fronting the sun, receives and renders back
His figure and his heat.

(Tudor Text, Player's Edition, Collins.)

   No Ajax, no Achilles even, can *be* the lord of anything, much less
know his own worth, save through resonance with others engrossed
in those same matters. No child, I wish to say, can gain competence
and knowledge, or know himself as competent and as a knower, save
through communication with others involved with him in his enterprises. Without a Thou, there is no I evolving. Without an It there is
no content for the context, no figure and no heat, but only an affair
of mirrors confronting each other.

Children are members of the same species as adults, but they are also quite a distinct subspecies and we want to be careful about not exaggerating the differences and not forgetting them, either. It seems clear to me that there are many complicated, difficult things they learn or can learn, and such learning occurs in an environment where there are other human beings who serve, so to speak, as a part of the learning process. Long before there were such things as schools, which are rather recent institutions in the history of our kind, there were teachers. There were adults who lived in the village and who responded to the signals that children know very well how to emit in order to get attention from adults. These adults managed, quite spontaneously and without benefit of the theory of instruction, to be teachers.

I really need a kind of electronic analogy here for what goes on in a child's mind. Think of circuits that have to be completed. Signals go out along one bundle of channels, something happens, and signals come back along another bundle of channels; and there's some sort of feedback involved. Children are not always able to sort out all of this feedback for themselves. The adult's function, in the child's learning, is to provide a kind of external loop, to provide a selective feedback from the child's own choice and action. The child's involvement gets some response from an adult and this in turn is made available to the child. The child is learning about himself through his joint effects on the non-human *and* the human world around him.

The function of the teacher, then, is to respond diagnostically and helpfully to a child's behavior, to make what he considers to be an appropriate response, a response which the child needs to complete the process he's engaged in at a given moment. Now, this function of the teacher isn't going to go on forever: it's going to terminate at some time in the future. What we can say, I think, and what we clearly ought to provide for, is that the child should learn how to internalize the function which the adult has been providing. So, in a sense, you become educated when you become your own teacher. If being educated meant no longer needing a teacher—a definition I would recommend—it would mean that you had been presented with models of teaching, or people playing this external role, and that you have learned how the role was played and how to play it for yourself. At that point you would declare your independence of instruction as such and you would be your own teacher. What we all hope, of course, is that as the formal, institutional part of education is finished, its most conspicuous and valuable product will be seen to be the child's ability to educate himself. If this doesn't happen, it doesn't make sense to say that the processes we try to initiate in school are going to be carried on when people leave school.

The image I want, then, is really the image Shakespeare is working with. You grow as a human being by the incorporation of conjoint information from the natural world *and* of things which only other human beings are able to provide for in your education.

I sometimes think that working in the style we like to work in—which is much farther along in English primary schools, I'm sorry to say, than in American schools—we forget the unique importance of the human role. We tend to say "Oh well, if children just have a good rich, manipulable and responsive environment, then everything will take care of itself." When you visit a class which is operating in this way, with a teacher who has a good bag of tricks, you're often impressed that the teacher doesn't seem to be very necessary. He can leave the room and nobody notices it. If *you* don't have that bag of tricks, you always rather marvel at what goes into it. After everything is accomplished it all looks as though it's very spontaneous. But, of course, that's a dangerous illusion. It's true only in those periods—in good schools frequent periods—when children don't need the external loop. When they do need it and there's no one around to contribute the adult resonance, then they're not always able to carry on the process of investigation, of inquiry and exploration, of learning, because they need help over a hump that they can't surmount through their own resources. If help isn't available, the inquiry will taper off, and that particular episode, at least, will have failed to accomplish what it otherwise might have.

Now, I'm speaking as one very much in favor of richness and diversity in the environment, and of teaching which allows a group of children to diversify their activities and which—far more than we usually think proper—keeps out of their hair. What seems very clear to me—and I think this is a descriptive, factual statement, not praising or blaming—is that if you operate a school, as we in America almost entirely do, in such a style that the children are rather passively sitting in neat rows and columns and manipulating you into believing that they're being attentive because they're not making any trouble, then you won't get very much information about them. Not getting much information about them, you won't be a very good diagnostician of what they need. Not being a good diagnostician, you will be a poor teacher. The child's overt involvement in a rather self-directed way, using the big muscles and not just the small ones, is most important to the teacher in providing an input of information wide in range and variety. It is input which potentially has much more heft than what you can possibly get from the merely verbal or written responses of a child to questions put to him or tasks set for him. When we fail in this diagnostic role we begin to worry about "assessment."

I think this is fairly obvious. It doesn't say that you *will* but that you *can* get more significant diagnostic information about children, and can refine your behavior as a teacher far beyond the point of what's possible when every child is being made to perform in a rather uniform pattern. But of course you will not get the information, or will not use it, if you are just sweetly permissive and limp, if you don't provide the external feedback loop when you think it is needed. We know children never do behave uniformly even when they're supposed to. When it appears they are, it's just because they've learned the trick of pleasing you—or displeasing you if they're all on strike!—and then you aren't able to make the needed discrimination.

But I think the real importance of teacher-intervention comes out in situations where a child is not involved in very many things, is not responsive to anything you provide. That child may be a problem; that child who doesn't give you much information, who is tight and constrained, often called "good." But you get little suggestions or inklings of interest and involvement, you get hunches about what might prove absorbing to him. If you have enough of these hunches and enough persistence you find *something* that works and when you do you have laid the basis for a new relationship between yourself and that child, and this is the thing that is really important.

The rest is good and important and not too hard to describe: when children are being diverse in what they're doing, selective in what they're doing; when you're giving them genuine alternatives—then you are bound to get much more knowledge of them from reading the language of their behavior. Of course, you certainly aren't going to succeed all the time with every child in this diagnostic and planning process. There are going to be several misses for every hit, but you just say, "Well, let's keep on missing and the more we miss the more we'll hit." The importance of this in the "I-Thou" relationship between the teacher and the child is that the child learns something about the adult which we can describe with words like "confidence," "trust" and "respect." You have done something for the child which he could not do for himself, and he knows it. He's become involved in something new which has proved engrossing to him. If he thus learns that he has a competence he didn't know he had, then you have been a very crucial figure in his life. You have provided that external loop, that external feedback, which he couldn't provide for himself. He then values the provisioner with the provision.

What is the feeling you have toward a person who does this for you? It needn't be what we call love, but it certainly *is* what we call respect. You value another person because he is uniquely useful to you in helping you on with your own life. "Love" is, perhaps, a perfectly good word, too, but it has a great variety of meanings and has been vulgarized, not least by psychological theory.

The relationship that develops with different children will be different just because they are different children. When *you* give a child a range from which to make choices, the choices *he* makes in turn give you the basis for deciding what should be done next, what the provisioning should be for him. That is *your* decision, it's dependent on *your* goals, it's something *you* are responsible for—not in an authoritarian way but you do have to make a decision and it's your decision, not the child's. If it's a decision to let him alone you are just as responsible for it as if it's a decision to intervene.

The investment in the child's life that is made in this way by the adult, the teacher in this case, is something that adds to and in a way transforms the interest the child develops spontaneously. If, as sometimes happens, a child gets particularly interested in a variation on a soap bubble theme that you've already given him, you can just happen to put nearby some other things that might not at first seem related to soap bubbles—some geometrical wire cubes, tetrahedra, helices, and wire with a soldering iron. The resulting soap films are almost bound to catch the fancy of many human beings, including children. What have they got? Well, they've got a certain formal geometrical elegance, they've got color; when you look at the films in the right kind of light you see all those marvelous interference colors. Such a trap is bristling with invitations and questions. Some children will sample it and walk on; but some will be hooked by it, will get very involved with it. Now, this kind of involvement is terribly important, I think. It's aesthetic, or it's mathematical, or it's scientific. It's all of these potentially, and none of them exclusively. The teacher has made possible this relation between the child and "It," even if this is just by having "It" in the room; and for the child even this brings the teacher as a person, a "Thou," into the picture. For the child this is not merely something which is fun to play with, which is exciting and colorful and has associations with many other sorts of things in his experience: it's also a basis for communication with the teacher on a new level, and with a new dignity.

Until the child is going on his own the teacher can't treat him as a person who is going on his own, cannot let him be mirrored there, where he may see himself as investigator or craftsman. Until he is an autonomous human being who is thinking his own thoughts and making his own unique, individual kinds of self-expression out of them, there isn't anything for the teacher to respect, except a potentiality. So the first act in teaching, it seems to me, the first goal, necessary to all others, is to encourage this kind of engrossment. Then the child comes alive for the teacher as well as the teacher for the child. They have a common theme for discussion, they are involved together in the world.

I had always been awkward in certain kinds of situations with young children. I didn't know them very well and I'd sort of forgotten that I'd once been one, as we mostly do. I remember being very impressed by the way some people, in an encounter with a young child, would seem automatically to gain acceptance while other people, in apparently very friendly encounters with the same child, would produce real withdrawal and, if they persisted, fear and even terror. Such was the well-meaning adult who wanted to befriend the child—I and Thou—in a vacuum. It's traumatic, and I think we all know what it feels like. I came to realize (I learned with a good teacher) that one of the very important factors in this kind of situation is that there be some third thing which is of interest to the child *and* to the adult, in which they can join in outward projection. Only this creates a possible stable bond of communication, of shared concern.

My most self-conscious experience of this kind of thing was when a few years ago I found myself with two very small tykes who had gone with me and my wife to the hospital to get their mother, who had just had a third baby. The father was ill and there was already some anxiety. With Frances Hawkins they were fine; indeed it was she who had earlier been my teacher in this art. They were perfectly happy with us two but they had never been with me alone. Suddenly the nurse announced in a firm voice that children could not go beyond this point, so my wife had to go in and we three had to stay. It was one of those moments when you could have had a fairly lively scene on your hands. Not being an adept, I thought quite consciously of the triangular principle. There had to be some third thing that wasn't "I" and the two children, otherwise we were all going to be laid waste. And there wasn't anything! I looked around and there was a bare hospital corridor. But on one wall there was a collection of photographs of some recent banquet that had been given for a donor, so in desperation I just picked them up, rushed over to it, and said, "Look!" That's a sort of confession, because I'm sure many of you would know how to handle this kind of situation: for me it was a great triumph and it was a demonstration, if an oddly mechanical one, of a consciously held principle. And it worked.

It seems to me that this kind of episode, which is in itself trivial and superficial, can symbolize a lot that is important in terms of the teacher-child relationship; namely, the common interest, the common involvement in subject-matter. Now of course, you never really deceive a child in important matters, so this interest can't long be feigned, as it was in my story. If you don't find something interesting, and try to feign an interest you don't have, the investment won't last. But if there is that common interest it may last and may evolve. You need to be capable of noticing what the child's eyes notice and capable of interpreting the words and acts by which he tries to communicate with you. It may not be in adult English, so the reception of these signals requires experience and close attention.

Visualize a long transparent corked plastic tube with water and other things in it, as fancy may dictate. Many years ago I would have thought that this was rather trivial, rather silly, and would have said, "What's there to be learned from that?" To tell you the truth, I honestly still don't know, there is so much! We can use a lot of words in physics that have something to do with it; or we can talk about color and motion and other things of some aesthetic importance. By now I've seen enough children involved in this particular curious apparatus to be quite convinced that there's a great deal in it—and I don't mean just this particular tube but many similar artifacts, as well as samples of the natural world. Such things can serve as an extraordinary kind of bond. The child is in some sense functioning to incorporate the world; he's trying to assimilate his environment. This includes his social environment, of course, but it also includes the inanimate environment; it also includes the resources of the daily world around him, which he's capable of seeing for the most part with far fresher eyes than ours. The richer this adult-provided contact, therefore, the more firm is the bond that is established between the human beings who are involved.

Finally, I'd like to mention something which is perhaps of special interest and which takes me into psychological theory. It has to do with how human beings come to attain the sense of objectivity, the sense of reality, with how they come to get a stable, reliable vision of the world around them and how, without losing their capacity for fantasy, they are able to make clear discriminations between what they know, what they have learned, what they merely believe, what they imagine, and so on. It has to do with how they are able to get straight the orders and kinds of belief and credibility. This is one of the most important accomplishments of a human being.

It seems to me that for some children and not for others this capacity for fitting things together into a coherent whole, into a coherent pattern, comes first mostly in terms of their relations with the human world, while for other children it comes first mostly in their relations with the inanimate world.

The capacity for synthesis, for building a stable framework within which many episodes of experience can be put together coherently, comes with the transition from autistic behavior to exploratory behavior. The first is guided by a schedule which is surely inborn, and is connected with satisfaction of definite infant needs. The second has a different style, and is not purposive in the same way, not aimed at a predetermined end-state. Its satisfaction, its reinforcement as a way of functioning, comes along the way and not at the end; in competence acquired, not in satiation. Both modes of behavior are elaborated through experience, but exploratory behavior is not bound and limited by a schedule of needs—needs which must, to begin with, have the highest priority. A child's first major synthetic achievements in exploratory learning may come in relation to the human world, but they may come equally, and perhaps more readily, in his exploration of the things of his surrounding physical environment, and of their responsiveness to his testing and trying. In either case, or so it seems to me, the exploratory motivation, and its reinforcement, is of a different kind from the libidinous, aimed as the latter is at incorporation and possession. And the child's development will be limited and distorted if it does not, by turns, explore *both* the personal and the non-personal aspects of his environment; but explore them, not exploit them for a known end. Most psychologists, in my reading and my more extensive arguing with them, tend to say that the roots of human motivation are interpersonal. They say that the fundamental dynamics of the child's relation to the rest of the world as he grows up stem from his relation to his mother, his relation to other close figures around him, and that these will be the impelling forces in his life. It is, of course, in such terms that Freud built up his whole systematic theory and although perhaps there aren't many very orthodox Freudians around nowadays this key feature of the theory persists, I think—the feeling that the only important formative things in life are other human beings. And if people pay attention to the non-human world—it may include animals and plants as well as the physical environment, enriched to contain bubble tubes and soap film—one tends to trace this to some desire to exploit the human world: for example, the child does something because he thinks it pleases you or because he thinks it displeases you, or because he's escaping you—but never because he wants wholeheartedly to do what he's doing. In other words, there's been a systematic tendency to devalue children's thing-oriented interests as against their person-oriented interests. It is assumed that the latter are basic, the former derivative. All I would like to say is that I think the interest in *things* is a perfectly real, perfectly independent and autonomous interest which is there in young children just as genuinely as the interest in persons is there.

And some children are *only* able to develop humanly by first coming to grips in an exploratory and involved way with the inanimate world.

We've certainly seen examples of children who very early have got on to the tricks which I suppose in some sense babies are born with but which infants can elaborate as they grow older, tricks for getting what they want from persons by planning how they shall behave. It's exploiting, and some very young children are already skillful at it. If you know such children as a teacher you'll know they're smarter than you are because they've put a lot more investment into this kind of thing than you have. You have to be very shrewd to cope with them.

One thing such a child cannot do is to get wholeheartedly involved in anything else; he has to be watching all the time to see what the adults and the other children think about it. But if you can set enough traps for him, if you can keep exposing him to temptations, if he sees other children involved and not paying any attention to the teacher, he's left out in the cold. So the temptations of bubbles or clay or sand or whatever it is are reinforced by the fact that other children aren't playing his kind of game. If such a child once forgets his game, because he *does* get involved in shaping some inanimate raw material, in something that's just there to be explored, played with, investigated, tried out, then he has had an experience which is liberating, that can free him from the kind of game-playing which he's got so expert at. He comes, after all, from a species that is called *homo faber*. If he doesn't get free of manipulating persons somewhere in his life, that life is going to be a sad one. In the extreme case perhaps it will even be a psychotic one. Children of this extreme sort are a special case, but being extreme, in a way they tell us a lot about what is involved in the three-cornered relationship of my title. They seek to get and to keep, but cannot yet even begin to give. For the verb *to give* has two objects and only the indirect one is personal. The direct object must be something treasured which is not I, and not Thou.

One final remark. It seems to me that many of us, whether our background was in science or not, have learned something about ourselves from working with children in this way that we've begun to explore. We've begun to see the things of the physical and biological world through children's eyes rather more than we were able to before, and have discovered and enjoyed a lot that is there that we were not aware of before. We don't any longer feel satisfied with the kind of adult grasp that we had of the very subject matter that we've been teaching; we find it more problematic, more full of surprises, and less and less a matter of the textbook order.

One of the nicest stories of this kind that I know comes from a young physicist friend who was very learned. He had just got his Ph.D. and of course he understood everything. (The Ph.D. has been called "the certificate of omniscience.") My wife was asking him to explain something to her about two coupled pendulums. He said, "Well, now, you can see that there's a conservation of . . . Well, there's really a conservation of angle here." She looked at him. "Well, you see, in the transfer of energy from one pendulum to the other there is . . ." and so on and so on. And she said, "No, I don't mean that. I want you to notice this and tell me what's happening." Finally, he looked at the pendulums and he saw what she was asking. He looked at *it*, and he looked at *her,* and he grinned and said, "Well, I know the right words but I don't understand it either." This confession, wrung from a potential teacher, I've always valued very much. It proves that we're all in *it* together.

Messing About in Science

There is a lesson for me in the fact that the essay which follows has by a factor of ten been more widely read, at least among teachers, than any of the others. The lesson is that one should try to recognize, in all discourse about education, what Philip Morrison calls "the logic of the concrete." Everyone knows that a readable essay needs a specific focus: a piece of chalk, a candle flame, a personal experience reflected upon. The essay has such a focus. But what counts is not the taste of sugar or the slipperiness of the capsule that takes down the otherwise unsavory pill or abstraction.

When we communicate together in the context of our work the particulars we are engaged with enter into the discourse, so to speak, as willing witnesses. Such things help us avoid the debasement of the language-coin and recall us to honest experience. The predatory hydra in his life space of a cubic millimeter, the salamander in his burrow, the rock which floats and the pendulum which willy-nilly does its thing, all these are guarantors in writing of what is otherwise not easy to come by, namely clear-cut meaning, the sense that you speak from within a shared ambient.

When it comes to writing one can, of course, only suggest this ambient. One cannot literally occupy it with a reader. The work on pendulums reported here was my first work, at all sustained, in elementary school classrooms (fifth grade). Eleanor Duckworth and I shared this trial and discussed it much between times. It was a relative success, I think, though not unqualified. I still remember one boy we could not involve except in "bombings" with those delightful spheres, steel or glass, on their string supports. It was he who reminded me that I was, after all, a not very experienced teacher of the young. A more experienced teacher would have worked hard to change the setting for that one, to find a pathway along which he could move from anger to accomplishment.

The one thing in "Messing About" which was not part of my experience, but conjectural, now seems to me the most dubious. It covers with a sort of formula—that of the need to prepare "work cards" for children who are ready to become more systematically involved in a subject-matter —what seems to me to be a far more basic problem. I was here proposing easy answers to a question which goes much deeper. Of course written guidance can be helpful in coping with the conditions of a "science lesson," three times a week with 30 to 40 children. And of course such guidance can be made more flexible than the usual thought-destroying one-two-three instruction. So far so good. But the problem addressed here is not to be considered as "solved" by such an artful contrivance as a file of good questions and suggestions. However necessary such materials may be on occasion, they surely do not go far to meet the need implied.

The more basic questions are questions I was not yet prepared to ask. I shall not try to ask them here, except to widen the field. For one thing science or any other "subject" does not have to come, by prescription, in three hourly lessons a week. That was a constraint we accepted at the time because we had to. And the same materials and array of questions do not have to confront all children at the same time or in the same context or sequence. Such an organization is one of many options which ought to lie within the control of a teacher.

Quite other kinds of options are, for the most part, more likely to support a teacher in helping children pursue an interest beyond the good beginnings. Not the least of these options is the opportunity to work intensively with one child, or a few.

And here we come, I think, to an option so basic as to affect the whole policy and pattern of our educational system: smaller classes for those who have mastered the art (or are learning it) of working with children as individuals.

The Coleman Report finds, by statistical analysis, that class size, along with a number of other variables (library size, academic level of teachers, etc.) makes little or no difference to standard academic attainments of students. Qualitatively similar findings were made in England.

As a characterization of the existing population of our schools such survey results are entirely persuasive and predictable. One hears conclusions drawn from such studies, however, that are illegitimate and false. It is indeed a sad thing to hear people cite the premise that "class size is unimportant" and argue from this to the gross economy of larger classes, rather than to the fact that few teachers have had deep and extended experience in the art of investing subject-matter with romance or dignity in ways matched to the momentary readiness of individual children. For that process there is never enough time, in classes of thirty, for a skillful teacher to reach more than a minority. What in current fashion is called "individualized instruction" is the very opposite—an affair of programmed texts and workbooks leading all children by the nose at different rates through the same collection of exercises.

The ideal of education expressed by the old story of "Mark Hopkins on one end of a log, the student on the other" was intended as a tribute to the humanity and skill of a teacher, not to those who could inspire one student no better than thirty.

In a rare kind of school, one inevitably lost in the jumble of global surveys based on large masses of cheap data, one finds such big differences, humanly and therefore statistically significant.

In good scientific investigation of such matters, one starts with the needle, not the haystack. Good statisticians know this, but unfortunately the data they would seek are very labor-intensive, and not cheap.

There is a sort of joke, or paradox, much puzzled over by formal logicians in recent times which perhaps illustrates the point. One wants to get evidence for or against the proposition that all crows are black. Now the proposition "All crows are black" is precisely identical in truth or falsity to the awkward proposition "All non-black things are non-crows." What we must do, therefore, is to start examining the whole abundant universe of things which are not black to see if we can find a crow among them. Why not?

Crows are rare in the universe, and looking for them is an expensive business. We are likely to find them "not statistically significant," however, if we find them at all by the method suggested.

Messing About in Science

(1965)

"Nice? It's the *only* thing," said the Water Rat solemnly, as he leant forward for his stroke. "Believe me, my young friend, there is *nothing* —absolutely nothing—half so much worth doing as simply messing about in boats. Simply messing," he went on dreamily, "messing—about—in —boats—messing—"

Kenneth Grahame,
The Wind in the Willows

As a college teacher, I have long suspected that my students' difficulties with the intellectual process come not from the complexity of college work itself, but mainly from their home background and the first years of their formal education. A student who cannot seem to understand the workings of the Ptolemaic astronomy, for example, turns out to have no evident acquaintance with the simple and "obvious" relativity of motion, or the simple geometrical relations of light and shadow. Sometimes for these students a style of laboratory work which might be called "Kindergarten Revisited" has dramatically liberated their intellectual powers. Turn on your heel with your head back until you *see* the ceiling—turn the other way—and don't fall over!

In the past two years, working in the Elementary Science Study, I have had the experience, marvelous for a naive college teacher, of studying young children's learning in science. I am now convinced that my earlier suspicions were correct. In writing about these convictions, I must acknowledge the strong influence on me by other staff members in the Study. We came together from a variety of backgrounds—college, high school, and elementary school teachers—and with a variety of dispositions toward science and toward teaching. In the course of trial teaching and of inventing new curricular materials, our shop talks brought us toward some consensus but we still had disagreements. The outline of ideas I wish to present here is my own, therefore, and not that of the group which has so much influenced my thinking. The formulation I want to make is only a beginning. Even if it is right, it leaves many questions unanswered, and therefore much room for further disagreement. In so complex a matter as education, this is as it should be. What I am going to say applies, I believe, to all aspects of elementary education. However, let me stick to science teaching.

My outline is divided into three patterns or phases of school work in science. These phases are different from each other in the relations they induce between children, materials of study, and teachers. Another way of putting it is that they differ in the way they make a classroom look and sound. My claim is that good science teaching moves from one phase to the other in a pattern which, though it will not follow mechanical rules or ever be twice the same, will evolve according to simple principles. There is no necessary order among these phases, and for this reason, I avoid calling them I, II, and III, and use instead some mnemonic signs which have, perhaps, a certain suggestiveness: ○, △, and □.

○Phase. There is a time, much greater in amount than commonly allowed, which should be devoted to free and unguided exploratory work (call it play if you wish; I call it work). Children are given materials and equipment—*things*—and are allowed to construct, test, probe, and experiment without superimposed questions or instructions. I call this ○ phase "Messing About," honoring the philosophy of the Water Rat, who absentmindedly ran his boat into the bank, picked himself up, and went on without interrupting the joyous train of thought:

"—about in boats—or *with* boats . . . In or out of 'em, it doesn't matter. Nothing seems really to matter, that's the charm of it. Whether you get away, or whether you don't; whether you arrive at your destination or whether you reach somewhere else, or whether you never get anywhere at all, you're always busy, and you never do anything in particular: and when you've done it there's always something else to do, and you can do it if you like, but you'd much better not."

In some jargon, this kind of situation is called "unstructured," which is misleading; some doubters call it chaotic, which it need never be. "Unstructured" is misleading because there is always a kind of structure to *what* is presented in a class, as there was to the world of boats and the river, with its rushes and weeds and mud that smelled like plumcake. Structure in this sense is of the utmost importance, depending on the children, the teacher, and the backgrounds of all concerned.

Let me cite an example from my own recent experiences. Simple frames, each designed to support two or three weights on strings, were handed out one morning in a fifth-grade class. There was one such frame for each pair of children. In two earlier trial classes, we had introduced the same equipment with a much more "structured" beginning, demonstrating the striking phenomenon of coupled pendulums and raising questions about it before the laboratory work was allowed to begin. If there was guidance this time, however, it came only from the apparatus—a pendulum is to swing! In starting this way I, for one, naively assumed that a couple of hours of "Messing About" would suffice. After two hours, instead, we allowed two more and, in the end, a stretch of several weeks. In all this time, there was little or no evidence of boredom or confusion. Most of the questions we might have planned for came up unscheduled.

Why did we permit this length of time? First, because in our previous classes we had noticed that things went well when we veered toward "Messing About" and not as well when we held too tight a rein on what we wanted the children to do. It was clear that these children had had insufficient acquaintance with the sheer phenomena of pendulum motion and needed to build an apperceptive background, against which a more analytical sort of knowledge could take form and make sense. Second, we allowed things to develop this way because we decided we were getting a new kind of feedback from the children and were eager to see where and by what paths their interests would evolve and carry them. We were rewarded with a higher level of involvement and a much greater diversity of experiments. Our role was only to move from spot to spot, being helpful but never consciously prompting or directing. In spite of —because of!—this lack of direction, these fifth-graders became very familiar with pendulums. They varied the conditions of motion in many ways, exploring differences in length and amplitude, using different sorts of bobs, bobs in clusters, and strings, etc. And have *you* tried the underwater pendulum? They did! There were many sorts of discoveries made, but we let them slip by without much adult resonance, beyond our spontaneous and manifest enjoyment of the phenomena. So discoveries were made, noted, lost, and made again. I think this is why the slightly pontifical phrase "discovery method" bothers me. When learning is at the most fundamental level, as it is here, with all the abstractions of Newtonian mechanics just around the corner, don't rush! When the mind is evolving the abstractions which will lead to physical comprehension, all of us must cross the line between ignorance and insight many times before we truly understand. Little facts, "discoveries" without the growth of insight, are *not* what we should seek to harvest. Such facts are only seedlings and should sometimes be let alone to grow into. . . .

I have illustrated the phase of "Messing About" with a constrained and inherently very elegant topic from physics. In other fields, the pattern will be different in detail, but the essential justification is the same. "Messing About" with what can be found in pond water looks much more like the Water Rat's own chosen field of study. Here, the implicit structure is that of nature in a very different mood from what is manifest in the austerities of things like pendular motion or planet orbits. And here, the need for sheer acquaintance with the variety of things and phenomena is more obvious, before one can embark on any of the roads toward the big generalizations or the big open questions of biology. Regardless of differences, there is a generic justification of "Messing About" that I would like, briefly, to touch upon.

This phase is important, above all, because it carries over into school that which is the source of most of what children have already learned, the roots of their moral, intellectual, and esthetic development. If education were defined, for the moment, to include everything that children have learned since birth, everything that has come to them from living in the natural and the human world, then by any sensible measure what has come before age five or six would outweigh all the rest. When we narrow the scope of education to what goes on in schools, we throw out the method of that early and spectacular progress at our peril. We know that five-year-olds are very unequal in their mastery of this or that. We also know that their histories are responsible for most of this inequality, utterly masking the congenital differences except in special cases. This is the immediate fact confronting us as educators in a society committed, morally and now by sheer economic necessity, to universal education.

To continue the cultivation of earlier ways of learning, therefore; to find *in school* the good beginnings, the liberating involvements that will make the kindergarten seem a garden to the child and not a dry and frightening desert, this is a need that requires much emphasis on the style of work I have called ○, or "Messing About." Nor does the garden in this sense end with a child's first school year, or his tenth, as though one could then put away childish things. As time goes on, through a good mixture of this with other phases of work,

"Messing About" evolves with the child and thus changes its quality. It becomes a way of working that is no longer childish though it remains always childlike, the kind of self-disciplined probing and exploring that is the essence of creativity.

The variety of the learning—and of inhibition against learning—that children bring from home when school begins is great, even within the limited range of a common culturę with common economic background (or, for that matter, within a single family). Admitting this, then if you cast your mind over the whole range of abilities and backgrounds that children bring to kindergarten, you see the folly of standardized and formalized beginnings. We are profoundly ignorant about the subtleties of learning but one principle ought to be asserted dogmatically: That there must be provided some continuity in the content, direction, and style of learning. Good schools begin with what children have *in fact* mastered, probe next to see what *in fact* they are learning, continue with what *in fact* sustains their involvement.

△ Phase. When children are led along a common path, there are always the advanced ones and always the stragglers. Generalized over the years of school routine, this lends apparent support to the still widespread belief in some fixed, inherent levels of "ability," and to the curious notions of "under-" and "over-achievement." Now, if you introduce a topic with a good deal of "Messing About," the variance does not decrease, it increases. From a conventional point of view, this means the situation gets worse, not better. But I say it gets better, not worse. If after such a beginning you pull in the reins and "get down to business," some children have happened to go your way already, and you will believe that you are leading these successfully. Others will have begun, however, to travel along quite different paths, and you have to tug hard to get them back on to yours. Through the eyes of these children you will see yourself as a dragger, not a leader. We saw this clearly in the pendulum class I referred to; the pendulum being a thing which seems deceptively simple but which raises many questions in no particular order. So the path which each child chooses is his best path.

The result is obvious, but it took me time to see it. If you once let children evolve their own learning along paths of their choosing, you then must see it through and *maintain* the individuality of their work. You cannot begin that way and then say, in effect, "That was only a teaser," thus using your adult authority to devalue what the children themselves, in the meantime, have found most valuable. So if "Messing About" is to be followed by, or evolve into, a stage where work is more externally guided and disciplined, there must be at hand what I call "Multiply Programmed" material; material that contains written and pictorial guidance of some sort for the student, but which is designed for the greatest possible variety of topics, ordering of topics, etc., so that for almost any given way into a subject that a child may evolve on his own, there is material available which he will recognize as helping him farther along that very way. Heroic teachers have sometimes done this on their own, but it is obviously one of the places where designers of curriculum materials can be of enormous help, designing those materials with a rich variety of choices for teacher and child, and freeing the teacher from the role of "leader-dragger" along a single preconceived path, giving the teacher encouragement and real logistical help in diversifying the activities of a group. Such material includes good equipment, but above all, it suggests many beginnings, paths from the familiar into the unknown. We did not have this kind of material ready for the pendulum class I spoke about earlier and still do not have it. I intend to work at it and hope others will.

It was a special day in the history of that pendulum class that brought home to me what was needed. My teaching partner was away (I had been the observer, she the teacher). To shift gears for what I saw as a more organized phase of our work, I announced that for a change we were all going to do the same experiment. I said it firmly and the children were, of course, obliging. Yet, I saw the immediate loss of interest in part of the class as soon as my experiment was proposed. It was designed to raise questions about the *length* of a pendulum, when the bob is multiple or odd-shaped. Some had come upon the germ of that question; others had had no reason to. As a college teacher I have tricks, and they worked here as well, so the class went well, in spite of the unequal readiness to look at "length." We hit common ground with rough blackboard pictures, many pendulums shown hanging from a common support, differing in length and the shape and size of bobs. Which ones will "swing together"? Because their eyes were full of real pendulums, I think, they could *see* those blackboard pictures swinging! A colloquium evolved which harvested the crop of insights that had been sowed and cultivated in previous weeks. I was left with a hollow feeling, nevertheless. It went well where, and only where, the class found common ground. Whereas in "Messing About" all things had gone uniformly well. In staff discussion afterward, it became clear that we had skipped an essential phase of our work, the one I am now calling $\triangle$ phase, or Multiply Programmed.

There is a common opinion, floating about, that a rich diversity of classroom work is possible only when a teacher has small classes. "Maybe *you* can do that; but you ought to try it in my class of 43!" I want to be the last person to belittle the importance of small classes. But in this particular case, the statement ought to be made that in a large class one cannot afford *not* to diversify children's work—or rather *not* to allow children to diversify, as they inevitably will, if given the chance. So-called "ability grouping" is a popular answer today, but it is no answer at all to the real questions of motivation. Groups which are lumped as equivalent with respect to the usual measures are just as diverse in their tastes and spontaneous interests as unstratified groups! The complaint that in heterogeneous classes the bright ones are likely to be bored because things go too slow for them ought to be met with another question: Does that mean that the slower students are *not* bored? When children have no autonomy in learning everyone is likely to be bored. In such situations the overworked teachers have to be "leader-draggers" always, playing the role of Fate in the old Roman proverb: "The Fates lead the willing; the unwilling they drag."

"Messing About" produces the early and indispensible autonomy and diversity. It is good—indispensible—for the opening game but not for the long middle game, where guidance is needed; needed to lead the willing! To illustrate once more from my example of the pendulum, I want to produce a thick set of cards—illustrated cards in a central file, or single sheets in plastic envelopes—to cover the following topics among others:

1. Relations of amplitude and period.
2. Relations of period and weight of bob.
3. How long is a pendulum (odd-shaped bobs)?

4. Coupled pendulums, compound pendulums.
5. The decay of the motion (and the idea of half-life).
6. String pendulums and stick pendulums—comparisons.
7. Underwater pendulums.
8. Arms and legs as pendulums (dogs, people, and elephants).
9. Pendulums of other kinds—springs, etc.
10. Bobs that drop sand for patterns and graphs.
11. Pendulum clocks.
12. Historical materials, with bibliography.
13. Cards relating to filmloops available, in class or library.
14. Cross-index cards to other topics, such as falling bodies, inclined planes, etc.
15.—75. Blank cards to be filled in by classes and teachers for others.

This is only an illustration; each area of elementary science will have its own style of Multiply Programmed materials. Of course, the ways of organizing these materials will depend on the subject. There should always be those blank cards, outnumbering the rest.

There is one final warning. Such a file is properly a kind of programming—but it is not the base of rote or merely verbal learning, taking a child little step by little step through the adult maze. Each item is simple, pictorial, and it guides by suggesting further explorations, not by replacing them. The cards are only there to relieve the teacher from a heroic task. And they are only there because there are apparatus, film, library, and raw materials from which to improvise.

☐ Phase. In the class discussion I referred to, about the meaning of *length* applied to a pendulum, I was reverting back to the college-teacher habit of lecturing; I said it went very well in spite of the lack of Multiply Programmed background, one that would have taken more of the class through more of the basic pendulum topics. It was not, of course, a lecture in the formal sense. It was question-and-answer, with discussion between children as well. But still, I was guiding it and fishing for the good ideas that were ready to be born, and I was telling a few stories, for example, about Galileo. Others could do it better. I was a visitor, and am still only an amateur. I was successful then only because of the long build-up of latent insight, the kind of insight that the Water Rat had stored up from long afternoons of "Messing About" in boats. It was more than he could ever have been told, but it gave him much to tell. This is not all there is to learning, of course; but it is the magical part, and the part most often killed in school. The language is not yet that of the textbook, but with it even a dull-looking textbook can come alive. One boy thinks the length of a pendulum should be measured from the top to what he calls the "center of gravity." If they have not done a lot of work with balance materials, this phase is for most children only the handle of an empty pitcher, or a handle without a pitcher at all. So I did not insist on the term. Incidentally, it is not quite correct physics anyway, as those will discover who work with the stick pendulum. Although different children had specialized differently in the way they worked with pendulums, there were common elements, increasing with time, which would sustain a serious and extended class discussion. It is this pattern of discussion I want to emphasize by calling it a separate, □ phase. It includes lecturing, formal or informal. In the above situation, we were all quite ready for a short talk about Galileo, and ready to ponder the question whether there was any relation between the way unequal weights fall together and the way they swing together when hanging on strings of the same length. Here we were approaching a question—a rather deep one, not to be disposed of in fifteen minutes—of theory, going from the concrete perceptual to the abstract conceptual. I do not believe that such questions will come alive either through the early "Messing About" or through the Multiply Programmed work with guiding questions and instructions. I think they come primarily with discussion, argument, the full colloquium of children and teacher. Theorizing in a creative sense needs the content of experience and the logic of experimentation to support it. But these do not automatically lead to conscious abstract thought. Theory is square! □

We of the Elementary Science Study are probably identified in the minds of those acquainted with our work (and sometimes perhaps in our own minds) with the advocacy of laboratory work and a free, fairly ○ style of laboratory work at that. This may be right and justified by the fact that prevailing styles of science teaching are □ most of the time, much too much of the time. But what we criticize for being too much and too early, we must work to re-admit in its proper place.

I have put ○, △, and □ in that order, but I do not advocate any rigid order; such phases may be mixed in many ways and ordered in many ways. Out of the colloquium comes new "Messing About." Halfway along a programmed path, new phenomena are accidentally observed. In an earlier, more structured class, two girls were trying obediently to reproduce some phenomena of coupled pendulums I had demonstrated. I heard one say, "Ours isn't working right." Of course, pendulums never misbehave; it is not in their nature; they always do what comes naturally, and in this case, they were executing a curious dance of energy transference, promptly christened the "twist." It was a new phenomenon, which I had not seen before, nor had several physicists to whom, in my delight, I later showed it. Needless to say, this led to a good deal of "Messing About," right then and there.

What I have been concerned to say is only that there are, as I see it, three major phases of good science teaching; that no teaching is likely to be optimal which does not mix all three; and that the one most neglected is that which made the Water Rat go dreamy with joy when he talked about it. At a time when the pressures of prestige education are likely to push children to work like hungry laboratory rats in a maze, it is good to remember that their wild, watery cousin, reminiscing about the joys of his life, uttered a profound truth about education.

The Bird in the Window

The order of these essays and talks is not chronological, but here a four-year gap is particularly visible. "Messing About" was written just after our return to Colorado from the Elementary Science Study in Boston. It is addressed to American teachers and deals with American school experience. "The Bird in the Window," like "I, Thou, and It" is an impromptu talk to an audience of British teachers. The difference is not only one of style and of 7,000 miles, but also in the practical experience of the two sets of teacher audiences.

For two or three decades British primary schools have been gradually (and very unevenly) diverging in style from a traditional pattern still dominant in the United States, a fact now much discussed and studied here. In the period 1965–69 I had been trying to bridge the gap in my own thinking and practice and to understand the historical roots of this transatlantic divergence. Then in 1968 we had a fellowship from my University and we used it to get more first-hand acquaintance with early education in England, which we had previously sampled only briefly. We spent the Autumn term at the Northumberland College of Education. I worked in the college while my wife volunteered in a superb nursery school in Newcastle-upon-Tyne, of which we made a film.*

In the Spring of 1969 we went to the University of Leicester and the Advisory Centre of the Leicestershire education authority. Leicestershire was one of the first English local authorities to be much talked about in the United States, and in this way gained the reputation for being the hub of progress in England. The facts are, of course, much less simple.

Our visit was, in a way, a stepping back in time—American time. It was a stepping back to the world surveyed by Lawrence Cremin of Columbia University's Teachers College,† of the boom of "progressive" schools and all the rest. For Frances Hawkins, as the talk will tell you, it was nothing

---

**Northumberland Children,* The Mountain View Center, University of Colorado, 1972.
†Lawrence A. Cremin, *The Transformation of the School.* Alfred A. Knopf, 1961.

radically new. It was a promising rebirth—on a larger scale, and on a steadier base.

The idea of progress has never been very adequately analyzed, and the genuine progress of British primary education, contrasted with our own regression, is a challenging example. When a small boom of interest in "British Primary Schools" developed in the United States, it was often taken for granted that there was some national plan guiding the new trend or some single center of radial influence. When on the other hand one actually hops about from one part of England to another one gains the impression that rather radical improvements, still fresh in the minds of teachers and heads, are seen as being almost entirely local and autonomous. Good teachers in the North Riding of Yorkshire, a county unsung elsewhere, were a bit irked by the suggestion that their ideas and practices had come from anywhere outside, let alone from a college in London or from some county in the Midlands.

One is confronted with two opposite habits of belief about progress, one tracing it to a central leadership, the other to sheer spontaneity. One reflects an authoritarian view of history, one a Populist view. And both are, in general, quite wrong. Good educational systems are like the good English classrooms discussed in the talk; they do not fit either simplistic model.

In the United States we have just lived through a decade in which authoritarian or technocratic ideas of educational progress have been in vogue. Improvement comes down from above or in from beyond. It comes from national curriculum development projects or from other forms of "educational R and D" sponsored by federal or private foundation grants. Progress is, in a word, engineered.

But of course the populist view is wrong too. In infant and junior schools in England one sees among the innovative ones a fair measure of similarity, often a bit too much of it. But the good teachers are in command of what they are doing. They want help but they have the bit in their teeth and no ring in the nose. The older ones have worked at it for a good many years and they are justly proud of their work. To a surprising extent they are not concerned about what is going on in another county or town.

But when one backs off one encounters a sort of professional network of local inspectors or advisers, national inspectors, college lecturers, headmistresses and headmasters who get around. Such persons spend real time working in schools, they are involved in intensive holiday courses for teachers, they get to some national and regional meetings. They constitute a sort of professional circulatory system. I don't want to eulogize them as a whole; my

English friends, conscious of their own needs, would laugh at me for doing so. But I think such advisers have a dominant attitude of respect for the independence of the teachers they work with. They see themselves as teachers also, and as facilitators. They have a great deal of personal authority, the best of them, but they are not seen as Authorities.

There are other important points of difference-in-similarity between our two systems of public education, but singly or jointly they do not in any obvious way add up to an explanation of our divergences. Every proffered explanation can also be seen, in perspective, as part of the very thing to be explained. That is an essential part of what progress means. It deals with matters too complex to be engineered or predicted; the best use of intelligence, and of theory, is to help us take part in them, not to "explain" them. It is not the "why" which counts in the study of evolution, but the "what" and the "how."

It was this matter of educational theory which concerned me in the talk that follows. One part of progress is a dissolving and recrystallizing of ideas to fit change, to guide it better and, above all, to allow for the formulation of new concerns and problems which that progress itself has begun to make visible. The old familiar framework of ideas has lost its cutting edge and remains only to hamper, a source of ideology and confusion.

The Bird in the Window
(1969)

The reason we made our way to England this year is that we had come, over a period of time, to believe that in England we could find more schools of the sort we wanted to look at, and more people to talk to who were involved in these schools, than anywhere else in the world. I think that is probably true. Since we've been here, since the autumn of 1968, we have, of course, had a chance to get over any romantic illusions we might have had about the trouble-free schools of your country, but on the whole, as far as we are concerned, the romance holds up pretty well.

I want to talk about a topic that I know is vexing many people nowadays. It vexes you because you have probably got the matter coming up soon and it vexes us because we are trying to start some battles in the United States. I think you will find yourself in a more defensive position, because you have done some things in primary schools which we've been trying, rather unsuccessfully, to get started in the United States. We're more on the offensive because so far we haven't made much of a dent, in terms of changing some of the rudimentary patterns of traditional school life, patterns which you are very familiar with from your own past. It's an interesting historical business. There has been some interchange over a long period between the United States and England, particularly with respect to primary education. I think there was a time about three or four decades ago when the slogans of progressive education were probably more resonant in the United States than in England, although in England there have been for a long time the traditions of progressive education, going back to the early influence of Froebel and others. Of course, we have had the same influences. We've produced some fraction of the materials, some of the components of infant school work of the kind that would be familiar to those of you who are infant teachers. You have produced a larger fraction of them, and some fractions have come from other sources. There's been a kind of international pooling of workaday ideas about the organization and the equipment of infant classes.

When we first walked into an infant class in Leicestershire my wife, who has been a kindergarten teacher for many years, sniffed the air, and said, "This is familiar, but I haven't seen it in the United States for a long time." What is now the tradition of a majority of your infant schools was the tradition in the United States of only one year of school, called kindergarten, which was as you probably know the year that was put in under the first grade of our schools, starting at age six. This five-to-six-year-old group was not introduced universally in the United States but did come about in many states as a result of this same progressive education movement which managed to get in under the establishment, so to speak. It created a new year of school which had a pattern quite radically different from the pattern which we call primary, a term which in the United States means the ages six to seven, seven to eight, and eight to nine. The kindergarten was almost without influence on the later years of school. In a typical American school of the 1930's you would see a kindergarten which you infant teachers would recognize as very familiar in style. Then you would go into a first grade which was very formal and almost completely lacking in concrete equipment of any kind, which was dominated by primers and pencil and paper, and which had the children sitting in neat rows and columns. The most extensive influence I know of from the kindergarten in the United States was that there was a great burst of progressivism which resulted in the unbolting of the desks from the floor. But that didn't mean they were ever moved! It was a symbolic achievement. Children were free to move but in fact they were not allowed to.

One of the things which we contributed to this movement was a rather good philosopher, John Dewey. Nobody *reads* Dewey very much but everybody knows how to say some things about him. I think actually John Dewey is very well worth reading, but not unless you're prepared to dig in and not unless you're prepared to argue with him, to try to recover the context in which he was talking, and to talk with your friends about it. Dewey is responsible for some good and very careful thinking which is almost totally unknown in most educational circles. When I was an undergraduate, students in education were usually required to read a book by Dewey called *How We Think*, which is a neat little thing he did for pedagogical purposes at some point. It classified thinking into stages and talks about the transition from one stage to another. It's dull, and the important ideas in the book are developed elsewhere much better, with much more sense of qualification and realism and with much more vitality. But there was at least a period in which Dewey was widely known in the United States and in which many people in colleges of education were devoted to him, at least in theory. But these people had very little influence on the schools. So neither the influence of the kindergarten nor the influence of the colleges of education was enough to make any real dent in the American public school system. This system isn't overtly authoritarian: it doesn't keep you out the way that schools in some continental countries might tend to do; it's just very resistant, it has lots of built-in feedback mechanisms for avoiding change. You can get in and you can do something and things will sail along very nicely but two years later you won't find much residue of effect.

Dewey was not only a very good, very thoughtful, very deep

philosopher in many ways, but he was also a man who had personal acquaintance with children and with schools. As you probably know, he was for a time involved in the operation of a school which was called "The Experimental School" at the University of Chicago. The record of that school is quite an interesting one. The pattern of what was generally identified as progressive education was dominant throughout the primary or elementary years. Dewey was a theorist, however, who didn't savor the practical details. He knew them, he learned: there's a quality in much of his writing which couldn't be there unless he was familiar with teachers and schools. But he loved to take off into realms of theory and polemic. He hardly ever illustrates what he is saying with any of the concrete stuff that would make a teacher say, "Ah, yes, I really know what he's talking about." So, he is a difficult person in his own way. Well, because of the battle we may have to fight—or the battle we would like to fight—I think that this level of concern and of theory, of getting our ideas straight and getting them into a form which we can verbalize clearly and which will hold up against neutral or even hostile criticism if necessary, this is an important thing.

I for one have found that since I've become practically involved in work connected with the early years I've acquired a great distaste for theorizing in the old style. I don't like to talk about general questions having to do with learning and teaching in the abstract, because I am so aware that when you do this you talk past people all the time. If they don't already know what you're talking about, if they're not already tuned to your wave-length, you can say things and then when they say them back to you you don't recognize what's happened. This is a very real difficulty, and it isn't a difficulty that has to do with the degree of academic training people have had: I think it's a difficulty in principle. Another way of putting this is to say that I think teachers—not all teachers but those who have a genuinely professional feeling about their work and who have learned and grown in their profession over a long period of time—do know more about things than is codified in any book. I think they know more about the psychology of learning than is written in the books. The psychologists, unfortunately—and I might be forced to name a few exceptions but I don't think there would be many—are unacquainted with this level of operation. They don't know children.

They don't observe children. They don't know teachers except as people they teach. They don't regard teachers as their instructors in psychology. To do so would turn upside down some sort of social pecking order and that would be almost unthinkable. But it may need to be done. More is known and understood on the practical level by people who work effectively and successfully with children than is codified in any of the books. And it's doubtful whether the codification which is in the books is for the most part particularly relevant to this level of knowledge and understanding. When you try to formulate ideas about learning and about education you have to get into the psychologists' league and play that kind of game one way or another. You have to try to make explicit, to find ways of verbalizing, things which you'd much rather just know in your bones and in your practice. Teachers are craftsmen, artisans, artists, whatever you want to call them, not theoreticians. And just as the good craftsmen of the Renaissance expressed themselves through the work they did and not through writing books about it (or research monographs) so teachers express themselves through the work that they do, through the human beings who have been their pupils, and not by writing little papers.

On the other hand, in the academic world the thing is geared the other way and the end-all and be-all of existence is that you write a little paper. Those of us who are in the academic world are very much torn. If we get involved in school work at a practical level we come to realize how empty a lot of the theoretical discussion is compared to the practice. We either struggle to express it—some of us are foolish enough to keep on trying to do this—or we acquire a distaste for our own academic ways of functioning. And I know that I myself am very much torn as the result of this. I want on the one hand to do battle with the psychologists and a good many of the American educationists, but that requires that I get into their league and read their papers and books and so on. But then I'm very dissatisfied because they're not talking about things I think are important, and I don't myself quite know how to talk about those things that seem to me to be important. So I'm in trouble. Everybody in this business is in one kind of trouble or another. Other people who haven't been in the academic world feel, often incorrectly, I think, that they don't have the means to express themselves, to develop theoretical ideas. In fact, I think they more nearly have the means than do the rest of us, because they have the raw experience, or, rather, the experience they have culled and analyzed over and over again to guide their practical work. What we want to do is somehow to get those ideas not only into practice but into the marketplace where they can be argued.

I want to try, with just one or two ideas that seem to me to be crucial, to talk about learning and teaching. It is said, and I think sometimes with justice, that the traditionalists in education have a more cogent rationale for the things they believe in than do the progressives, with whom I would identify myself. We are people who talk in vague generalities and don't really have any consistent theory at all. When we are called on to discuss something we tend to point to particular concrete examples rather than to develop tight, consistent logical positions. I think this is often true. But it has also been true in the past in other places, and the places I know best are in the history of science. I think it's always true in principle that when new ideas are in the process of development those who are devoted to them and who are trying to bring them to definition have a very hard time expressing themselves, whereas those who represent some established order have a very easy time because the language patterns which have been worked out fit their ideas, against which the innovators are reacting. And the language the innovators have to use is, therefore, the language of their opponents, so to speak. You can find many examples of this in the history of science. For example, consider the very slow acceptance of something like the germ theory of disease. People who advocated this point of view were simply laughed out of court because the way they had to talk was in a framework of ideas which made the notion of little, invisible micro-organisms something that just had no reality at all. There weren't yet words for the things which are now part of the established pattern in, say, medical education. You had to coin words, and you had to use words in a new meaning, words that meant something else to other people.

This, I think, is very much our situation now. So, for example, I have said on various occasions that it seems to me a fundamental aim of education to organize schools, classrooms and our own performance as teachers in order to help children acquire the capacity for significant choice, and that learning is really a process of choice. If children are deprived of significant choice in their daily activities in school, if all their choices are made for them, then the most important thing that education is concerned with is simply being bypassed. Children have to be encouraged, supported in self-directed activity. And that means that you give children certain kinds of freedom. But now you're talking a language which has a lot of emotional loading. So, if you believe in giving children a lot of freedom this means, in terms of the emotional loading, that you are withdrawing discipline. To say the child is free is to say you are not coercing him and if you think of discipline as coercive then you are not imposing a discipline on the life of the child in school and that means you are turning him loose to do whatever he wants to, and now we're on the merry-go-round of the old, familiar argument.

It's very clear, isn't it, that in traditional ways of thinking the opposition between freedom and discipline is of this kind. Discipline is an externally imposed mode of acting under the influence of something called "authority" and authority is something externally imposed and coercive. Look the word up in the Oxford English Dictionary if you don't believe me. There is no other primary meaning of "authority" except that of constituted authority, legally constituted authority or the authority of a person who has power because he has status or because he has special knowledge or something of the sort. Now, if that's what authority means and if discipline is something which is imposed by authority, then freedom in the usual sense is simply negative, and that means you're getting rid of authority. So the stereotype of progressive education is, "Turn the children loose and let them do whatever they want to." If you don't do that then it means you are imposing structure, order, discipline, and so you have this dichotomy between two things which are inalterably opposed: that's the way our common, everyday marketplace language works. Whenever you get into a futile, frustrating argument with somebody about education, you recognize that this is the pattern you have allowed yourself to fall into. The interesting thing is that you get annoyed at the other person for pulling this trick on you, but you also get annoyed at yourself because you've let yourself get trapped in it. You don't want to say something, but he's made you say it, and you've had to assent because that's the way the ordinary language works. What is sometimes called "ordinary language philosophy" has sometimes been used, illegitimately, to support such arguments. One just rings the changes on the ordinary stereotypes of English speech and forces you into a corner. He doesn't force you very hard and you may not be much impressed but he thinks he's forcing you. If you take *his* meanings of the words then everything is pretty clear and cut and dried and people who talk the language of progressivism are mushy and unaware of the logic of their own language.

So I think we are in a difficult position because we're trying to say something that's rather genuinely new, and I don't think that our ordinary modes of expression allow us to do this without falling into traps. We have to think very carefully about what we're saying, how we're saying it, and what kinds of illustrations we use to pin down our meanings. It's a difficult task to argue and to reason cogently at a level which corresponds to the understanding of many practicing teachers. "Authority" is a particularly interesting case. If you look at the practice of the best primary schools (I'll reserve to myself the privilege of saying which ones they are but I think you'd probably agree with me) one of the important roles of the teacher in those schools is something that could be described by the word "authority." I think it is a different meaning of the word, and one which isn't in the Oxford English Dictionary, or if it is, it's buried in some special context. Authority is a way in which human beings are related to each other and it is connected with the word "respect." If someone plays a role as an authority in your life this means that you respect him. His activities or contribution to your existence you value because it has proved itself to *be* valuable. If you respect and trust someone you may follow his suggestions or his style, knowing that you are getting something that you will come to value even though you don't yet know enough to develop it for yourself.

In other words, authority is one of the primary sources of learning. To be an authority in this sense, to be a teacher whom children honestly respect because you give them something which helps them on the way and which they know they couldn't get for themselves, is to be a teacher. If you are not that kind of authority, you are not a good teacher, you're not functioning properly as a teacher. Therefore the word "authority" is very important, but if we let it get captured by that kind of opposition which is arguing against the primary importance of encouraging children's autonomous, self-directed learning, then we don't have any way to talk about this important part of teaching.

There's another way you can look at this which is very familiar. The polarity that is in the ordinary language reasserts itself between two stereotypes of the classroom, and I think many of us are guilty of these stereotypes ourselves. There's the old, authoritarian classroom—notice the word "authority" again in the same sense: an authoritarian is one who advocates or who imposes, who believes in the propriety of imposing discipline by authority, and that means by coercion. The word has a disparaging tone. So there's the authoritarian classroom and in opposition to it there is the permissive, *laissez-faire* classroom. Get a lot of good, stimulating environment for children and turn them loose in it and seven years later they'll come up with the requisite education. Or at least they will have been expressing themselves, they will have been creative—and all the other "sloppy" words that the philosophers object to. So, again, we're in this trap. How do you devise ways of calling to people's attention that there *is* such a trap? You can say to an opponent in an argument, "Look, I don't want to accept this dichotomy, this is not what I'm talking about." But then you have to have some general ways of describing what you are doing. You can give illustrations, but your opponent will say "Yes, that's very nice, but you can't build a whole school on that basis." Or he'll say, "Yes, but that's an unusually good teacher and after all we must be prepared for the ordinary sort of teacher who can't do that." These arguments are all so stale, so repeated, so rehearsed that you can hardly mention them in any audience without getting a lot of people smiling because it's in the experience of all of us. Well, let's try.

One scheme that I've tried is to say, here is the authoritarian classroom, the stereotype: children are doing things in unison, they're told to open the spelling book at page 23 and do the following and when they're busy doing that the teacher goes and gives some similar busywork to other children or perhaps has *all* the children doing the same thing at the same time. I won't develop that, we all know what it is; it's a conventional stereotype of a classroom. Many classrooms have approximated it and still do. Then there is the permissive classroom in which children are running wild and running out of steam, which they will inevitably do if they're given a good environment and then not given any kind of reinforcement and help; they'll try all the things that are tryable by them at that stage, they'll exhaust the possibilities and then the possibilities will get narrower and narrower. Finally they won't have any choices left and they'll get into the same kinds of troubles that children get into who live in the authoritarian classroom because both of them are now bored. Children who are bored exhibit similar symptoms no matter what the cause of the boredom is. You have behavior problems and discipline problems and all that sort of thing.

So, how can you break out of this contrast? Well, one way of doing it is to think of a triangle. The authoritarian classroom is at one corner, the permissive classroom is at another and at the third is a classroom which isn't either of them. It's as far off that axis as you can be. Because you have that contrast of teacher direction versus child freedom sometimes you look at this classroom from one point of view and it will look authoritarian and other times you will look at it from the other point of view and it will look permissive. In fact it isn't either of them and it's a distortion of the classroom to describe it in this language at all. So, how will you describe this third alternative? Well, one thing I certainly don't want to do is invent a label for it. God help us, I think we ought to get along without labels for things that are really important. Maybe that's a mistake, maybe you have to have a label but I, at any rate, don't intend to invent one. It's a classroom in which there are two kinds of choices being made, one kind by children, the other kind by the teacher. So it isn't either the teacher making all the choices or the children making all the choices. It's a more complex situation, and we all know that it is. We're trying consciously to break out of the stereotype.

Sometimes children are making decisions because the classroom, the atmosphere of the school, the behavior of the teacher are such that they're encouraged to make choices and they have alternatives before them that are meaningful to them: you can properly say they are making choices. The teacher is observing what they are doing, following what they are doing and interpreting what they are doing, diagnosing their state, their level, their special problems and thinking of ways of making provision for them in that situation. This is now the choice, the freedom, of the teacher. What a teacher does in this way is just as genuinely a matter of choice as anything the children do. So it's absurd to say that this is a classroom which is permissive. A teacher may in such a classroom make a choice, sometimes quite properly, which involves a very firm use of the adult role. "Why do you make me do this?" "Because I'm bigger than you are and let's not argue about it." If that was the only kind of choice the teacher was making it would be pretty bad, but it's quite another thing to say that no good teacher ever makes choices of that sort, because this is patently false. There are times when coercion in particular is a very salutary thing. There are times when it's the only *educational* thing that you can do.

We know a young man who told us in great detail that the first time in his life he thought he might be a normal human being was when a teacher whom he had struck caused him to be arrested and put in jail. This was a vital component of his education. To say that you could have had the same effect with sweet reasonableness is just plain false. He'd had sweet reasonableness all his life and that in fact was the chief malady he was suffering from. On the other hand, a teacher may at other stages be consciously withdrawing, consciously be non-interventionist, may give the child complete freedom with a perhaps anxious calculation that the only way in which that child is going to get over a particular hump is to be entirely on his own in confronting it. These are contrasting kinds of decisions made by the same teacher under different circumstances for different children. So the whole range of choices is there. Some are very like the authoritarian model and some are very like the permissive model, but they are quite different in character because this is now a teacher operating, dealing with human beings and using observation, interpretation, wit, strategy, to play the role in reinforcing the self-directed learning of children. It can't be put more simply than that because it isn't any simpler. It seems to me that such a description has to be made and it has to become familiar. I probably don't do it right. I'm only making a rough cut at it; there are lots of qualifications, lots of filling in of detail, lots of discussion about how you know when to do this and that and the other thing. It's a very complex matter. But these are questions that can be solved in practice to some good approximation, otherwise we wouldn't have good teachers. There may not be an elegant theoretical formulation about it but it's still possible to describe the range of considerations that are involved in a teacher's making intelligent choices.

Once you are committed to the belief in the primacy, the priority, of children's choice-making capacities as the main thing that education is after, then there are many things that follow which likewise run afoul of the traditional stereotypes. Once you accept this basic aim of education you discover some other things that come along with it that are vital to the process. For example, if a teacher has children doing things, or ostensibly doing things, that are pretty much according to a pattern which he has laid down, then the opportunity for significantly observing the child's behavior is very much diminished. If you tell a child to do a set task and there are many ways of failing and one way of succeeding—solving a particular kind of set problem that has a unique right answer, for example—then essentially the only thing you can observe is the success or failure of the child in doing that particular task. This will divide children into categories, but no more. There may be some incidental observations you make along the way—some children groan when set the task; others try to act cheerful about it and so on. But you don't really learn much from the success or the failure of the children in a situation where you are requiring uniformity of behavior from every child. Whereas, if you encourage diversity, which you're bound to do if you encourage choice, then you will observe that much-too-large number of human beings doing different things. The range of choices they make is very wide and therefore the amount of information you get about them is much greater. It is just common observation that if you watch a child working with a particular kind of material quite successfully and avoiding everything else, you're learning something about that child which is a much more important guide to your behavior as a teacher than his success or failure in particular set tasks. If you give a child a choice, for example, and he does nothing but work with paints and acquires a certain status in the class because he does have something of a flair in painting that other children don't have, but he's a total failure in everything else—he simply avoids everything else, he doesn't read, he doesn't write, and so on—then you know a great deal about the child that is relevant to you as a teacher. What strategies you will use now will be very much determined by your knowledge of the way this child has homed in on one activity and avoided a lot of others.

I still have very limited personal experience in teaching primary school children, so I speak only as an amateur. My experience has been with college students. I do believe they're not really so different under the skin, but there are some differences. Mainly, college students have learned very well how to avoid giving you important kinds of diagnostic information. They know how to look bright, alert and to pretend they've turned you on when in fact they've turned you off fifteen minutes before. Nine-year-olds don't know how to do this or at least don't care to do it, in my experience. So I learned much more about myself as a teacher as soon as I went to that age. And even more when I first, with fear and trembling, got involved with four- and five-year-olds. One of the things that became very clear to me was that when children were engaged in a considerable diversity of activities, I had no trouble at all remembering what they were doing and no trouble recalling information about their behavior and what it probably signified. Whereas when they were all doing the same set piece I'd have to go around and make records all the time in order to keep up with them. In fact, I think the familiar phenomenon called "The Test" is largely a crutch to replace the good means of evaluation we have when we don't suppress children's capacity for choice. Children simply distinguish themselves individually when they're working at different tasks in different ways. You get so much more information you don't have trouble remembering.

Many teachers in the United States who've become involved with us and are somewhat interested in the things we are doing and think maybe they will try some of them bring up this question: "Yes, but how will we test them, because they'll all be doing different things?" And again, that's part of that stereotyped pattern. How can you test? If people are not doing the same thing you can't compare them. And you say, "Yes, that's true, isn't it." But that's terribly unsatisfactory, because there's that hole left there, that demand for evaluation. Of course you're evaluating much more effectively, in another meaning of the word. But you've got to say what that meaning is, because it isn't the business of putting people on a linear scale. It's a much richer scale you're putting them on, with many dimensions to it.

You're saying, "This child is best at telling stories, this child is best at numbers and this child is best at catching frogs!" These are three dimensions and each of them gives a different permutation of the children. That's the way human beings really are. It is not the way the traditional demands of education have seen them and therefore we have real problems in meeting the traditional demands; that is, in meeting the people who make the traditional demands with the kind of information we want to give them. So, there is a very close and important relation between children's actual level of choice-making in the classroom, or in the field if they're in the field, and our own ability to interpret and diagnose, but it's not the kind of thing that will yield information on a paper and pencil test of any kind that anybody I know has ever devised. And I doubt in principle whether it can be devised because the paper and pencil test imposes a set of criteria which are preconceived by the tester and this reduces not necessarily just to one but to not very many dimensions of comparison. The teacher who is skillful at this kind of observation can tell you a great deal that's quite important about a child but will not give you numbers on scales because the nature of the thing being measured is not a lot of little points along a line; it's a lot of points that are in different directions defined by completely different qualities and attributes. Many of these are not in any catalog. They are too numerous to catalog.

The demand for testing is bound to be one we have to confront, to think through. I'm not making any recommendations for how to cope with this on the practical level. I'm just saying that I don't think the demand for this sort of thing on the practical level should confuse us about our basic thinking, as I'm afraid it sometimes does. We say, "I would like to think that way but it isn't practical." Nonsense! In thinking, the only important question is whether it's true or not, not whether it's practical. When you're making decisions about how you're going to behave, you may have to make compromises, but for heaven's sake, let's not start shading our beliefs in order to make an uncomfortable situation more comfortable to live in, because that doesn't really make it more comfortable.

Another thing that comes up here has to do with the business of curriculum. There was a time, I think, when the word "curriculum" didn't mean what it means now. I'm not sure what it means in

England. In the United States a curriculum is apt to mean the whole works—curriculum, syllabus, timetable—because in the United States many groups of people who have been involved in curriculum development have in fact spelled everything out at a level of detail that amounts almost to giving daily instructions to the teacher about what to do next. This means that the choices are not available to the children: the choices are not even available to the teacher unless the teacher is bold enough to disregard the curriculum guide. The choices are made "up there" by somebody. The word "curriculum" used to mean a general outline of subject matter and areas of competence that children were supposed to be systematically exposed to. You wanted them to understand arithmetic, for example. You didn't list 25 number facts for the first three months. That wasn't curriculum. That was something that some teacher might do, but it was no concern of the adult community, because the curriculum was primarily a set of decisions by the adult community about what children ought to be learning and how the general aims of education could be made more specific in terms of areas of competence and skill, subject matter and so on.

Dewey, for example, is very strong in asserting that The Experimental School, which he ran for a time, had a definite curriculum and there was no freedom to depart from this curriculum. This was imposed: it was a pattern which could be argued about, it wasn't sacrosanct, but at any given time there was a curriculum and everybody understood what it was. Within this framework, teachers were *enormously* free to pursue these general subject-matter situations in any way they wanted to. It was quite clear also, to many of them at least, that an important group involved in making those decisions was the children themselves. I don't know how romanticized they are—it's hard to tell at this distance in time—but if you read some of the accounts of what some teachers and some children in that school did you can see that they were having a great good time making their way through some aspect of the curriculum but diverging all over the place. They were diverging into other areas which were also on the curriculum. Nobody regarded it as a waste of time, therefore, if in the process of studying some primitive society they got heavily involved in the craft of pottery, because that also was part of the curriculum. So there was great freedom within a general framework that was rather clearly spelled out. I think today we would find this framework to be a bit special and narrow and would perhaps accuse Dewey of being a bit of a traditionalist about some of it. But it was very interesting for me to discover that Dewey in no sense subscribed to the *laissez-faire* belief that the curriculum was up to the children, so to speak. These were decisions made in the patterning, the organization of the school itself, and in the provisioning of the school. Well, we all make such provisions, don't we? We can't dodge the responsibility for the things we put in classrooms. These are not put there at the request of children—they may be added to at the request of children, they may be subtracted from because children don't use some of them, but that represents our learning and not the direct decision of the children.

The other problem that we face, however, is that as soon as we talk about self-directed learning this implies—correctly, I think—that we cannot lay out in advance a track that children are going to follow, because we don't yet know the things we will learn by observing them that will cause us to make decisions we haven't yet thought of. Therefore, there is an essential lack of predictability about what's going to happen in a good classroom, not because there is no control, but precisely because there is control, of the right kind; precisely because the teacher is basing his decisions on observation of the actual children in their actual situation, their actual problems, their actual interests and the accidental things that happen along the way that nobody can anticipate. A power shovel moves in next door to the school: this throws all your plans for studying batteries and bulbs into a cocked hat—or it should! But, you say, there are many aspects to science and this is also part of the curriculum. You can't anticipate those things. Everyone knows that the best times in teaching have always been the consequences of some little accident that happened to direct attention in some new way, to revitalize an old interest which has died out or to create a brand new interest that you hadn't had any notion about how to introduce. Suddenly, there it is. The bird flies in the window and that's the miracle you needed. Somebody once said about great discoveries in science, "Accidents happen to those that deserve them." If the bird coming in the window is just a nuisance you don't deserve it, and in fact it never happens. If you deserve it, the bird *will* fly in the window or there'll be a door that opens into the jungle. There will be some romance around the corner that will be there to be captured. This is again something very different from the stereotype of the permissive classroom because what's involved all along is a teacher who is making educational capital out of the interests and choices of children and out of the accidents that happen along the way, as well as out of his own cleverly designed scheme for getting something new into focus. He fails part of the time but sometimes he succeeds. When the school year is over, you say—or at least I used to say in my college teaching—the best times were when we got off onto something that had no relation whatever to the timetable, something that wasn't envisioned but that turned out to have a lot of relevance to what the course was really about. I just had never had the wit before to see this: it came up accidentally or it came up because of some question or some argument with a student and we got off on a new track, and that's when things really came to life. We all know that this doesn't happen successfully all the time or even very often, but we all also know, I think, that when it does succeed it's worth a great deal because in fact far more is learned under those conditions than under conditions of routine presentation of subject-matter.

One of the other things one has to fight against is the belief that because the central priority is self-directed learning there is never any value in instruction or didactic teaching. There are times when a group of children is very ready to be instructed about something, or to engage in a set task which might even be rote learning under certain circumstances. Their readiness to do this means that it has become for them a significant choice, and it is therefore by no means violating the principle of choice to say there is room, and sometimes a significant amount of room, for quite formal instruction.

I think the people who advocate formal instruction greatly exaggerate its relative importance in terms of the learning of subject-matter. For example, in mathematics as far as I can see, the set pattern of the text, whether it be old mathematics or new mathematics, makes very little difference. Some people really believe that the set pattern of the text is *the* way mathematics is to be learned. Or they might grudgingly admit that there are three or four alternatives, but all of them would be carefully sequenced, outlined series of steps. They say, "But you can't *possibly* understand multiplication before you understand addition." You *can* of course double or treble a collection of pennies; *we* see this as a special case of adding, but a child doesn't have to know the general case first. That's the logical order and you expect children to come to it; but it's not always where they start or should start.

Addition and subtraction are a more obvious case. How can you subtract if you can't add? Well, subtraction, I would suspect, is the more primitive of the two operations. It's easier to think of taking something away from a collection than it is to think of putting two collections together, which is a rather artificial activity that we don't often engage in, whereas we've very often taken candy out of a box—we're depleting a collection by taking things away. There is a logical objection here too—you have to stop when the box is empty, whereas you can always go on adding. "The set of natural numbers is closed under addition, but not under subtraction." A reasonable child might object that you have to stop when the box is *full*, as well as when it is *empty*. Whose logic are we consulting here? The child's logic may be limited but it will guide him; our logic is more adequate but can easily confuse him. When his logic leads him into trouble, *then* is the time to help him expand his logical framework.

We all know that learning doesn't have any very close or intimate connection with adult logical organization. The order in which children come to understand such a logical pattern is not by following it from the beginning. They don't have it yet so they can't follow it. You can lead them by the nose, but that also means they can't follow it. We all agree there is some body of connected ideas and propositions that we can call mathematics. Nobody has ever written it all down but it's there; all the logical connections that exist among all the ideas in the area which we agree to call mathematics. There isn't any linear order among them. They're connected in a very complex sort of network and you can make your way through them along thousands of different paths, depending on your momentary readiness, your understanding, your fund of analogies and your interests. You can get into it in many different ways. The obvious thing from the point of view of teaching is to say, well, we want to find that way which is optimal for a particular child at a particular time. This will be in terms of all of the things which characterize him as an individual. We don't know how to do this, we're not omniscient, but one of the very practical ways of getting on with it is to give the child himself some choice. This doesn't mean that he will always, unerringly, choose the way that is best for him but it means that you will get evidence from his choices that will help *you* to define a pattern for him that will probably be much more effective than a standard pattern that is distilled out of mass instruction of the past.

Just as a personal comment about mathematics, I feel very strongly that there are two things the word refers to. One is mathematics and the other is the pedagogical tradition, and they don't necessarily have a very close relation to each other. Mathematics is what mathematicians do and it's what people do when they're being like mathematicians, solving problems of various kinds, bringing certain kinds of understanding to bear on these problems. I don't want to try to define mathematics. But the pedagogical tradition is something not very closely related to that, because the pedagogical tradition is one particular slice, one particular pathway through this network of ideas, or through part of it. "Through it" is the wrong phrase to use because you never get through it, you get into it. You don't cover it. You get into it by many paths, and some of these have been standardized because they have a certain average level of effectiveness, I suppose, and because they happen to appeal to the taste of people who have been engaged in the teaching process under certain kinds of conditions. But I think many people in education think that mathematics *is* what is in that syllabus. Therefore they talk about going through it because you get to the last page in the syllabus and you're through it. But this isn't the nature of mathematics. Mathematics is infinite and it has this kind of structure and complexity, which means you can't reduce it to the linear order of words in a book. There are just too many cross references. You can't put it on a computer, which can cross-index a lot more than a book can—the organization is too rich for that. People are forever discovering new paths in very old mathematics. Only four or five years ago a very able mathematician found a new method for proving that there are infinitely many prime numbers. He just went back and looked at this old problem from a fresh point of view. That's not very important, but it is the nature of mathematics that it should be this way. The thing that is really important is the capacity to function as a human being in this domain. You acquire this capacity for functioning by functioning. Along the way there are many disciplinary elements which you may decide to accept or which you may have imposed on you and completely reject—and which of course we know that most children, in terms of the habits of the disciplinary pattern, have in fact rejected. Or they have very cleverly invented a way of accepting these elements only as far as necessary to get through something called an examination, being careful to protect their minds from contamination in the process.

So, the disciplinary argument is really a very weak one. It implies that we progressives are just cutting loose, not giving children the strict order and discipline that is really necessary to become competent in mathematics, when in fact, the practices of the past have created almost universal failure. It isn't very hard to beat the past record. We shouldn't pat ourselves on the back very much just because children are doing a little better on the eleven-plus as a result of some new mathematics program. That's a cheerful thing, but it's almost unimaginable that they would do worse, not given three months, but given five or six or seven years of work in the style I think we could recognize as that of present-day progressive tendencies (which we can certainly vastly improve on). But given the opportunity to get children repeatedly exposed to the development of mathematical interests and given lots of material which does in fact embody a lot of the things which we regard as basic to mathematical understanding, they won't do worse. It's almost unimaginable. If you set children to memorizing the multiplication table on day one, then on day thirty they will do better on a test than will children who have not been memorizing the multiplication table. That's perfectly obvious, if the test is a test on multiplication tables. But we're not interested in one-month results; we're interested in, let's say, seven years. And here—and partly I'm safe in saying this because the seven-year test hasn't been made yet—it does seem to me almost unimaginable that people could point and say, "See? It's a disastrous failure; they don't know mathematics the way they used to."

If children will not know mathematics the way they used to it will be because they know it differently, and better. I and many others have had many—indeed most—freshmen coming into college with two or three years of secondary school mathematics who are nonfunctional with respect to any interesting use of it, applied either to practical activity, to science or to itself. They were not inducted into the art of using mathematics to develop more mathematics.

I have chosen school mathematics for my illustration because of all the curricular subjects it is the most "disciplinary." If we can demonstrate that this discipline, better understood, gives us a wider range of choice and context to match different children's experience and power, then the whole argument about discipline will be turned around, which is the way it should be.

I have tried to pick a few central terms in educational theory and to suggest ways in which we can start to "turn around" some of the traditional issues, can begin to say what is important without falling into traditional traps. *Freedom* is related to opportunities for significant choice in the optimization of learning. *Discipline* is related to the very nature of subject-matter; it is accepted and prized as it is seen to extend the power of the learner, to increase his range of significant choice. Freedom and discipline together imply an environment which is rich in the opportunities for their exercise. A curriculum becomes functional in proportion as it is reflected in the material provisioning of that environment and as teachers grow in the art of matching those provisions to children's own changing valences and capacities.

Two Essays on Mathematics Teaching

The two talks which follow continue the discussion of school mathematics. They were addressed to mathematics teachers in England, "Mathematics —Practical and Impractical" at a national conference, "Nature, Man and Mathematics" at an international congress. A new treatment of both the experimental roots and the emerging formalities of mathematics has been one of the leading edges of progress in British primary schools, and there is good reason for that. From the point of view of sheer testable competence of a conventional kind there is probably no subject which is taught so inefficiently to most children. From a purely tactical point of view it is a good subject to start reforming if you know how. Without exquisite effort you can probably match or improve on the traditional performance.

A major problem lies in the fact that teachers of the young have typically been handicapped in their own mathematical education and this creates a vicious circle which many acknowledge but feel powerless to break out of. A second handicap is that many teachers of mathematics are victims of a tradition which does not value and even does not understand its own spontaneous sources within experience. A decade of curriculum development in the United States has gone in the direction of carefully reconstructing the formal textbook development of the subject, making it more logically acceptable to formalists and often, at the same time, more inaccessible to teachers and children. This is not uniformly true, however, and some of our projects have broken fresh ground in exploring new mathematical subject-matter and new ways of teaching it, ways which give credence to the faith that children are all, if their interests and opportunities lead them that way, potential mathematicians. Even the majority effort, which I think has moved in a direction to compound a long-established failure, gives us a broader platform from which to begin than was available ten years ago.

This failure of direction is not easy to correct, and if it were it would make a mystery of our state. It is a failure which goes to the whole style of the elementary school environment, whose barrenness creates a constant pressure toward the use and manipulation of symbols, of the mere notational integument of subject matter. Now while mathematics is inescapably tied up with written symbols and in some ways, indeed, incorporates them into its very essence, it is also true that the symbols are nothing without the perceptual and manipulatory intuitions which bring them life and meaning. The experiential roots evolve as a product of children's exploration of their environment and, by reflection, of their own emerging practical competencies. This is the part we have unknowingly neglected. Like Euclid of old we have taken as a self-evident starting point what ought to be the principal challenge. Where this intuitive grounding is well evolved mathematics becomes home territory, easy or challenging. Some children bring such grounding with them, but only a small minority. For the rest an almost exclusively formal style of instruction produces an intellectual tissue-graft which, by a kind of antigen-antibody reaction, is sooner or later rejected. Perhaps the metaphor is too extreme. The mind has sometimes an extraordinary capacity to store and sometimes to retrieve useless skill and information. When teachers who have been turned off by mathematics belatedly get on to good tracks of early learning they are often able to retrieve and revitalize some of that early and unused track of school arithmetic or geometry, still somehow there in the files, though till then marked for dead storage. I was a borderline case and can speak with feeling. I took a calculus course in college which I mostly, and barely, rote-learned. Four years later I was lucky enough to meet it, unexpectedly, along another track, and discovered the few simple central secrets. I do not blame my teachers, who were patient and humane explainers. Such secrets cannot be explained, the explanations are at least as secret as the things explained. Until, that is, a mind is prepared to use and examine its own experiential store. A bad environment can frustrate this process, and a good one amplify it many fold.

Mathematics—Practical and Impractical
(1967)

The five-year-old child of a friend of mine, riding one day with his mother, asked out of the blue, "Mummy, what *is* the biggest number?" It was a serious question, not to be ducked or counter-questioned; it was, she must have judged, a time and a place for adult commitment. "There is no biggest number," she replied. There was then a silence as they drove along, and finally she looked across at her son—looked to see a great tear rolling down his cheek. In my own daughter's case the episode had a different dramatic quality, comedy rather than high tragedy. Friend Cindy had asserted that a "trillion trillion trillion" *was* the biggest number. The question came home, and we were noncommittal: "What do you think?" A visiting physicist friend, with characteristic outlook, answered: "No, Julie, the biggest number is 10^{39}." After a day or two of silence we were told, "Cindy just thought that a trillion trillion trillion was the biggest number that had a name, and Bob knew a name for a bigger one, 'ten-times-to-the-thirty-nine.' But what they *said* was wrong, wasn't it?" "Why do you say that?" And now, with great solemnity, "Because you could *always* add *one more*."

I am sure many of you can duplicate these stories, which I tell to make a starting point—the distinction between computation and mathematics or, in Greek, between logistic and arithmetic. The distinction is a vital one, but it has been the focus of endless rather unattractive snobbery and, more importantly, of confusion in philosophy and wickedness in teaching. Among the Greeks, and some say once upon a time among the the British, it was almost a class distinction: computation and mensuration were vulgar, banausic, befitting the life of an artisan or tradesman. What was wrong, of course, was that the *connections* between the practical and the impractical had to be played down, for example so that Archimedes had to keep secret the method of the unequal arm balance. Our own schools—being a guest I speak only of America—carry on in this great tradition, and have concealed very successfully the fact that mathematics has anything to do with anything very much. Of course much of the older curriculum did have to do with computation and mensuration, but never, except for the vocational stream and the "retarded," was it evolved *out of* the arts in question. Nowadays we have New Mathematics, which is intrinsically better in its intent, much of the time, than the old. But the capsule is often even more insoluble than before, I believe; conspicuously so in a characteristic preoccupation with a pointless rigor, premature abstraction, and with the dullest of all mathematical subject-matter, the elementary algebra of finite sets—which is the algebra human beings learn earliest in their spontaneous experience and last have need of in conscious formulation.

I should like to look a little at the particular case of my two stories, the discovery of infinity. I think it shows in a simple early form a characteristic of much mathematical subject matter. Let me see if I can set forth the elements and the levels. First there is the level of perception of discrete things; things grabbed, mouthed, smelled, pushed and pulled, thrown or dropped. Then there is the process of taking things apart and putting them together, of the serious business of *homo faber*. Out of a vast and essential redundancy of such practices certain mental habits are precipitated. By calling them *mental habits* I don't mean to imply that they are not physical, overt habits; I only mean to imply that they are human habits, evolved out of conscious intercourse with the physical environment. I am going to flag such a system of habits with a technical word, *schema*. *Schemata* are ways of going at a subject-matter, strategies. The child learns words that belong with the *schemata* he builds up, and first learns them just as unreflectively. He counts and he says "count" as well as "one," "two," "three." Now I want to think of all this kind of performance, in relation to concrete particular situations, as one achieved level of functioning and learning, and I want to come back to it. But there is a second level, quite new and different, which comes when the *schemata* or strategies the learner has acquired are transformed, by the learner, into vehicles of a new kind of meaning and interest. The schema for counting, a pretty elaborate one, is not merely used, but rather is rehearsed, enjoyed, and reflected upon. It is perceived as a sort of matrix within which are first revealed the *entities* we call *numbers*; it is so, I think, that arithmetic matriculates.

When a child makes the transition from the practical schema as a tool to the reflection upon that schema, to looking at numbers and not merely using them, *he* first experiences that kind of many-one transformation which Plato immortalized in the allegory of the cave. But what he sees behind him, casting these shadows, is *not* just number in the abstract.

There is a third story to tell here, from Frances Hawkins, about a group of four-year-olds, in which all the sand in a sandbox, seen via the hand lens, is suddenly known and discussed as fitting the schema of number, even though you couldn't count all the grains. This was the insight they gained. They lost it again, and then regained it, and the whole process makes Platonism seem thin. This story is not simple in the telling, a single episode out of context. But it is a story of a kind that can be foretold—and not just told—as the characteristic outcome of a certain sort of teaching in a certain sort of school. The sandbox was, first of all, an early culmination of much involvement with numbers—in matching and ordering, in nursery rhyme, and in such stories as Wanda Gag's *Millions of Cats*. Like all early culminations it was fragile, and the insight *was* lost and regained, and regained again. Until finally one day there was that marvelous episode of the cattails, which expand so manifoldly, when a pinch is removed, into the individual winged seeds. One child threw back his head and announced, "Now we can say hundreds of cattails, thousands of cattails, millions and billions and trillions of cattails!"

If I read all of this correctly, it says that the transition from *schema* to insight, from operation to conception, involves a sort of experience you would misdescribe unless you underlined its *aesthetic* quality. To know the universal in its own right is first and foremost to enjoy it as an achievement. In my particular three stories the emotional quality is that which used to be tagged with the name of the sublime—Kant called it the mathematically sublime. It is the experience in which our grasp of things suddenly outruns our imagination, like the vastness of space and time. More properly: we catch ourselves in the act of going—of knowing—beyond imagination, and thus we first know ourselves as knowers. For the younger child, this sublimity may be evoked, in seeing a sandbox, or a cattail, under the aspect of number. For the older children (a whole year older!) in facing up to the simplest infinity. But does this mean that they are now ready for the sober sequential development, putting away childish things? I think not—not without a great and crucial loss. For these stories only mark some early passage through a door into a new country, a new ecology comparable in importance to the continental surfaces they encountered when our remote ancestors first crawled out of the sea. Number is only a small part of this new Platonic ecology, and my stories only sample a small part of it—but let me stay with it a while longer. The schema of counting mirrors it, when children have learned how to look. But what they all too seldom get is the associative richness, the sense that the world around is suffused with numerosity. The *schema* leads to the concept, but the concept in turn leads back to the world of sense and imagination, and thus to the invention of new *schemata*. I think particularly of the long evolution of number codes, to a point where they can rank the seeds in a cattail, the sand in a sandbox, and the stars in a galaxy. The changes from practical exploration to *schema* to conception and back to new explorations and new *schemata* are many and varied, and perhaps never twice the same. If we talk too easily in terms of *stages* of development (in the manner of Piaget) we shall miss this frequent switching, by which even as adults we return, again and again, to the most immediate and primitive level.

The particular point I want to make about this new level is that it is a second story which must be supported by the first; and too seldom is. The nursery school child in my wife's tale had a glimpse of this second story and found it rewarding—aesthetically rewarding, literally wonderful—full of wonder. To have a momentary grasp of "a sandboxfull" as the name of a number is not to *use* the schema merely, as in ordinary counting, I repeat, but to see the sandbox suddenly from a *point of view* which requires some previous mastery of the schema. But that means to become aware of the tool as something more than a tool in use; it is a tool mastered and at the moment it has become, rather, a power, a transforming principle, a kind of philosopher's stone. I wonder (parenthetically) how many of us can give other names to the order of number I called a sandboxful? Is it more, or less, than all the stars in the galaxy? Than the letter symbols (tokens) in a library of books? Than the number of seconds in a lifetime, or the cattail population of the world? There was a classroom of ten-year-olds a few years ago in New England which had almost spun itself into a cocoon of paper tape, with a foot to the hundred thousand years of geological history. This was a second start, the first having given a foot to the century; and I think they were about to invent logarithms. The starry heavens may dwarf the imagination, as may a sandbox, but the truth is we have resources to stretch the imagination. The *schema* of logarithms was in fact invented a long time before Napier, again as use precedes theory. The essence was there in the practical invention of the power series number code, the Mesopotamian code which preceded the arabic. You can get to the sandboxful by successively halving it—twelve steps, say, from the whole box to a core drilled out with a piece of water pipe. Then another series of halvings, with test-tubes and plastic straws, gets you to a number you can count on paper with a pin. So we come out with a total of some thirty-two partitionings, and that's about all the stars in the galaxy. One group of children called such logarithms *jars,* because their partitioning of beans or rice or sand was done with jam-jars. So they found that rice was ten more jars than sand was; translating to a factor of ten powers of two, or a thousand.

Of course this is only the beginning, and I won't go on to the rest except to say it would be nice to know that what we start in school is only a beginning, and not an ending. I can summarize one pathway with a pretty classification, which some of you may not have heard, of the learned professions. It classifies them acccording to the range of numbers they use. Teachers are low men on the totem pole of course; they go only from zero to one hundred. Economists work in the range of millions to billions. Physicists have the range up to my friend's 10^{39}, or possibly a bit more—a ratio of two physical quantities, the largest and smallest quantities of the physical quantity called action, is the cube of that, or 10^{117}. Then come the experts in permutations and combinations, who might mention 2^{320} geometric combinations, and the number theorists who sometimes need larger numbers as the famous Skewes number which as I recall is $10^{10^{34}}$. Then of course we come to the theologians who think they are tops with infinity as their domain. They never seem to have understood that concept, however; their stronghold completes the circle; the only really essential numbers for them are one, two, three and sometimes zero.

We could anticipate here by preparing a notation for numbers much larger than anyone has so far had any reason to employ. You have probably heard the challenge, to write the biggest number you can, using only nine 'nines.' Let us start off adding,

(1) $9 + 9 \ldots + 9 = 9 \times 9$

which might not be hard to beat with

(2) $9 \times 9 \ldots \times 9 = 9^9$,

or the slightly larger 999,999,999, which leads someone to say he can beat that with

(3) $9^{9^{9^{\cdot^{\cdot^{9}}}}} = 9_9$

which looks like a really big number, much bigger than any I have previously mentioned. But then it occurs to someone that the above stairs step is really relatively small, although it can hardly be distinguished from its own square root and just barely from its own logarithm. For it occurs to someone to write it, as I have, as 9_9, and then of course we have

(4) $9^{9^{9^{\cdot^{9}}}}$

But now the game is almost gone stale, because we are just repeating a trick, and have only done it four times. So let's do it nine times and call this 9*9. Repeating the same trick not nine times, but 9*9 times we have what seems like a really big number; until the humbling thought occurs to us that none of these tricks will get us to any number that is properly a large number; for they are all vanishingly small compared to most numbers. Thus we finally come back to the perception that there *are* no large numbers; *all* numbers are small, and the theorem is only an adult way of discovering what those two five-year-olds were concerned about—going around in a much bigger circle to get there.

When we come back to the sandbox there are other directions to jump. We pour water into it and the water disappears. Where did it go? Well, the sand is wet now, and it piles up differently, it looks different. After we've finished making rivers and valleys we collect the water back again with a piece of stretched plastic in the sun. Where was the water? One has surely not seen all the offshoots of this. One, for example, has gone into soil analysis and the growth of plants. Two adults I know were led back into their school geometry after some experimental measurements. How much space is there between closely packed spheres? They tried to do it by school geometry, but kept getting different answers. So they hit on another method, to build a regular tetrahedron, "a three-sided pyramid," out of glued marbles, with N marbles on an edge. For a way to count the total they got into Pascal's triangle, a considerable detour; but they came out with a first approximation of $N^3/6$, and then there was the problem of the *volume* of a regular tetrahedron. Here Archimedes came to the rescue, with another detour into the weighing of areas and volumes on the unequal arm balance. Thus they knew the volume of the tetrahedron, *and* the volume of all the spheres in it; so the fraction unfilled was theirs, and lo! it confirmed the experimental result, the rough quarter of the volume they had found by direct pouring into rather uniform sand. Then there is the next step, two years later in time perhaps but still hard on the heels of this one, when the sand is salt and solution occurs—again with no apparent increase of total volume—where are the holes now? Is it conceivable that water has holes in it? How many are they, or how big? All of this kind of exploration will take time, and at any moment, looked at from the outside by an unsympathetic school-inspector, will appear inefficient, diverse, and he will call it the *dis*integrated day. But I want to rob him of one argument, which is implied in a division of opinion which an English correspondent has put to me: "Many of us are concerned about some of the work now being considered at Primary Level, particularly where the fostering of abstract thinking seems to be very much in the background." I don't know your debate much at first hand, but let me guess.

I would guess that a cross-classification has been collapsed into a single one, and that two issues are being debated as one. As I listen to such debate I sense that "abstract" thinking means two things. One of these meanings I have already touched on: it flags the mode to which we shift when we shift attention from dealing with the concrete particular to the schema by *which* we deal with it, and to the universal concepts latent there. This meaning is of course essential to the nature of mathematics, which is not directly concerned with the empirical order of nature, but *is* concerned with the schemata which prove fruitful in *dealing* with that order. The other meaning of abstract is "detached, cut off, looked at apart from all but a carefully delimited context." It is in this sense of "abstract" that we may be dealing with things when we construct formal rationalized schemes of operation, whether in practical affairs or in the mode called theory.

When people were first inventing Cuisenaire rods or Dienes blocks or balances or Poleidoblocs they wanted to avoid the first kind of abstraction initially; dealing with concrete particulars of a sort that were not mere symbols, but concrete examples of number, of addition, or sequential order, or base 3, or what not. But as we know, such materials are very heavily stylized—the intended concept is pretty unsubtly there, if you already know the secret, while all the other inevitable properties of the concrete object are de-emphasized by standardization. The blocks are smooth and regular, the colors are stark and stereotyped—not color for color's sake, but mere elements of a formal code. Thus also the Dienes balance, the "equalizer," is carefully designed to home in on a whole-number version of the law of moments. A child who had worked with it in the intended way would never connect it with the see-saw, much less rediscover the *physical* insight of Archimedes, except by an unruly act of genius. So it turns out that this material is abstract in both my senses, heavy with conceptual intent *and* cut off from nature's variety and interconnection. Fortunately the concrete style has one consequence that is good. Children are in fact playful and eolithic, and can find more unintended uses for the concrete math materials than they can for printed tokens, crayons and work books. I use the word *eolithic* in memory of our remoter ancestors who had to start life with objects not intended for *any* purpose, but who after picking up the stone, for example, invented uses for it. The first invention was not the object—but the purpose. By now you see, I hope, my answer. When we speak of "abstract thinking" do we mean thinking that is in an insoluble capsule, unrelated to the wealth of experience that can make it come alive? That can be done with Cuisenaire rods and geoboards as surely as with paper and pencil—or almost as surely. There is a time for such thinking, of course, but it should be very late—as late as a child's readiness to grasp the partial isomorphisms between concrete reality and formalized systems of signs. Or do we mean the cultivation of intuition, of analogy, of the mind's power to order and schematize? No time could be too early, I think, for that. At least one five-year-old who could conclude that all numbers have successors had been ready three years before to ask (looking at a necktie dangling over the bath): "Do *all* daddies have neckties?" We know little about these subterranean developments, but surely we know they don't come from capsules.

Nature, Man and Mathematics
(1972)

Several years ago, when I had brought home a new microscope designed for children's use, we had the opportunity to observe the first recognition, by a five-year-old, of the world of size and scale. Or perhaps it was not the first, beginnings are hard to catch; and this fortunate young girl was already deeply involved with fragments of that world, at least—with dolls and furniture to scale, with pictures and maps of her own and others' drafting, and much else besides. But the *world* of size and scale is something else again, it is a recapitulation and a surmise; a glimpse of generality and of closure. At that young age the eyepiece of a microscope is first a shiny object and then, with luck, a sort of peep-show or television screen in miniature. At any rate we did what we all three, Christa, my wife, and I, called "looking at" various objects. Some, which Christa brought for this new occupation, were ten or fifty times too big to fit between object and stage, and one saw a young child's perceptual unreadiness to make use of what might be called the transitivity of congruences.

But one evening Christa brought to the microscope a tiny bit of lint from the floor. Here for the first time there seemed to be recognition, the lint was seen as lint though transformed a hundred-fold in scale. But the next day confirmation came in full measure, pressed down and running over. Our young friend came trotting from our bedroom carrying a small souvenir of London, a red Corgi double-decker bus. Halfway to the microscope she hesitated, then smiled at us a rueful smile. Touching the outside steps with her finger, she said, "Wouldn't it be nice if there were little people going up and down?"

It was not a statement one could call theorematic in the usual sense, but it took us suddenly to the world of Leeuwenhoek and Robert Hooke, of the life cycle of the flea, and of Jonathan Swift and Voltaire. In all previous history we find no evidence of such liberation of imagination and even today it is known only to some happy few. In our work with children and teachers you and we have had many opportunities to observe how poorly developed, in most humans today, are the intuitions of variation and invariance to scale. I suppose this is because we and the things around us are often undergoing translations and rotations, but very seldom shrink or expand. Confronted with the question whether a jar full of pebbles or a jar full of sand will absorb more water, even most adults are in the kind of trouble which Piaget has made famous concerning children's perception of invariance in number, area, and volume. This one concerns invariance to scale, one of numerous topics which should be proposed for similar investigation.

E. T. Bell once observed that while we might admire the ingenuity which led historically to more and more accurate approximations of pi, the greatest admiration should go to that unknown genius who first gave this ratio meaning by recognizing that it was a pure number, invariant to scale.

Lacking well-consolidated intuitions which could bring alive the space-groups of transformations, we also seem to lack the conceptual means for getting to a zero-th approximation understanding of natural phenomena on the scale of the very large, the very small, and the very complex. Conversely, our failure to assign dignity to children's exploration of this world of scale robs us of a powerful resource in the teaching of mathematics.

I thought to begin this talk with the example of scale transformations because they are, perhaps out of the whole of mathematics, among the most simple and most illuminating in their relevance to the diversity and nature of the material universe, and to the habits of thought with which mathematical education sometimes is and more often ought to be concerned.

In the United States at least one finds that this glorious topic of size and scale comes first into students' ken only when they are struggling with the equations of a physics text. My own first-year university students have almost uniformly been amazed to discover that a two-centimeter cube has four times the surface area and eight times the mass of a one-centimeter cube, a discovery I have often shamed them into with a gift of sugar-cubes. And even this discovery left them unprepared for the argument that single cells cannot in general be as big as birds' eggs or Lilliputians as small as mice. Dimensional relations in general are black magic to most students, mainly I think because such topics have never been considered to be proper mathematics—despite Hassler Whitney's elegant demonstration of the formal simplicity of dimensional numbers. But even if such topics had been woven into the earlier curriculum they would almost certainly, I fear, have been effectively divorced from the simple empirical and practical sources of their appeal and power. Yet (as I shall argue) such matters as dimensional analysis, whether at the level of five-year-old Christa or at the level of theoretical physics, are very nearly ideal examples of mathematical art.

From such examples one is led toward two questions which I wish to raise in this paper. One concerns the teaching of mathematics. The second, intimately connected with the first at a philosophical level, concerns the nature of mathematics itself.

The first question has to do with the range and repertoire of a teacher who knows success in leading children into the mathematical domain. If such teachers are rare they are all the more worthy of support and study if we hope to make them less rare. Let me therefore say a little more of what is involved in their art.

There are two aspects of this art which are inseparably connected, and this connection leads me from the consideration of teaching to the nature of mathematics as a teacher must grasp it. It commits me, I find, to the view that such a rare teacher has within his grasp a privileged source of information concerning the nature of mathematics. I think this view might scornfully be rejected in some circles.

The working perspective of a teacher allows him—though unfortunately it does not always compel him—to make many observations of those acquisitions and transitions in intellectual development upon which the growth of mathematical knowledge depends. But such a teacher is of course not only an observer; he would indeed be less of an observer if he were not also a participant: one who, because of the way he shares in and contributes to that development, can earn the privilege of insight into its details and pathways. The ideal work of a good teacher has then these two aspects inseparably combined: that of diagnosis and that of providing in accordance with the indications of his diagnosis. As a diagnostician the teacher is trying to map into his own the momentary state and trajectory of another mind and then, as provisioner, to enhance (not to replace) the resources of that mind from his own store of knowledge and skill.

It is clear to all of us, I think, that teachers who approximate this ideal are rare indeed. We do not educate most of our teachers very relevantly to such a way of teaching, and we hamper their potential fluency of performance in a hundred ways, not least the incredible burden of managing active children in too large numbers and in too sterile surroundings. So my ideal teacher is approximated only as we get out to the tail of the distribution of teaching opportunities and teaching styles which prevail today. Circumstances which allow and encourage good teaching are rare, though we can make them less so. At any rate the teacher I speak of is a presupposition of my argument and does exist, though rarely. He is, so to say, a kind of existence theorem.

For such a teacher a limiting condition in mapping a child's thought into his own is, of course, the amplitude of his *own* grasp of those relationships in which the child is involved. His mathematical domain must be ample enough, or amplifiable enough, to match the range of a child's wonder and curiosity, his operational skills, his unexpected ways of gaining insight. David Page once remarked that when children are seriously attentive they seldom give wrong answers, but they often answer a question different from the one we think we are asking. A teacher-diagnostician must map a child's question as much as his answer, neither alone will define the trajectory; and he must be prepared to anticipate something of what the child may encounter farther along that path.

It is obvious, I think, that in many respects a teacher's grasp of subject-matter must include far more than what we conventionally call mathematics. It must include what a child sees, handles, plays with; miniatures, for example, such as cars, lorries, bricks, dolls and doll houses; more generally the great and the small. It must include finished materials and raw, sand and water and clay as well as batteries and wire and globes. It should include rocks, plants and animals, mirrors and crystals. It should include all those things which in serious play with them contribute to children's grasp of orderings, of number and measure, of pattern and structure.

It goes without saying, of course, that mathematics as conventionally understood may include, on the other hand, a great deal which a teacher of children need not have mastered. Otherwise we would ask the impossible. But a teacher of children, of the kind I postulate, must be a mathematician, what I would call an *elementary* mathematician, one who can at least sometimes sense when a child's interests and proposals—what I have called his trajectory—are taking him near to mathematically sacred ground. There is a delightful report of Edith Biggs concerning a ten-year-old who noticed and became intrigued by the fact that in the graph he had made of area against linear dimension, the curve was *locally* a straight line. That child then was supported in extensive investigations along what one can only call the trajectory of Isaac Newton. A teacher who lacked any feeling for the calculus would almost certainly have failed him. In the same way one has seen children's curiosity about the individual properties of numbers leading straight toward the great problems of number theory, but likely to miss them without a teacher's recognition and support.

If a teacher's grasp of subject-matter must extend beyond the conventional image of mathematics, we must then face the question of definition in a new form—what is at stake is not the nature of the end-product usually *called* mathematics, but of that whole domain in which mathematical ideas and procedures germinate, sprout and take root, *and* in the end produce the visible upper branching, leafing and flowering which we here all so value, and which wither when uprooted.

In this way I find myself compelled to extend the domain of mathematics so that it will provide room, provide closure, for all the mapping operations of a teacher. Mathematics so considered will obviously overlap with other parts or aspects of the curriculum. A child tracing the flow of colored water through a transparent siphon is not thereby being a mathematician, or physicist, or town engineer, nor simply delighting in the intuition of color and motion. What he is being is a matter of his momentary trajectory of learning. A good teacher will diagnose the child's involvement as related potentially to all of these or other important educational concerns, but will not identify it as any of these too soon or too simply. In that sense the curricular divisions overlap in all the childhood praxis of learning, as they do in the practical existence of society. The child has not yet chosen a career—except in passing.

So by closure of the mathematical domain I mean not to partition mathematics off from other educational concerns; on the contrary I mean to define the mathematical domain in such a way that it does not *exclude* any situation of learning *merely* on the ground that the latter might also be described under social or scientific or aesthetic categories. I use the mathematical term "closure" as particularly apt—recognizing that as mathematicians use the word, it implies removing barriers, not building them. Ideally any concrete involvement of children, any relationship with the world around them in which they are caught up, will link up with mathematics among other things and in that sense is part of its extended domain.

The extension I propose can be justified, I think, in two ways. The first is that persons called teachers are particularly susceptible to intimidation by persons called mathematicians. Teachers often feel constrained by the opinions of the higher sect, constrained in particular to narrow their own views and their own practice to conform to such opinions, rather than to explore more widely beyond the implied barriers. A deliberate effort to extend the domain of mathematics is inseparable, I believe, from any practical effort directed toward the deepening and enrichment of mathematics teaching. We must aim to convert the higher sect.

We have recently enjoyed a small report of an American teacher, Dudley Hunt, who involved a group of ten-year-olds in an extensive project around the partitioning of regular hexagons. Her original aim was to provide a matrix for experience in the addition of fractions, but as the project ramified, one might equally have described it as a study of the geometry of the hexagon, of symmetry, or of decorative design. This teacher happens to be a mathematician herself and does not need the approval of the higher sect, and indeed many individual mathematicians would be delighted by such work, even though their own "official" view of their subject-matter, translated in terms of texts and syllabuses and work-books throughout the world, would imply disparagement of some part of it occurring, so to speak, in the wrong part of the syllabus. In my country the only respectable part, I fear, would be those boring unmotivated work-book pages of symbolic problems, $\frac{1}{3} + \frac{1}{2} = \square$.

It is for such reasons we must speak about the nature of mathematics itself—we will not otherwise give teachers the license and support they deserve in teaching mathematics, and we will not see the work of serious adult mathematics in its deep inner connections with the world of childhood.

The second justification is therefore that the proposed enlargement gives us the possibility of a view of the nature of mathematics which, regardless of pedagogical motives or implications, may be worth pursuing for its own sake.

In speaking of an extension of the mathematical domain to provide a kind of closure for the mapping of the potential range of children's mathematical learning I am appealing, of course, to a heuristic principle which has been important in the history of mathematics. I shall call it the Principle of the Extended Domain. It is based upon the fact that a problem can arise *within* a domain which nevertheless proves too restrictive to allow an adequate solution of that problem. Indeed I think this principle lies very close to the heart of what might be called the mathematical style, to the secret of mathematics.

The most familiar major historical example of a successful application of this principle is, I suppose, the development of the number system, which only in the complex domain gives full closure to all the elementary operations of arithmetic. In his essay on *The Essence of Mathematics* Charles Saunders Peirce uses chess as a sort of counterexample. "Chess is mathematics, after a fashion; but owing to the exceptions which everywhere confront the mathematician in this field—such as the limits of the board: the single steps of king, knight and pawn; the peculiar mode of capture by pawns; castling—there results a mathematics whose wings are clipped, which can only run along the ground." G. H. Hardy, in his *Apology*, uses the example of chess also, as a kind of mathematics which he says is not *serious;* he says of it that its problems cannot be generalized in such a way that their solution links them significantly with the rest of mathematics.

Serious mathematics then must be able, as Peirce says, to fly. And it can fly only as it can generalize. Hence, he says, "a mathematician often finds what a chess-player might call a gambit to his advantage; exchanging a smaller problem that involves exceptions for a larger one free from them." That is, he extends the domain. It is interesting in connection with this counterexample of Peirce and Hardy, to consider the rather major gambit later engineered by John von Neumann in the theory of games, by which chess becomes only an example of the most elementary form of game. The mathematical theory of games flies *so* high it can hardly distinguish chess from tic-tac-toe.

But the use I wish to make here of the principle of the extended domain is a different one. What I wish to urge is an extension of the domain of mathematics itself, as usually conceived, so that mathematics in the extended domain will provide something like logical closure to the diagnostic mapping and resultant planning of a teacher. I shall argue that this extension, although motivated by a primary concern for learning and teaching, is at the same time entirely consonant with the traditions of Archimedes, Newton and Gauss. It is dissonant, I think, with dominant pedagogical traditions of the past and present.

In proposing to extend the domain of what we call mathematics and therefore of what teachers conceive their mathematical commitments to be, I have no wish to blur the disciplinary distinctions. Indeed, the challenge is to widen the domain of mathematics with analytical care. We want to make its essence more intelligible, not to dissolve it.

Let me be explicit. The domain is to be consciously expanded to include all those junctures in the lives of children, in their working contact with the great world of nature and of human society, out of which mathematics in the usual restricted sense can be seen to evolve. Only so will educational closure be possible. But it now becomes a question as to how the mathematical treatment of this shared domain can be characterized—what its essence or genius is, what are the invariants across this enlarged domain, of aim and style. Clearly there will be some sacrifices from the point of view of one confined to the restricted domain. Explicitness of symbolic definition and of generality will not be among the invariants, nor will formal argument. Eight- or ten-year-olds working with the Archimedean balance will sometimes come to isolate those moves, those operations, which maintain the state of balance, sorting variables and gradually isolating the underlying relations which characterize the balance. Their discourse will be mostly limited to the concrete context, they will not think to offer formal statements. Their investigation is surely not deductive, but highly empirical. As children continue this process of sorting and isolating, as they come closer to a grasp of regularity and symmetry, they move toward a more analytical and deductive style. Where a teacher can support and provide, can dignify with pertinent curiosity, children will sometimes reach the law of moments empirically, and less easily a simpler fact underlying the famous theorem of Archimedes: the invariance of balance to any pairwise symmetrical displacement of equal weights—the law of the equal-arm balance.

Let us look at these two results, not crammed down children's throats, but supposing each to be achieved with some inner illumination: the law of moments and the law of symmetry. Logically, when put in a proper formal context, these are equivalent, if one supplies a premise which Archimedes failed to state, the conservation of weight. But they are not equivalent in heuristic value. The law of moments for the unequal-arm balance is a part of empirical science, and its formulating could be called "applied mathematics" if we assumed that the algebra were already available for application. The symmetry principle is on a different footing; its use in characterizing the invariance of balance is not applied mathematics; on the contrary it *is* mathematics. It is also theoretical physics, to be sure, but I warned that the extension of mathematics would produce overlap, if not require it. First of all the second formulation, that of symmetry, is simpler and deeper than the law of moments. It is a type of formulation which, in Hardy's term, has more "seriousness" than the law of moments, useful as this is in many other contexts. It is an example, perhaps the simplest one, of the whole family of logical tools whose nature was first discussed by Leibniz, who related it directly with the principle of causality, of sufficient reason. If we assume that nothing else matters but mass and length of arm, then with equal masses and equal arms, any argument that the left side would descend is *eo ipso* applicable to the right side, and all such arguments will cancel each other by contradiction. It is a deep thing that this symmetry is still sufficient, though hidden, to define the unequal-arm balance, that the special case implies the general one. One should add in passing that with an unstable balance, the symmetry argument gives us equal *probability* for the two possibilities —an example of what Bernoulli called the principle of *non*-sufficient reason. Modern theoretical physics would be unthinkable without such arguments.

But to return to the ten-year-old: much of this is still remote from him, far along on his current trajectory. But even within his own reach a symmetry-argument has seriousness, it relates to his growing manifold of perceptions and intuitions of symmetry and of choice. It provides him with a way of thinking which, though it will not automatically or easily transfer to different situations, will be available as an analogy. It will be a potential cross-link in his intellectual file, when he has worked out what a teacher can recognize as similar patterns of thought in other situations.

That is my reason for dwelling on this example from Archimedes. The symmetry formulation of the balance provides a clear-cut example of something very close to the essence of mathematics— closer than the axiomatic method, closer than the ideal of deductive rigor—and which holds up, I think, across its extended domain. Archimedes showed us something of its power in his argument from the special case of the equal-arm balance to the general case of the unequal-arm balance. And he deepened the demonstration by his use of the balance in those extraordinary extensions of plane and solid geometry which bear his name.

In the essay I referred to before, Charles Peirce offers a definition of mathematics which is helpful; namely "the study of what is true of hypothetical states of things." It is not clear to me that this definition as it stands is adequate to my extended domain. In any case it seems also too broad. As a definition it could well apply to the novel, for example, which invents hypothetical states of things and tries to discern what is true of them. Since the nature of the novel is at least as problematic as that of mathematics, it may be well to restrict the definition, while bearing in mind a genuine family resemblance.

Peirce does in fact narrow his definition. Mathematical investigations are distinguished, he says, by resort to what, following Immanuel Kant, he calls a *schema*. A schema is a kind of artifact or model constructed to satisfy the conditions of a hypothesis, about which we then notice that it has thus and such additional properties not obviously entailed by the hypothesis. The kind of schema Peirce has in mind is the use of drawing and auxiliary construction in synthetic geometry. Though the hypothesis may be universal and abstract, the schema which fits it is particular and concrete, produced by the hand and observed by the eye. In the absence of such motor-perceptual transformation no amount of sheer reflection about the hypothesis will produce a mathematical investigation or argument. If you make a triangle out of rigid rods and rotate one of them slightly about some point, you can directly *see* that the sum of angles remains unchanged. Such action and observations are intrinsic to the mathematical style, which thus never loses touch with what Piaget has called the concrete operational *étape* of thought. The symmetry principle applied to the unequal-arm balance is another kind of example. We establish the general case of balance by starting with all mass at the center and then, by using only symmetrical displacements, produce any arbitrary balance configuration in the general case.

I should like to give two more examples of schematization at a relatively adult level before proceeding further. Martin Gardner recently reported the following story of a reader's reflections about a tin of beer, American style. About to put it down at a picnic on uneven ground, the thought occurred to him that if he drank some beer first it would be less likely to tip over. On further reflection he observed that if he were to drink all the beer the center of gravity would be back up to the center of the tin. *Ergo* there is a minimum, a liquid level of maximum stability. Now, of course, any mathematician or physicist immediately thinks of expressing the combined center of gravity of the tin and its contents in terms of the variable amount of liquid, then taking the derivative and finding the point where that derivative vanishes. But the author of this tale thought of another way of finding the answer, which I leave to you, with only a hint that your non-standard solution would delight the heart of Archimedes, who had not yet been taught the calculus. All I need say about this example is that once again the schema of balance is brought into view. In solving the problem by either means one performs an act of abstraction, of cutting away all features of the realistic problem except those that fit the schema provided by the unequal-arm balance—cutting to reveal the hidden symmetry. This is the kind of step which Peirce saw as so characteristically mathematical.

But the first solution is again after all—once one sees it correctly —a standard bit of applied mathematics. The non-calculus solution is more interesting in terms of my general thesis, as I think you will agree when you see that solution.

My last example is of a different kind, but I think it also illustrates the significance of Peirce's thesis. It also comes from chess. There is a stop-rule in chess which says that a threatened king may not simply move back and forth between two squares. In a typically mathematical spirit G. A. Hedlund and Marsden Morse proposed and solved a slightly more general problem. Suppose a king were confined to three adjacent squares a, b, c, from any of which he could move to either of the others. It is assumed that all of these moves would avoid checkmate. Clearly the defensive player could avoid such a pattern as *abab*, which would save him from the usual stop-rule. Morse now proposes a more general rule, namely that the game ends if the player directly repeats *any* sequence of moves—such as *abab; abcabc; abcacb; abcacb;* and so on. The question arises whether under this rule he can still play an unending game. I do not give Morse's affirmative solution but a different and more special one which Walter Mientka and I happened to find, and of which I therefore know the genesis. Mathematicians seldom let us in on such secrets. In an unending sequence of three letters one must avoid all direct repetitions, double blocks of any length, and those very long blocks get troublesome. It is easy to avoid direct repetitions of pairs or triples, but the farther one goes the longer become the blocks one has to avoid repeating. As with testing for prime numbers, the testing keeps increasing in difficulty.

Now at this point we would all recognize, I think, that a step is needed which does not follow from the hypothesis by any amount of reasoning of the kind outlined in logic texts and it is, somehow, a uniquely mathematical step. The step is, I shall say, a search for a schema. Because one does not find a "standard method" the problem cannot be called applied mathematics. One does not even know in advance whether this might turn out to be serious mathematics in Hardy's sense. A search for analogies, therefore, is the next step. I happened to find one in the procedure of substitution, as when one replaces a simple element by a complex one, each element in a pattern by a pattern of elements, a noun by a noun clause, a variable by a function. That was my schema. If one replaced each *letter* in a block by a corresponding *block* of letters, each block guaranteed to be repetition-free, one might then have a much longer block which was equally impeccable. The answer is: almost, but not quite. I shall not go on with the details, but with suitably chosen blocks *A, B, C* the method does work, and the substitution can be iterated endlessly, producing an infinite sequence without repetitions. In Peirce's language, it flies. I still do not know that this is very serious mathematics, although there are many unsolved problems about such sequences and they link up in possibly interesting ways with other parts of number theory. The point of the illustration is that new mathematics—new to a child, new to an amateur such as myself, or new to a professional mathematician—takes off and flies through a successful search for schemata available in one's repertoire, for patterns of construction which one has previously mastered, which *may* provide guidance in building a new variant suited to new situations encountered in nature or in mathematics.

As this process is successful it served also to enrich the repertoire, the store of useful schemata. As is true of all knowledge, the growth of mathematics lies always in some *use* of mathematics—not primarily in providing premises for an argument, but in providing schemata for the guidance of thought.

When we search in our repertoire we sometimes find what we call an algorithm, a standard schema which fits the conditions of a new problem, and leads directly to its solution. In such cases we can speak of applied mathematics, whether the problem is one of everyday life, of science, or within mathematics itself. The implication of the term "applied mathematics" is often slightly pejorative. You can imagine the other kind of mathematician, called "pure," offering his discipline for use but not—as mathematician—expecting to learn anything new in the process. *Noblesse oblige*. But as I have suggested, this case of the standard schema shades over into the schema by analogy, where no standard method is available but where those that are available *suggest* ways of looking at a problem which may make it at least partially tractable. This may still if you wish be called applied mathematics but whenever such a problem is solved it does, in principle, add new mathematics to the general repertoire. Finally, there are cases where problems cannot be brought under existing schemas, and where even the power of analogy fails. In such cases we resort to direct induction, to numerical examples, or to various other related, but easier, investigations: and very often the problem waits. If it is a serious problem it waits on a special shelf of fame, such as the list of Hilbert's problems. Whichever case we consider, the general conclusion is clear—that in a proper sense all mathematics grows out of the use of previously schematized knowledge which is itself explicitly or potentially mathematical—in that sense *all* mathematics is "applied mathematics."

I have at least sketched the case I wish to make concerning the essence of mathematics. There is a sort of corollary, however, which I would like to develop. Mathematics has evolved historically into a large and richly interconnected system which is not only a mirror of the world of nature but which has many internal mirrors—morphisms of one kind or another—which sometimes generate, in turn, new mirrors for the world of nature, new analogies of structure, new schemata. But running pervasively through this whole system there is a common implicit style which in general human terms is both a strength and a limitation. When Peirce talks about mathematics which can fly, this metaphor refers, I believe, to the generalizing power implicit in the structure of the domain, a power which depends essentially upon a certain monotony, a certain iterative character, both in its objects and in its perceptions and arguments. The number system evolves from such monotony, though each step generates novelties which are in turn a challenge to new investigations. The method of Archimedes, like early calculus, depends upon those results of infinite iteration, called infinitesimals, which the great of the eighteenth century used fluently, which physicists have in fact perversely used all along, and which formal logic has recently, after long doubt, declared absolutely rigorous.

From Archimedes to the recent past the assertion that the method of infinitesimals is not rigorous is now known to be a non-rigorous assertion, indeed a false one! I should mention again the wide sweep and great power of the schema of iterated substitution revealed, for example, in logic, in geometry, in the statistical theory of branching processes, or in the elegant and very "serious" theorem of Kolmogorov, that a function of many variables can always be expressed by composition from functions of two variables only. This schema, with its imagery of branching trees, has many delightful uses within the range of children's arithmetical explorations—although it seems to find no place within the official repertoire, curriculum, or race course.

The iterative or monotonous character of mathematics, so deeply embedded in the nature of its domains and so profoundly exploited in its style of thought, is often noticed by outsiders and given as a reason for a certain repugnance by persons whose special cultivation lies in other fields. Words like "mechanical" and "abstract" enter in. Consider for contrast the visual pattern of a painting such as Gauguin's *Maternité* or the thematic patterns of Mozart's Second Horn Concerto or of Beethoven's Eroica. Structure there is, even structure which is repetitive, iterative; but the interesting part typically connects with just that deviation from simple-minded regularity, just that surprising use of ambiguity which mathematics will avoid. Though a computer can compose music which is recognizably Mozartian, it does not compose Mozart which is musically interesting. It does not know when to depart from an algorithm.

So with a great novel, such as *The Magic Mountain, The Red and the Black, Crime and Punishment,* there is a formal structure but it is never maintained at the expense of those unique non-recurrent or even discordant details which win our trust and convey to us the higher levels of order and significance which lesser works fail to capture. Picasso's Don Quixote presupposes a precision of anatomical knowledge, yet the anatomist despairs of him. To be *that* kind of mirror of the world, a different kind of structure and order is necessary, one which stays far longer in the domain of concrete intuition and which requires a very different, though *not* incompatible, sort of cultivation of education from the mathematical.

Yet structure is never absent, even (at some level) a kind of structure which can be abstracted and schematized. Whereas random music, like Borges' Library of Babylon—to which I shall return—can produce no surprises. Departure from regularity presupposes regularity, and significant irregularity implies order on a higher level. So when we are working with young children we should not be surprised that they wear what may seem to be seven-league boots, and that the cross-connections they can make may go easily from mathematics to science or to decorative or dynamic art. My idealized teacher will not sorrow, but rather rejoice, when the dissection of hexagons leads to crochet patterns or visual fantasy, or when Fibonacci numbers lead to a new interest in rabbits or the growth of trees, or *vice versa*. From the time of Froebel and Montessori to that of Cuisenaire and Dienes, too much of our move toward the mathematics of the concrete, invaluable as that has been, has had such deviant possibilities puritanically designed out of it.

I wish now to return to the perspective of a teacher of children, and consider the extent to which my case holds up. My argument is one which seeks to make it plausible, when mathematics is extended in meaning to include the roots as well as the branch and the flower, that mathematical subject matter is potentially the whole of experience. Its differentiating mark is not primarily one of subject matter, but of style. This style is not defined by reference to the deductive as opposed to the empirical, by the formal as opposed to the concrete, by the axiomatic as opposed to the intuitive, but rather by a characteristic more generic than these, which I have called, following Peirce, schematization. But let me first reassure you that I intend no disparagement of these admirable, but secondary, stylistic features. I am only saying that as one looks at mathematics in its extended domain, these features are *not* invariant across that domain. As one looks more deeply to the roots one sees these nice distinctions tending to dissolve. They characterize branches of mathematics, or leaves and flowers, but not the whole of it; they characterize these products as finished products. In the process of being born, whether among children or among amateurs or professionals, no mathematics is yet rigorous, or fully deductive, or axiomatic; but its style *is* that of schematization. In the process of being born mathematics is a searching out and delineation of structure, guided by those analogies of structure which have already been consolidated within the minds of the searchers. Its final format is intended to convince, but that is only one stable product of mathematicizing, not its essence.

I believe that I owe here a further debt to all the modern efforts which have gone into the process of differentiating between mathematics and empirical science. As a young philosopher I was raised up surrounded by the belief of Frege and Russell and the Viennese positivists that all of mathematics is somehow a vast tautology, thus sharply and finally distinguished, and pedagogically separable, from empirical science. Although, they said, our natural language is full of ambiguities and confusions, there is possible a rational reconstruction of that language (we were assured) which will make clear just where the dividing line occurs, and thus rid us of the besetting sin of supposing that mathematical truth owes anything to the nature of the world we live in. This philosophical movement rode partly on great new developments in mathematics going back to Descartes' invention of analytic geometry, to the invention of non-Euclidean geometries, and to the foundations of arithmetic initiated by Peano and Frege. These discoveries revealed the fact that at least major parts of mathematics, and presumably all of it, could be faithfully mirrored within the domain of arithmetic, while arithmetic itself could be reduced to, or mirrored within, a suitably clarified and formalized system of pure logic. Not only was this true of traditional mathematics, but it proved true also of those parts of empirical science which had been sufficiently developed —rational mechanics, for example, the theory of elasticity, or more recently (as in the work of Ulam and Kolmogorov) the theory of probability, long suspect, like the calculus, as to its precise mathematical status.

By such developments, it was hoped, the contribution of rational analysis could be sharply differentiated from all questions of empirical truth involved in the description of nature. What was somehow overlooked or treated arrogantly was the fact that these powerful and impressive mathematical structures had been evolved through constant intercourse with the domains of science, practical life, and engineering. It was also overlooked that they could be *re*applied in those domains only by *informal* rules of interpretation which carried within them all the philosophically interesting problems which had supposedly been banished by the new program.

What tended to be overlooked also was the fact that this whole development failed in one crucial way to explain the specific content and form of existing mathematics. If we define mathematics merely as a system of propositions organized according to the axiomatic method and rules of deduction, this is rather like defining a book as consisting merely of a few hundred pages of printed marks; like defining a sculpture merely as any form carved out of stone or cast in metal. Jorge Luis Borges' fantasy, to which I referred before, is about a library which turns out to be the library of all possible books. The inhabitants of this library spend their lives in a search for meaning among its volumes. A book is defined here as—merely— any 400-page sequence of letters (and spaces) from the alphabet. If you calculate the number of books in Borges' library it turns out to be about two to the power 2^{20}. My students and I once estimated the number of the subset of such volumes which consist of recognized words organized grammatically into sentences, and this vastly reduced library, at a few volumes per kilogram, was still incomparably more massive than the known physical universe. I do not quite know how to estimate the number of distinct self-consistent formalized axiom sets of not unreasonable complexity, but I would guess it is at least large enough to use up a galaxy or two at the modest rate of 2^{48} kilograms/galaxy of printed paper.

We are in no different position with respect to sculpture or music or any other art. In one way we are in a worse position with respect to the development of mathematics: these axiom sets, though stated in a few pages, will entail an infinity of theorems from which we can in fact deduce only some selected finite number.

The view that mathematics is somehow only a vast tautology, that truth in mathematics has no relation to the order and connection of nature, is thus a misinterpretation of its schematic iterative style. If deductive formulation is necessary to its final formal product, this criterion alone does not enable us to distinguish between deductive sense and deductive nonsense. Defenders of the philosophy of Frege admit this criticism, indirectly, but by adding another criticism, one embedded in a doctrine of art for art's sake. From among the infinity of potential mathematical structures one picks for development only those which are aesthetically pleasing. Mathematics is, so to say, another genre of art, its products free creations of what is somewhat eulogistically called the human mind. No art is free except within the bounds of some discipline; the discipline of mathematics is the deductive mode. But otherwise—the argument goes—it is free. This view has been held by some first-rate mathematicians, notably by Hardy, just as the corresponding view in painting or literature has been held by some first-rate artists. The work of the mathematician may, on such a view, throw light on the world of man and nature, as if by chance. If so, again, *noblesse oblige*. T. S. Eliot produced, as an example of what might engross an artist fully, while lacking all practical utility or moral relevance, the following remarkable image—an eggshell on an altar. Unkind critics might seek to match this from some corners of contemporary mathematics. Surely, Hardy did not go so far as Eliot. His criterion of seriousness precluded that.

I think, however, that we can take one important lesson from this view. Whatever else it may be—and I have argued for much else—mathematics as my ideal teacher sees and lives it is unthinkable except as a kind of disciplined art. It is unsuccessful in the teaching or learning of it without that interplay of aesthetic tension and release involved in all creative activity, and which rewards all the intervening discipline which creativeness requires.

What is wrong with the doctrine of *art pour l'art* is that it makes a mystery of any kind of discipline at all. The essential art of mathematics, if I am right, is that of investigating hypothetical states of things through the discipline of schematization.

But I have only illustrated this Peircean doctrine, not developed it in detail. In particular I have not discussed the epistemological and historical origins, or the systematics of those basic mathematical structures we know and seek to regenerate in our teaching. Fortunately the subject is very much alive today, thanks in large measure to the work of Professor Piaget. In closing I can only comment on certain aspects of that work. From my own point of view, at least, Professor Piaget has brought about a long-overdue revitalization of the philosophical framework of Immanuel Kant, who developed the first coherent account of knowledge as the product of a self-regulating synthetic activity.

With respect to the proto-deductive style of mathematical thinking, Professor Piaget has made an important theoretical argument which is thoroughly Kantian in spirit, though grounded also in his own empirical studies of intellectual development. This argument concerns the origin and nature of our sense of logical entailment or necessity. Like Kant (and Hume), Piaget argues that contingent generalizations derived from factual observation can never, of themselves, give rise to this idea of necessity.

This sense of necessity is first operative, Piaget argues, in the habitual use of those schemata by which infants and children develop, with increasing competence, their ability to control and transform their material surroundings by systematic means. In still later intellectual development the distinction between the necessary and the contingent gains recognition by a kind of reflective abstraction; our knowledge can be traced partly to perception and partly to a growing awareness of our own active transformation of that experience into a stable and organized system of intellectual resources. Thus, for example, the space-group of translations and rotations (as Kant also long ago suggested) is developed first through the empirical fact that these are reversible operations whereas other changes, those which we describe only temporally, are not. It is not our direct perception of spatial properties which gives rise to our idea of space, but our reflection upon the operational or manipulatory schema which we have been busy developing since infancy at a motor-sensory level. In the same way our schema for counting and number evolves not from a direct perception of different degrees of numerosity, but from more primitive operations of matching and sequencing. In both cases a process of reflective abstraction, appearing in the fullness of time and experience and education, raises these schemata from the level of use to the level of *objects* for conscious scrutiny and analysis. When we have thus begun to be aware of what are in fact our own operational commitments; we find that they, so to speak, lead a life of their own; the number system or the nexus of geometrical relations as it were imposes its will on us, we are not free to imagine that there is a largest number, that seven has two immediate successors, or that there are spatially unconnected localities. But unlike Kant and Kant's predecessor Hume, Piaget has taken seriously the complex developmental nature of these ideas, and has brought it home to us naïve adults that our obvious necessities of thought are often disconcertingly absent in the thinking of young children, who typically make sense of their world in ways we have abandoned and can retrieve only with great imaginative effort. When I was speaking of a teacher's capacity to map the trajectories of children's thinking, I was referring in part to these way-stations of logical thought, which along with other childish things we have long since, most of us, put aside.

With all due respect to the theoretical perspectives and empirical studies of Piaget, I wish to emphasize what Piaget himself has often asserted, that this developmental framework is not directly relevant or adequate to the practical and theoretical perspective of a teacher. In particular there is a certain danger in the unimaginative use of Piagetian interviews to check off children's conceptual "attainments" and thus provide a sort of profile of individual developmental level. It would be very poor credit indeed to the thought of a great investigator if such very limited diagnosis became a sort of administrative substitute for the widely abused IQ, which, in turn, was poor credit to the early great investigations of Binet.

But more basically we must reserve judgment about inferences from the average behavior of groups of children of different ages to the actual pathways of individual growth. As we know from the theory of the comparative method, we can sometimes construct a fair description of the developmental stages of single organisms by observing samples of similar organisms of different ages. The means and variances obtained by this use of the comparative method are however significant only to the extent that we are sampling from populations which are uniform in essential respects—in some degree of approximation, for example, in the case of gross physical growth. If on the other hand we are interested in the common dynamics of growth in populations where individual development pursues different pathways, the means and variances of a composite picture may entirely mask the essential dynamics of the process.

When, for example, individual learning is in reality all-or-none, a group average may produce the standard continuous learning curve. And since children are in fact diverging in humanly important ways toward different careers, different competencies and insights, different talents and interests, a method which looks only at those common conceptual nodes which most biographical trajectories sooner or later traverse is likely to miss the most interesting part of the theory of learning and development, and the part most crucial to education. It is likely to observe the fine structure and the dynamics of transitions, differing from individual to individual, under such low resolving power that these are seen as little more than a residual statistical variance, what Piaget calls *décalages*.

None of this is said by way of criticism of Piaget's work, which in common with many others I both admire and learn from. What is at stake is that human creative capacities are only weakly inferrable by testing for the presence of those widely relevant schemata which —*because* they are widely relevant—we all do more or less competently develop, along one pathway or along another. The epistemological perspective of a teacher is one which is closer to the dynamics of developmentally significant learning, whereas this potentially vital role of a teacher is diluted out by the comparative method. In education as in biology the absence of a theory based on detailed study of specific transitions leads away from science toward orthogenesis, toward belief in the automatism of progress. One of the more enthusiastic of Piaget's adherents allegedly once said, "You don't have to teach, just wait a while." But that is a remark which cuts both ways; all cats look alike in the dark. On the other hand, the overwhelming mass of studies which deal with the effects of teaching deal with short-run reversible learning, of no particular educational significance. The really interesting problems of education are hard to study. They are too long-term and too complex for the laboratory, and too diverse and non-linear for the comparative method. They require longitudinal study of individuals, with intervention a dependent variable, dependent upon close diagnostic observation. The investigator who can do that and will do it is, after all, rather like what I have called a teacher. So the teacher himself is potentially the best researcher, if only we would offer him strong intellectual support and respect his potentialities as a scientist: lighten his mechani-

cal burdens, join him more frequently in his association with children, argue with him, pick his brains.

In the meantime the very existence of such a teacher as I have
described—and he does exist, though all too rarely throughout most
of the world—is a challenge to all the narrowing preconceptions and
practice of mathematics teaching as that art is usually described and
practiced.

Development as Education

In the summer of 1965 I was a guest of the Nuffield Junior Science Project in Britain. Its Director, Ronald Wastnedge, had visited the Elementary Science Study two years before, and we had discovered both bonds of common purpose and differences of style, the latter reflecting the divergence of British-American experience I have already discussed. In the earlier part of that year Frances Hawkins had been to Nigeria, involved in the beginnings of an African offshoot of the Elementary Science Study and its parent organization, Educational Services. She and I then met at a summer workshop and conference in Entebbe, Uganda. Through such associations we gained some first-hand acquaintance with primary school reform efforts brewing in other parts of the world. In all countries except Britain these efforts were confined to relatively few persons. Among these however, there appeared to be a basic consensus and kinship. We were strongly reminded that universal public education was a movement which, though scarcely a century old, had spread, without basic alteration, throughout the world. We were reminded also that everywhere its original promise had fallen far short of the high aspirations of its founders and promoters.

In economically poor countries particularly the politically irresistible demand for universal primary education has resulted in a widespread adoption of a European-American style of schooling. In most cases the meagerness of curriculum and the mechanical style can only be very partially offset by an unquestioning faith in its efficacy, the devotion of many teachers and the esteem in which they are held. Almost nowhere has there been any serious recognition of a challenge to evolve new educational patterns, even where the opportunity has existed. In many countries under colonialism schooling was, of course, deliberately engrafted in a way which was ignorant of or ignored local educational traditions, often rich ones. Intended or not, such schooling became a means toward the dislocation of traditional societies and the creation of petty bureaucracies and of urbanized wage labor.

In most parts of Africa, for example, schools will touch perhaps half of the

132

children, of whom some two thirds will leave before the completion of the primary years. Of those who complete primary school some very small percentage will "pass" and go on to secondary schools. Of these, in turn, a fair fraction will gain some special training, for example as teachers, or will go on to a university, at home or more rarely abroad.

For the overwhelming majority of children school is thus a cultural pathogen or antigen. Their "literacy" is often mechanical and useless, and fades away almost as rapidly as it was acquired. Thus of all the UNESCO statistics those on "literacy," considered as a measure of a country's educational level, are the most cruelly meaningless. As school leavers before secondary school the youth are "failures," though already often dissociated from family and village life and unequipped, at the same time, for the productive life of the city which school has seemed to promise. The graft is rejected, again, and in its disappearance leaves behind a mass of unorganized social tissue, in Toynbee's phrase a "cultural proletariat" who participate in neither the traditional society nor the new.*

Inadequate by European-American standards, and surely inadequate and inappropriate by any standards which are intrinsically defensible, such schooling accounts for a very large fraction of governmental budgets. Measured by any reasonable measure of effectiveness per quality unit of education (averaged over negative as well as positive outcome) schooling under such conditions is monumentally inefficient. It tends to create, moreover, a steep gradient toward those cumulative social ills already so familiar in our own world of rural and urban poverty, and minority existence. Indeed, the African picture only gains in significance for us when we consider it as a mirror—warped here and there, but still a mirror—of our own past and recent history.

And of course it is tempting to believe that when faced with such realizations, the new polities and governments of developing countries will increasingly initiate and support a radical re-examination and redefinition of their whole educational commitment. If they can do so they may well "leapfrog" —as Jerrold Zacharias once put it—over the developed world, an educational Macedonia to our Athens.

It was against this background, and in the context of a conference on economic development in the Arab world, that the ideas which follow began to

---

cf. Julius Nyerere, "Education for Self-Reliance," in *Freedom and Unity* (New York: Oxford University Press, 1967).

assemble themselves in my thinking. I was not yet acquainted with the polemical arguments and proposals of Ivan Illich or the reflections of Paulo Freire.* I do not think they would at all have swayed me from the position I took at the time, though they would surely have helped in my education. Perhaps here I should say again that the aim of my own thinking in these years has been to learn more about learning and teaching, and only from such a base to turn social critic. Illich condemns the modern institution of schooling as a wholly inadequate and stultifying one, and proposes to solve the problem by getting rid of schools, as we know them, altogether. In the course of his argument he is forced to imagine how a society like ours could expand its informal educative capacities to replace our present formal system and be rid of its inadequacies. This solution is what I would call a mathematical solution—an unreal solution which, however, can help us to define the problem better. A richly educated society would educate, at any rate, by easily evolved networks of informal and decentralized human associations. Like all "revolutionary" solutions to complex positive problems, this one generates a sort of Zeno's paradox of motion: how to get from here to there with resources that will only there be available. In the meantime the very effort to revitalize our schools, whatever its outcome, represents the kind of practical and intellectual work upon which the future of education, in school or out, depends. And in the meantime such efforts should join forces—the schools themselves should join forces—with those who like Ivan Illich seek to increase the educative potential of all our associations and institutions.

The kind of modest advisory system proposed in the following essay, a system which aims to bring more of society's scarce educational potential into the schools, is also if you wish only a "mathematical" solution. What makes its claim to realism is that it can start small to match that scarce potential and can grow by its successes. It is not true, as Spinoza said, that all noble things are as difficult as they are rare. But apparently they have to begin that way.

---

*Ivan Illich, *De-Schooling Society*, (New York: Harper & Row, 1971); Paulo Freire, *Pedagogy of the Oppressed*, tr. by Myra Bergman Ramos (New York: Seabury, 1971).

Development as Education: A Proposal for the Improvement of Elementary Education
(1967)

The American economist Kenneth Boulding recently remarked in an informal talk on education that what economists mean by the word capital is, in essence, knowledge. Economic growth is, by the same sign, learning.

In spite of certain objections which a literal-minded critic might make to this identification, it comes from an eminent economist who was by no means joking, and it is surely suggestive and deserves attention. Professor Boulding commented, in passing, upon the speed with which Germany and Japan, possessing much capital in this sense, have been able to recover from large wartime destruction.

When we reflect further about the nature of economic wealth, we are led to recognize that all productive processes are governed by systems of technology which have, so to speak, a double function. One function is the direction and execution by which material embodiments of knowledge and skill are constantly produced. Another is the reproduction of that very knowledge and skill which, in an expanding economy, must be reproduced at an expanding rate.

Concerning the two processes, the production governed by technology and the self-reproduction which governs technology, a very simple consideration suffices to rank them. They are related roughly as type to token. For each human embodiment of the technology and skill, of the type or archetype, there are many physical embodiments, or tokens, produced. Another way of saying the same thing is that the time scale of reproduction of the technology is long compared to the average time scale of production. Thus in even a mechanical sense the human reproduction and growth of technology is a limiting factor upon the physical production processes of a society. Value in the classical real-cost sense of the term, the embodiment of human labor in material form, is premised upon skill and understanding which is not itself produced in the same sense, but transmitted through the processes of culture; through the play of young children, the apprenticeship of work, and the special channels of formal education. When we examine the totality of conditions under which this reproduction of labor skills occurs, it is co-extensive with the entire life of the society. An American Indian friend of Ruth Benedict spoke to her of a cup which the gods made for every people, to hold their lives. And he added, of the life of his own people, disappearing amid the invasion and indifference of neo-American life: "Our cup is broken."

The picture I suggest is in effect one of two levels for economic analysis: the first level includes appropriation from nature, production, exchange and consumption of goods and services, including the replacement of fixed capital, exports and imports, etc. At this level we may consider economic growth, balanced or unbalanced, the construction of new physical capital, and of technical services, indigenous or imported. Superimposed on this level, with its implied framework of public and private ownership, markets, financial institutions and exchange, we have another level, the human and cultural matrix which, while depending upon the material economy for the short run, in the longer run limits and shapes that economy.

In the literature of economic development education is considered as very important. It is recognized as a key factor in the growth of an exchange economy and a literate middle class, in the creation of skilled labor power and a scientific and technological elite. But the educational system is treated as if what went on in it was a sort of standard production process with well-defined inputs, outputs and fiscal requirements. It is assimilated to the lower of my two levels, of no more intrinsic interest to the theorist of development than the inner operation of an oil refinery. Its function is conceived as that of producing a population increasingly ready to embrace and further the new industrial technology which development requires.

This view of education, and of economic development, is I believe profoundly wrong, for it hides from view the relationship between the material economy and the general culture. The very reason for insisting upon a two-level conception of human economics is that the terms of economic analysis in the narrow sense presuppose a social nexus within which the equations of technology and distribution are definable at all, but which itself is not susceptible to analysis in economic language. This cultural nexus is too complex and too historically rooted to yield to mechanistic analysis. To forget this is to forget that *ordre naturel* within which the *tableau économique* can be isolated for study. For Quesnay the *ordre naturel* was something fixed and given. For us, confronted with the instabilities of all contemporary cultures, this cannot be so. No culture today can reproduce itself except in altered form, and the cup that is not refashioned will indeed be broken. Thus to treat education as a mere matter of stocks and flows, of routine services and predictable transformations, is both a moral and theoretical error. It is a moral error if education is not seen first as the way in which a culture can assimilate new knowledge and new interests, seeking continuity and integrity in the transformations it must then embrace. For then otherwise the living culture, rooted deeply in a pre-industrial past, will continue to stand as a massive hindrance, as an interminable source of "inefficiency and corruption," corroding away the very machinery of progress including that of formal education. It is a theoretical error to see formal education as able to detach itself from the living culture except relatively, except as a current within the culture. In what follows I shall be concerned to define this relativity more carefully and thereby also to suggest for it a more effective role than it now plays.

Under the term "education," therefore, one must understand all the social influences, evolved and designed, which bear upon and foster learning from the time of birth. Of these influences the special institution of school is an essential but dependent one, and it is to the aims and problems of schools that I speak. If one examines the history of school education—which began not far from here in the urban society of ancient Mesopotamia—one sees it as having had a special character, centering on the very arts and skills which still define its dominant content of reading, writing, and arithmetic. In that ancient society the school was an instrument to mark off and instruct a special division of labor connected with functions of priesthood and bureaucratic management. It was by no means a substitute for the informal education of family life or village life, but began with such education fully presupposed, being thus an informational superstructure built on foundations taken for granted.

Throughout the history of education, until very recently, this foundation has still been taken for granted, presupposed but unexamined. In modern societies whose economic development has pushed ahead in recent centuries, spreading north in Europe from medieval Mediterranean civilization, the content of formal education has evolved and branched impressively. Yet only in very recent times has it come to the place where the educated world has begun to look seriously at its own foundations in the life and learning of children.

The demand for universal formal education, school education, is only a very few generations old in any country. I think it may safely be said that in no country, at the present time, is it a reality even by fairly minimal standards. The mere condition of literacy, widely taken as an index of minimal education, is a very poor one on which to base any serious and reflective consideration of the problems we face. Literacy is implied, to be sure, by any level of formal education above the most rudimentary. But literacy must be accompanied by other forms and conditions of learning before it can possibly be thought of as a stage sufficient to open doors even to higher primary or secondary education. In the United States at the present time, for example, there is a substantial minority of children who, although literate by the most rudimentary definition, are in a state which makes virtually the whole of our present primary and secondary education, considered with respect to its substance, inaccessible to them. These are our school leavers, our dropouts. They are carried along to the legal age limit of compulsory schooling but the care bestowed upon them is essentially custodial. And accompanying this pattern, with its endlessly repeated frustrations and failures, is a loss, a negative education, which I for one believe outweighs any accompanying benefits.

We see the limitations of the traditional style and content of formal education most clearly where it has become most prevalent and is, in that sense, most successful. What we see is that an essential part of the learning of children, which our schools are supposed to bestow, in fact comes before the school or alongside of it, and comes to different children very unequally. In the past we have accepted this unevenness either without question or with easy assumptions about the variance of biological endowment—and the "we" who have accepted this view have, of course, been of the favored minority. It is also true that if we look to the conditions favorable to success in our schools, the *preponderant* conditions have to do with children's early exposure, indeed since birth, to a social environment in which the fruits of formal education, in the previous generation, have already been enjoyed and assimilated. In other words, the most powerful force for education in the *content* which schools prize and foster has been, if I may phrase it so, in the folk-culture of the well educated. Children who have lived and flourished in this culture are on the whole able to take from school that which will advance their learning. And I say "take *from* school" advisedly, because this implies a basis of learning that in reality lies outside the school.

What has happened in the United States is that the growth of education is far slower than the growth of schooling, and also slower than the changes in our economic and cultural life, which demand a higher level of skill and understanding than in fact our society, through formal and informal means, can provide. The result is a widening gap which becomes more and more visible. It is the awareness of this gap which underlies much of our recently renewed concern about the quality of our elementary and secondary schools.

In speaking about such matters in the context of the present conference it is my aim to express a point of view, and a hope—a rather wry hope. The point of view is one which suggests the need to re-examine some quite fundamental assumptions about primary education. The hope is that in so-called developing countries this re-examination may lead to the exploration and development of quite radically new patterns for schools to follow, in both curriculum and instructional style, that will enable such countries, as they devote increasing budgets to universal education, to by-pass serious mistakes inherent in the established European and American school systems. Perhaps our mistakes could not *easily* have been anticipated, although they have in fact been seen by a long minority tradition, illustrious but practically ignored, from Rousseau to John Dewey. It is my hope that as these mistakes become even more obvious and well defined, countries not yet fully committed to them will avoid them and thus become leaders rather than followers.

One problem is nearly universal, I think. Everywhere in the world people have seen in education a great hope for the betterment of life, and this hope has seized the imaginations of all. But in many places the European and American patterns of schools, so closely tied to the new learning of science, mathematics and industrial technology, will not easily fulfill its promise, even when accepted with the greatest enthusiasm. For it is also tied to what I have called "the folk-culture of the already well educated," and there have lain its traditional and impressive successes.

I can only speak of the developing countries from some knowledge of Latin America and Africa, but at least in those regions there is a pattern of early school leaving which is a source of major concern. These school leavers are fitted neither to return to the life of their childhood nor for the new life which education itself has seemed to promise. The result is a large body of youth who are doomed to an unproductive and alienated existence, and indeed bearing a strong resemblance, in spite of superficial differences, to the North American youth of whom I spoke earlier. In many of the new countries of Africa, in particular, it will be a long time before even universal primary education is an accomplished fact. Yet the schooling which is received may be sufficient to disorient many from the life they came from, while *leaving* them unfit for the new life of a more urbanized, commercial and industrial society. It would be an oversimplification to say that the schools are the sole vehicle of such dislocation, towards which many other social forces join. But the schools are such a vehicle, and a strategic one.

Under these circumstances one is forced to re-examine the foundations I spoke of, and it is to that which I wish to devote the remainder of my paper. This needed re-examination moves, as I see it, between two poles, universal and particular. At one pole attention must be directed to the human infant and child, and here we may hope to benefit by research and practical experience that transcends cultural boundaries. At the other pole we must look to the resources of children's environment—human and natural—as providing the essential material of their education. It is material which will not be twice the same, in different countries or even in different regions. In the minority tradition of European-American education, supported now by clinical research and by early practical success in some countries, notably England, there is mounting evidence to support the belief that the most basic learning processes are entirely dependent upon a *two-way* interaction between the learner and his material and social environment. That is one basic statement. Another is that teaching, conceived narrowly as the transmission of verbal structures and instructions, always presupposes an antecedent learning of perceptual content and conceptual operations which are effected *first* at an essentially non-verbal active level. When we take these two propositions together we are ready, I think, to see why and how the out-of-school aspect of education has always been so crucial, and why its deficiency has tended to limit the value of schooling in an almost *a priori* fashion. For schools have never been organized on either principle, but have put the child predominantly and from the beginning in the role of a passive recipient of symbolic, verbal instruction.

A third basic statement about learning, coupled to the above two, is that it is an active process not only in the sense of motor-sensory coupling between the learner and his environment, but also in the sense of being self-organizing, not subject to direct external control or command. Because children differ in constitution and temperament, and also in the history of their previous learning, each child will assimilate experience and knowledge *selectively* from his environment, in accordance with *his* momentary readiness and *his* unique individual style. This has, of course, always been widely known, but has been regarded more as a perversity of child-nature than as a ground for criticizing educational patterns which ignore and fail to exploit it. The development of the child, like that of the culture, must come from within.

When we examine the implications of these three basic propositions, they lead to a practical conclusion. This conclusion can best be stated in the form of a description of a classroom which differs, in important respects, from prevailing classrooms all over the world.

First and quite basically, the room contains many kinds of materials and equipment available for children's use. There are written and printed materials as well, and these permeate every aspect of the work, but they are not detached and they do not dominate. A child learns to read and write about matters which have seized his imagination, through practical work and discussion. Where literacy has been a major goal the tools of reading and writing have often pushed everything else out, thus stimulating and utilizing only a minute fraction of the child's abilities. There are hard economic questions connected with the well-stocked classroom, one that readmits the world into the classroom, and not just the book. To which I shall return.

A second feature of the good classroom is the role of a teacher, and the role of children, in working with and teaching each other. The teacher very seldom is addressing a whole class; that is only *one* of several important phases. More often the work is decentralized, and children are directing their own work, choosing both *what* they will work with and *how* they will work. Here the teacher's role is to diagnose the needs of individuals and provide materials for choice in accordance with this diagnosis. Such decentralization is possible only because of the wide variety of materials provided. This makes it possible for the teacher to intervene directly with individuals and small groups, where readiness and need is greatest. To give each child a larger fraction of personal attention for a smaller fraction of the total time is to make possible two beneficial results. First, the child is more often using his own resources or those of his fellows, which thus are cultivated. And second, the teacher can meet a single child or a small group with far greater relevance than when dealing with a whole class at once.

A third characteristic of such classrooms is that children are free to move around in their work and to talk about it in the process, thus constantly raising the level of their discourse to that of the important subject matter—intellectual, artistic, practical—with which they are occupied. And this raising of levels is in turn coupled to their writing and reading. The teacher's authority and discipline are not threatened by such informality, because that authority does not *depend* on having the only voice. The discipline is that of workmen engrossed in work, not that of adult coercion.

It is quite evident that such a classroom requires not only ample materials and supplies, but also a very competent and perceptive human being as teacher. To many persons these two conditions imply that the school I speak of is utopian. This is the common reaction we have to such proposals in the United States. In countries where budgets are smaller and teachers receive on the average less formal education, it may seem utopian indeed. But I believe it is not so. My reasons for saying this lead me now to the other pole of my description of a better education. This concerns the continuity of the curriculum with the world outside the school, which we must conceive broadly as the physical and biological environment, the social environment, and the environment of ideas.

A large part of the material and equipment in the classroom will not be purchased at the insufferable prices of school supply firms, but will represent concrete materials from the city market, the village, the farm or the nearby forest or hillside.[1] Plants are grown from seeds and cuttings, there is an aquarium in a cheap plastic bowl. And there are microscopes, costing if necessary nothing at all—a piece of suitably cut and folded cardboard, a drop of wax and a drop of water will suffice. Small animals of the vicinity find their way there too, for study of their food habits and behavior. There are torches, candles, mirrors and a water prism. Mechanics is represented by inclined planes, unequal arm balances, springs and weights, and pendulums. There is water and sand. Geometry and arithmetic are represented by an abundance of concrete materials—pebbles, marbles in cups, small tiles from the market, wire frames for dipping in soap solution to study their colors and shapes. There are books, some having been written by children, with pictures, to be read by other children. And what of the arts? Clay and other plastic materials are provided, as is paint for the easel, yarn for the loom, and the tools of cutting and carving.

I could extend the list; what I have mentioned is only an illustrative sample. My point is that many of the essential materials already exist largely in the surrounding milieu, and are familiar to the adults of the surrounding community. Indeed they are often more familiar to the relatively uneducated than to the "educated"—yet these are the concrete embodiment of all the essential beginnings of the higher culture—of science, mathematics, literature—as well as the common practical arts.

It is true that such materials can serve only with the guidance of skilled teachers. But who is the skilled teacher? I think of two Kikuyu teachers, in the Ngong forest of Kenya, with primary schooling plus two years of secondary; one would not trade them for very many B.A.s. To be a skilled teacher in primary school is to satisfy criteria which higher education very seldom aims to bestow: to be easy and attentive with children, to find them fascinating bundles of capability and potential; to love the world around, and to wish to induct children into the exploration of its marvels and mysteries; to know enough of the disciplines to be able to learn more, sometimes with children rather than ahead of them. All of this lies within the capacity of rather simple people—simple, that is, from the point of view of the academically sophisticated like ourselves, who are somehow seldom sophisticated enough to rediscover the breadth and depth of the childhood world, or to applaud the talents of those who can.

But none of this "old-new" mode of education for children will develop by itself. One component is needed, one kind of catalytic agent must be supplied and given economic support. And in general, so far as I know, this component is in scarce supply. What is needed is a new kind of organization and staff which unites the world of higher education and the world of children and teachers in schools. This organization will serve multiple functions. In some respects it will resemble that of school inspectors or supervisors, but the essential role will be advisory rather than supervisory, working with teachers rather than above them, bringing new ideas and materials to a school, and staying long enough to induct a teacher or two in their uses.

But where will such ideas and materials come from? One person who works in that role gave a short answer: "By blowing sparks into flame." To do this an adviser must have both wide knowledge and wide sympathies. Here is a teacher who has thought it worthwhile in instructing children about the clock, for example, to introduce a sun-dial. The adviser is one who knows a little about the central place of this instrument in the history of astronomy, and suggests an investigation of light and shadow, making shadows in the school yard through the day, working indoors with sticks, torches, mirrors, pinhole images, and all the rest. Many of the phenomena are familiar to children and adults, but have never been invested with educational value for either. Yet out of just these phenomena came beginnings of cosmography, of geometry, and of that extraordinary history which leads from ancient Mesopotamia and Egypt to Athens, Alexandria, to the court of Harun al-Rashid, Toledo, and in the end to landings on the moon and Venus. But it begins in the school yard and returns there repeatedly to catch new phenomena, new discussions, new involvements—because, as we say, that is where the action is.

Another crucial advisory function is to make what teachers and groups of children do visible, harvesting what has proven its worth for others, helping them to assimilate and adapt, thus findng new pathways and new linkages with other significant subject-matter. What evolves in this way is not imposed from above and does not arise spontaneously from below. Teachers, advisers, scientists and scholars all have a contribution to make; but the children, ignored in most educational invention, will be the main contributors—for they, and they alone, can tell us what is for them exciting, absorbing and liberating.

At this stage I want to mention and dwell on one other source to feed the evolution of education, namely the adult community from which children are not yet separated except by the school door, which is too often closed. Just as is true of the natural world, there are deep sources of education within any human community whether urban or rural. Consider first the variety of skills and arts practiced there—of construction, of weaving, of mechanics, of song and instrument and dance. Such arts are typically learned by apprenticeship, not in school. Yet children's early encounter with them, when invested with educational value, can bring to the fore aspects and implications of these arts which are now for the most part lost—aspects of mathematics, of physics, of chemistry, of economics and history. In all of this potentially rich subject-matter there is a strong continuity with community life and also a certain discontinuity—for what is practiced and passed on in the life of the community may also, when brought into the school, be examined and investigated on another level, relating it to the world of the sciences and humanities. But it cannot be understood in the full sense, and cannot be a starting point for exploration and curiosity, except as it is pursued on *both* levels, by participation as well as by observation, discussion, reading and writing. A crucial point arises here relating to the alienation of children from their own background which has been so conspicuous in our changing societies. In moving schools towards a far greater use of local resources, including human resources, children's already acquired strengths are brought to the fore and are directed back upon the lives they lead outside school, rather than by-passed as in standard curricula at present. But because of the simultaneous levels of work possible in schools, the life of the community can be *both* valued as a possession *and* criticized from a wider and more detached point of view, bringing to bear upon it new knowledge and understanding.

It is my thesis that the deliberate and planful establishment of the advisory, catalytic function I have outlined is a way, and so far as I know the only way, leading out of the relative sterility and failure of modern mass education. But I am all too well aware that when you search for persons of the requisite talent and education for this role they are few indeed. Yet I think that here again there is an answer, which lies in the willingness, the necessity, to start on a very small scale but with extra resources, on that scale, for rapid growth. Persons already competent—and competence includes the capacity to learn—must have their own apprentices, drawn carefully from the younger people of universities and training colleges, who in a very few years may then graduate to more independent status.

In the beginning, working on a small scale, advisers can work only in a few localities, picking first the liveliest and best teachers; "finding the growth points," as one adviser put it. As these teachers' work becomes visible it must be helped to spread. That will not happen spontaneously, but it is easier than the first beginnings. Clearly the advisory staff must grow, but only with its successes; and success can powerfully help in the necessary shifts of budgetary priorities. Such talk may sound overoptimistic, but I believe early successes and growth on the small scale, with proper staffing and proper political support, is quite predictable. One is after all not competing against educational patterns that are already effective; often indeed even rudimentary gains are very visible. Profounder and less reversible gains will not come fast, and I make no claim to chart their course—only to say that there are good beginnings, and that we should indeed begin them. One *knows* the kinds of first steps I have outlined are good. One *believes* they can be made self-propagating through the guidance of thoughtful and devoted advisers. One *hopes* that in such a context of educational development it will prove possible to dig deeper into the problems of learning and teaching than has been possible heretofore. Early small-scale development can be rapid, and can provide the capital—the living knowledge—for further growth. In the United States we have often insisted on "starting big," with the result that quality is compromised at the outset.

There is one skeptical objection to the process proposed, based on past experience. Why is it, one may ask, that the existing educational superstructure of the schools (principals or headmasters, supervisors or inspectors, and training colleges) have not *already* brought about such changes? The answer I have is a plea of ignorance, tempered by one major piece of evidence and the conclusions it suggests. So far as I know Britain is, at the present time, the leading country of the world in bringing about just the changes I have spoken of. No documents, alone, will convey the style and content of the best British Infant and Junior Schools today, but the Plowden Report[2] is required reading for those who would learn more from a distance. British successes in major educational reform are still far short of the possible, but they are impressive. And there has been one major condition satisfied, I think almost uniquely, in the British context. This is precisely the existence of the advisory staffs around which I have built my case. One should mention, first, the HMIs, the National Inspectorate. This Inspectorate was created originally to examine pupils and see that the schools were "measuring up to standards." But later, with increasing local and school autonomy, the Inspectors began to transform their function from supervisory to advisory, and lost their threatening mien as omniscient judges of performance. Decentralization robbed them of one power and granted another, that of supporting and discovering the creativity of teachers and making the ideas and inventions of these teachers visible to others. In many cases this advisory function has evolved also within local school systems and training colleges. A rather consistent feature of the whole process is that advisers are not involved in the line organization of school systems. They thus do not have coercive powers, but only persuasive ones. On the other hand they are independent, not themselves subject to coercive control with respect to the content or form of their advisory work. And it goes without saying that their role is understood and supported by the Ministry or the local authorities. From one case such as the British, however plausibly supported by general wisdom, one cannot sustain the conclusion that the British pattern is the only one. Still it is a real case, and we should study it carefully.

Here ends my sketch of a possible plan for the development of early education to new levels of quality and productivity. I shall not follow the argument back to my beginning, in which I suggested the identification of economic growth with the intensive cultivation of human resources for learning and inquiry on the widest possible scale, beginning with the earliest school years. I am content to let that identification stand for examination and argument.

But it is proper to close by reiterating the suggestion that education in developing countries is intrinsically able to evolve more effective patterns of teaching and learning than is easily possible in the so-called developed countries, where the resources of wealth are so heavily committed to massive school establishments. Perhaps Britain, with a backward look at Empire and a foreward look at grave unsolved economic problems, might once more be classed as a *developing* nation! In the perspectives of education that declaration might have a very positive ring to it.

But our concern is with the developing countries as usually defined, which surely lack the resources of the great industrial nations, Britain included. What I have tried to argue is that childhood education is a key to the future of the former countries, and indeed the latter as well, in a sense far deeper than is usually understood. I have not followed the argument to its implications for secondary or higher education, but I do not think the cases to be made are different in essence. At any level such formal education cannot succeed as a pattern superimposed upon and against the common culture, but only as it roots itself and evolves, within that culture. In this essay I have tried to suggest a way by which existing resources in developing countries, each with its own special traditions, pressing problems and sources of strength, can grow to meet and feed the needs of an expanding material economy without losing, as is so tragically possible, its distinctive style and genius, without breaking the cup that holds its life.

REFERENCES

1. In British Colonial Africa the frogs for dissection in the biology course had to be imported from England, to fit the drawings in the textbook—African frogs did not

measure up! Much of our school equipment has a comparable history. That is what happens when a system is imposed, either by empire, by foreign experts, or by the home-grown variety.

2. *Children and Their Primary Schools: A Report of the Central Advisory Council for Education (England)*, 2 vols. (London: HM Stationery Office, 1967).

On Environmental Education

In the fall of 1969 we returned to the United States after a year's absence and became aware of a rather startling change. Long-standing concerns of environmentalists had at last begun to seize the public imagination. The protection of the physical and biological environment had become, at least superficially, a political issue.

During the previous year or so we had been making plans for an expanded Center at the University of Colorado, a center devoted to advisory work with teachers, offering professional help of a kind too seldom and too little available. Unlike our previous work in curriculum development, this center was to be an example, we hoped, of badly needed professional support for the most strategic part of the entire educational process—teachers.

A minor problem was that of titles and labels. The old label seemed debased coin, "progressive" education. "Open" education seemed equally undescriptive, and "informal" education—a label more often used in England —seemed unenlightening. One substantive feature of the kind of educational progress we had seen and wished to advocate kept coming to mind. It was a major emphasis on the importance of a rich material environment as the context—the indispensable context—of children's learning and growth. I have tried elsewhere to spell this out in some detail. Suffice it to say here that we wished to emphasize the needed richness of the material environment within the walls of a school, and the school's readiness to use the educational potential of its immediate geographical and human surroundings. So we had been led to the term "environmental education" as suggesting what we stood for. Our major emphasis was not on such negative aspects as pollution and contamination, but on giving children opportunity for engagement and enjoyment of the great world around them. Except against such a joyous childhood background the looming ecological problems of human existence would fail to gain esthetic, moral or intellectual substance.

So there is a broad and narrow view of what "environmental" education means. Our belief about the right relation between these two views was

150

reinforced by the fact that our initial financial support came jointly from the Ford Foundation Office of Public Education and the Office of Resources and Environment, who shared our opinion that the "narrow" issues of environmental protection, adequately understood, must sooner or later lead to a recasting of the whole pattern of public education, indeed of our culture as a whole. As one of our co-workers, Ronald Colton, has put it, education for the environment must be education through the environment.

At any rate we didn't intend to use a catchy title, and we are not very much interested in field trips up the hillside to look at the smog-layer when these might miss the trees and the birds and the fossils to be found along the way.

Such is the background of the testimony which follows.

On Environmental Education*

(1970)

As a college teacher of philosophy and of science and mathematics I have long been acutely and sometimes frustratingly aware of the fact that education, like politics, is an art of the possible. What this means, to a teacher, is that the young human mind is not an open filing system in which teachers can store the fruits of society's wisdom, but a highly reactive and selective affair which accepts, reorganizes or rejects what we offer in accordance with its own inner program of readiness, need and motivation.

If frustration is the inevitable consequence of thoughtful teaching, the other side is delight—delight with the inventiveness of the young mind, with new perspectives and connections, and so with the opportunity to learn while teaching. Good teachers are those who learn to steer themselves by these responses and so maintain the freshness of subject matter and of their own minds.

I make these remarks at a time when there is widespread and varied criticism of our educational system. The United States has been one of the great traditional leaders in universal elementary and secondary education, and there is deep puzzlement as to why a

*Testimony before the Committee on Labor and Public Welfare, U.S. Senate Education Subcommittee, May 19, 1970.

system, of which we have been so justly proud in the past, should now receive such devastating criticism for its failures. Somewhere between the changes of our unique North American social scene with its propitious racial mixtures, the changes of the schools themselves, and the changes in our own perceptions, a gap has appeared and widened rapidly between what is and what ought to be. This need not be considered a negative state of awareness.

On the contrary, I think the evidence shows clearly that part of the change is a new recognition that we have indeed never done very well by a large fraction of children and youth. I refer to the army induction tests and other large-scale studies restricted, as they mainly have been, to rudimentary literacy and other such narrow skills and understanding. A second part of the change is that there has been increasing dislocation in the lives of many of our children—in suburbs and slums for example—which among other serious symptoms has led to a widespread alienation from traditional neighborhood school patterns and programs. Many children not only drop out—educationally speaking—but never drop in (with their minds) in the first place. Our real educational needs have increased and not just our subjective awareness of past failure.

The traditional offerings of school, including kindergarten, do not match the limitations *or* the strengths of many of these children whose families are new to the "school" educational scene, and there begins a long and dreary process of boredom and failure which dooms them to further alienation from the early days of what we call "their" failure. Thus also there is a new challenge to be met.

Another aspect of the widening gap affects children even from well-educated families as the lengthening years of childhood, adolescence and "young adulthood" swell the numbers of human beings who are in but not of our working society. These demand a new sort of involvement and relevance in their lives which they fail to find in school and have not yet found in the apprenticeship of work. From them also a need to learn, which was once more adequately met outside of school, brings challenge to the educational system.

Let me add another to this catalogue of woes and opportunities, necessarily a matter of personal interpretation. In spite of hard and devoted work by many of our nearly two million elementary and secondary teachers, there is a sense of frustration and demoralization widespread among them in the face of public indifference, neglect or lack of imaginative awareness of the needs teachers have in order to grow and change with new developments in society. This demoralization has existed for a long time in urban systems, and the outcry of newly developing constituencies—of urban blacks and Indians and Mexican-Americans in particular—has made it more widely visible. While bond issues fail, economic needs increase in our urban school systems, and we are in mounting trouble.

The central aspect of education I single out, in all of this, is a need to carry forward the initial promise of American education—but with a new emphasis. One of the signs of demoralization most conspicuous from the inside is an increasing acceptance of the belief that teachers are not really professional persons who are accorded the freedom and dignity of planning their own work with their children, of learning themselves. Traditional "canned" learning aids, useful to teachers as adjuncts to their work, are developed more and more ambitiously—not as adjuncts, but as replacements of the teacher's work, "teacher-proof" materials. Teachers are very often hemmed in by inflexible timetables, by inflexible system-wide "adoption" of textbooks and guides which pre-program the daily work, sometimes literally even putting words in their mouths—and, amazingly, their children's. All of this work is of course much tried and tested, but I have yet to see an evaluator's report which says, in effect, "this program is no good."

Such beliefs and practices tend, of course to be self-confirming. Teachers who are not treated as professionals often fail to grow professionally, and often themselves drop out after a very few years. The rapid turnover of elementary school teachers is usually attributed to a stereotype of the young girl college graduate who only intends to teach for a short time until, allegedly, she finds the right man and settles down to being a happy homebody with no further professional life. The truth is, I believe, that many of our potentially best drop out from discouragement and fatigue as a result of being treated like cogs or ciphers. And the result is that we keep for long terms only the very hardy best, or those insensitive enough to regard teaching as a routine job.

Thus it is that all three explanations of the newly visible gap are partially correct. First, our schools have never evolved to the place where they were adequate to the task of universal mass education, especially that of children from poor and poorly educated backgrounds. It is only some four generations, after all, since the time when schools were mainly for the literate and well-to-do, and their progress in style and content has not yet adapted them to the century-old need and opportunity to expand into new areas. Second, the problems of early education have intensified in several ways. Deprivation in the lives of children from new-old slum, new suburbia, old Indian reservation, forces us to re-examine the old presuppositions underlying the curriculum, to ask anew what various groups of 5- and 6-year-olds are really like, what their early learning and development really equip them for as a springboard, and in what *kind* of schools they are ready to function well.

Third, there is a new demand, and a new promise, in childhood and adolescent education which makes us see more clearly than ever before the inadequacies of the old education and the reasons for its failure in the lives of so many of the children of today.

It is from the perspective of this third partial explanation that I wish to speak about the importance of a new turn in the evolution of schools, and about what I would mean, in particular, by the phrase "environmental education."

I believe that funds which might be appropriated in support of environmental education will be looked at in two rather different ways. There will be a majority view, I fear, which will see the existing school system only as an available means for advancing the cause of sensitizing or rote "teaching-learning" of new generations to a concern for the preservation of the environment. Then there will be a minority view, with which I strongly identify myself, which sees the new concern about the welfare of our environment as a way of advancing the more general cause of education. Froebel's perception of school as a *Kindergarten*, a child's garden, must be deepened and rescued from its nineteenth-century parochial limitations. The planet is our ragged garden and children who grow to honor it must first live well within it—for us they are the central core of *our* environment. This second view shares a deep skepticism that we will face and welcome the new problems of our relation to Mother Earth unless we reorient our whole culture and conception of what education is and ought to be.

The central point in this needed reorientation, then, is a conception of education as environmental in style. The adequate development of the human mind and character depends on the learner's personal involvement with the world around him. In and through this involvement a child is able to assimilate knowledge and tradition as these match his own growing perceptions and needs.

From this point of view there is a basic inadequacy in the conception of school which fails to value, provide for, and in all ways encourage children's active involvement in understanding and exploring the world around them. On the other hand, it is a romantic fallacy to suppose that this sort of activity—for which children come well-equipped at birth—can be sustained, enjoyed, deepened, and made lifelong merely by benign adult permissiveness and provisioning. This is a fallacy indulged in by some of today's radical critics of our schools, as though all one had to do were to get out of children's hair. Good teaching is a many-sided professional activity which indeed often leaves children on their own resources—partly to discover what those resources are. Knowing those resources, on the other hand, good teachers sometimes intervene actively to redirect the work and sometimes join in an investigation as partners in the enterprise. The over-riding purpose is that children can grow in knowledge and organization, discipline, and independence of mind and character. There are occasions for coercion, but in good schools these are infrequently and decreasingly needed.

To be very concrete about the meaning of environmental education, imagine first an elementary-school classroom which you visit on a Saturday morning. There are no teachers or children around, and you are required to infer from your inspection just what has been going on in the lives of those children in the previous days and weeks. In classroom after classroom you will find a few wall charts, a few neat displays of all-rather-similar paintings, a few rows of workbooks and books, some pictures of astronauts, and perhaps, for example, a chart declaring the dependence of all living things on sunlight—but few living things. What you will scarcely find displayed are any samples of the *immediate* unique environment in any profusion, any evidence of individual investigations in progress, children's own graphs, maps, written summaries, shelves full of jars, wire, simple tools and apparatus, experiments with seeds and plant cuttings, a microscope or two, animal cages, rocks from the local geology, or rubbings from the old gravestones in a nearby churchyard. Nor will you find a sizable display of books other than a few textbooks—there exists an increasing array of small inexpensive monographs and story books which represent some of the best and most exciting children's literature. Some of these are in a school library if the school boasts one, but they are not often available for reading and study in the place where the action might be, the classroom. One could add to the list of missing items a tape recorder, a film-loop projector with a file of loops in a corner carrel, a Polaroid camera. But books above all can be the great storehouse, the stimulus to enter a world beyond the immediate, and except for a few primers and texts we exclude them from the rich imaginative uses which a classroom could provide. "Reading" as practiced in most elementary schools is in essence a mechanical instruction in unmotivated decoding or translation, the aim and savor of which is lost on all but those happy few who learn elsewhere the real romance of all those little marks on paper. Writing is similarly mechanical for the most part, in which spelling, sentences and paragraphs are valued but not the intent of a child's potential for fresh and vivid communication about his own world. Our schools predominantly neglect the concrete stimuli to thoughtful and imaginative communication which could be the context for strongly motivated reading and writing. In pursuing a curriculum which minimizes children's direct investigative contact with the world around them, we make everything depend on an abstract symbolic medium which in that very process is drained of vitality and meaning. During the past eight years I have spent all or part of my time working in and around our elementary schools and have been a visiting teacher in many schools here, in Britain and in Africa. I have come to the conclusion that there is one really hopeful pathway of progress. In various places I have seen the beginnings of it, and in a few it is well along. Progress lies in the evolution of a style of school and classroom organization which engages children far more and far more actively than at present with the natural and human world around them—not just in the context of science or social studies, but also as fresh subject matter for artistic expression, for mathematical analysis, for astronomy, history, for reading and writing.

Such a thoroughgoing shift in emphasis can be evolved through a many-sided effort by teachers, principals, coordinators, and with the understanding and support of local authorities and parents—again the art of the possible, but with essential steps already known and described, and at least as feasible and challenging as the exploration of the moon.

One crucial step, partly charted, is that which helps teachers to rescue themselves for new levels of work and insight. In workshop situations many teachers become involved with environmental subject-matter that is tangible and fresh, and discover in a very personal way what one teacher expressed in delight—"I have a mind!" The occasion was one of capital scientific discovery, that a soap film spanning a twisted wire frame will contract to a shape with minimum area. She could have been told this in 30 seconds, but it could not have brought insight or new mental power without her considerable work or play with the fascinating shapes and colors of the Plateau surfaces. In her eyes, moreover, it gave new dignity and potential to children's endless fascination with an ancient toy—that after *such* pleasures the mind is in a new state of readiness to organize and reason.

The three R's should be woven into every activity of a proper environmental education, not kept aside in separate periods unless a time is ripe for separation. The curriculum is a system including subject matter objectives, as always, but it is fulfilled in different ways for different children and groups. It is planned and organized for diversity and for openness to specific topics and enterprises which a manifold environment and a teacher's guidance will bring forth.

If what teachers need is not canned "programs," except sometimes as points of departure or anchors to the wind, then what? A rich array of supporting resources—concrete materials, tools and instruments, written guides which talk about ways of exploiting typical situations and materials, time, material provision to explore—for example, the school's own city block. One time it might be grasses in the pavement ecology, fossils in a limestone wall, the erosion of steps by human feet—for age-determination of a building or for estimates of each footstep's share—and a story about Lucretius' estimate of the size of atoms from the toe of an old statue, worn by the kisses of supplicants. Another time it might be the architecture and age and previous use of old houses, once grand and now crowded with a slum's tenants—a small corner of history come alive.

Teachers need help also with the mechanics of a classroom erosion table or with the making and uses of maps. They need time—paid professional time at least in part—for the exchanges of experiences and ideas, for discussion of children's capacities and ways of fostering these. Some of this can come with books and film, much must come through personal discussion with other teachers and with advisers. We know of one large system which provides a half-day a week set aside for such programs, another which offers short-term "fellowships" for teachers bent on studying new educational research and new subject matter. Such practices are a minimal recognition of a professional status for teachers.

Such manifold changes cannot in general come quickly, but they can come at a rate which arouses new interest and new morale, sustained by early partial successes. A reading corner with good and enticing books will not lower anyone's reading score on the formal tests, and here and there will dramatically liberate a child who goes to it with fossils to identify and who stays, reads, and writes a "book" about *where* his fossils were formed. He stays because the corner is valued. He learns something about books that is not *in* books—that they are his home and not, as so often is the case, enemy territory.

The history of the last decade has brought new groups into the field of elementary and secondary education, and has established a pattern in which there have been many national projects working to revise and modernize curricula and, more recently, to investigate some aspects of instruction and what has come to be called instructional technology. I refer to the curriculum groups supported by the National Science Foundation and by the Office of Education, to the Regional Laboratories and many other projects in and out of schools of education, federally supported or otherwise.

My own way into the field of elementary education was through the first-named of these. As a generalization, we of that period (in my case scientists and mathematicians) had our virtues and our vices; on the one hand a fresh view of subject matter and a willingness to try radical innovation; on the other, ignorance about children—and thus about the art of the possible—and arrogance about teachers' difficulties and schools' failures. From the combination we, many of us in fact, accepted very conventional ideas about the proper use of textbooks, timetables and lesson plans. Some of us were saved, I think, because we had the wit or innocence to go and try to *be* teachers of the young. A few good teachers stood up to us when we went wrong (we were already called "experts") and we had some successes, heady stuff. So I value the period very much and think it has produced some good curricular ideas and materials. But it did not really come face to face with the deeper problems—and we still must.

Along with or some time after us who were content-oriented, there has grown up another sort of expertism having to do *not* with subject-matter primarily but with programming, testing and evaluating of curricular materials, teaching strategies and educational technology. While professedly concerned only with the effectiveness of means, the *modus operandi* of such groups often reinforces the existing narrowness of aims as well. Valuable as much of this work may yet prove to be for special purposes, it has often had the effect I spoke of before, of rigidifying the behavior of teachers and children even further by a very detailed daily charting of their course and thus robbing *them* of the very initiative and planning which education ought constantly to induce.

Good teaching involves much planning, but "lesson plans" evolve along the way. Since local opportunities will always loom large in the operation of environmental education, it will therefore vary radically from time to time and place to place, though always within a curriculum of suitable scope and organization. Ten-year-old children mapping a magic island found there a river "which rises nowhere." I leave it to the reader to find how this is possible—in the instance I mention the discovery was an open door to a wholly new exploration of the world of maps, a high level of curiosity and insight. Can you map the *ocean*? The magic world, the real world and the world of maps came together for these children on that day as a source, as a new way into the world of rivers, lakes and oceans.

Under such circumstances, proposals to give Federal support to environmental education and to define this support in terms of now-established patterns of curriculum development, testing, evaluation and teacher training, seem to me in danger of over-reliance on instruments inappropriate to the job. This pattern may result in some valuable ideas and materials, but it does not touch the vital nerve—for the basic innovation we need to support is that of exploring, with and through innovative teachers, all the means through which children can be brought into a different way of learning. The very phrase "teacher training" implies a style of innovation in which teachers are being shown the way when in fact teachers must be part of every effort to find the way—with help, with moral and material support, through teachers of teachers who value their minds and respect their innovative capacities, who are prepared to receive as much as they give.

Nowhere is this more true than in our present inner-city environment, which "environmental education" will neglect at its peril. This world of children in the slums needs the profoundest exploration by skillful and perceptive teachers newly awakened to the need and potential of environmental learning, and with all the support we can give them. Detached study by sociologists or psychologists or linguists will help, of course, but can only lead to dubious panaceas and formulas if it is not measured against much creative detailed working experience to seek out the manifold resources for learning which can be found there by discerning eyes—butterflies and beetles are to be found there and not only the lamentable rat; and there are streetside rivers and lakes which rise somewhere when the rain comes.

What I fear is a narrowing of the broad intent, so that "environmental education" comes to be one more didactic package, carefully designed and suitably evaluated, which joins a company of others labeled "new math" or "new science" or "new social studies" and which in spite of its original intent fails to alter the "ecological imbalance" of present education. At the worst I see sheafs of environmentalist Sunday sermons for the young, and in that case I almost hope they play hooky in favor of field and stream or city streets. But we can do far better than either of those alternatives.

It seems that we may pile up mountains of abstractions and try to "pass them on" while forgetting the primary motivating qualities of our learning—of perception, engagement and enjoyment. Many of our college students are trying, I think, to tell us this, though their own confusion sometimes makes it sound like and becomes a repudiation of learning itself—which, as we ourselves have unwittingly taught them, is seen as dreary and irrelevant to life. We have not invested, as we must, in helping our young become engaged to the world rather than alienated; in being marriage-brokers toward lifelong union. Without this, nature is left a prostitute. Unless education leads the young to "love, honor, and cherish" the planet from their own direct experience, and to value *themselves* as its custodians, it won't lead them beyond our own previous record of ignorance and indifference.

John Dewey Revisited

No one today—as I have said before—can discuss education well without acknowledging that Dewey has been there already, and without at the same time facing the insistent question as to Dewey's almost negligible influence in our educational theory and practice. In my own view the correctness of Dewey's major positions in the theory of education is, or ought to be, beyond any basic dispute. A philosopher has always two related commitments. He must work to be right, and he must work to be listened to and understood. These commitments are not incompatible, but their joint fulfillment is rare. To break fresh philosophic ground is to risk unintelligibility, while intelligibility can be all too easily achieved by saying only what an audience expects to hear.

Dewey is not graced—except rarely—with a high philosophical style; he is relatively easy to read until you try to paraphrase and argue, and then he can be pretty elusive. Like all genuine philosophy since Plato, Dewey's is something we must share before we can criticize it, and that is how philosophy can progress. It takes time. Perhaps half a century is not enough.

John Dewey Revisited

(1968)

Every achievement of philosophic thought is a product of special times and personal circumstances, yet it has or gains significance only by tests applied in other times and other circumstances. John Dewey has not joined the immortals, but in the United States his influence is still visible and may, indeed, be once more on the increase. In the philosophy of education, in particular, his work is now undergoing what promises to be a vigorous re-examination. Works out of print or previously unprinted (like his 1899 *Lectures in the Philosophy of Education*) are coming off the press, and several commentaries have appeared or been announced.

It has always been clear to those who read him that Dewey was no mere inventor of systems or methods or panaceas in education. He far transcended the movement that called itself Progressive Education. Dewey was a powerful figure, and the leaders of that movement were powerfully moved by him. It is not easy to sort, in that movement, the chaff from the good grain, nor to measure his philosophy by the one or the other. Nor is it any longer very relevant. There is a different and more contemporary point of view from which to examine Dewey's thought and his practical work: it is our own recent re-acknowledgement, thin and sporadic still, that our public educational system is grossly deficient and that our resources of educational theory have dwindled, in this hour of need, to a low level of vitality.

Let me begin by supporting the presumption of Dewey's enduring importance. Considered as a philosopher—if you wish, as a philosopher's Philosopher—Dewey ranks among those few dozen who, since Plato, have seriously and systematically tested their basic insights against all the major areas of human experience. I mention particularly his *Ethics*, his politics (*The Public and Its Problems*), his esthetics (*Art as Experience*), his *Logic*, his philoosphy of nature (*Experience and Nature*). I for one would not place him among the very greatest of systematists; that company is pretty select. But since education is also—ought also to be—concerned with all the major areas of experience, Dewey counts here as he might not for other philosophic interests. Indeed there is no major systematic philosopher who has looked so long and so carefully at education. Plato comes closest, and he is a more acute philosopher. But Plato suffers from what I shall call the innocence of adulthood, which Dewey, with some success, sought to lose. If one is to take ideas seriously, as more than passing conveniences, the presumption of Dewey's importance is very strong.

There are two independent tendencies in Dewey's thought. One tendency is that of modern Naturalism, oriented toward the physical and the evolutionary sciences. The other is that of phenomenology, of the analysis of self-consciousness, of human praxis, stemming from Hegel. The orientation of phenomenology is inherently humanistic, an orientation to which nothing human—nothing recurrently important in experience—is alien. Dewey's joint aim is to look at science humanistically, and to look at the human situation scientifically.

If there is one practical enterprise which most requires this synthesis of scientific knowledge about man with man's own self-conscious analysis of his experience, it is education. If there is a scientific enterprise which most requires such guidance, it is the inquiry into the human capacity to learn. An educational practice which fails to nurture the practical and esthetic capacities, or which treats knowledge as merely a matter of verbal structures to be "transmitted" to children, stands condemned in the light of such a philosophy as Dewey's. And so stands the conception of learning, still dominant in schools and among many academic psychologists, which divorces it from the child's own self-conscious probing and exploration of the world around him.

Dewey's philosophy of education (cf. the *Lectures* mentioned above, *Democracy and Education, School and Society, Experience and Education*) begins with an emphasis on the biological fact of prolonged infancy in the human species, during which the assimilation of culture is paced by physical development. Education is not something invented during human history, but something necessary to its history as human. The *institutionalizing* of education, the school, is a late, partial and still problematic development. In his 1899 *Lectures*, Dewey states a general thesis which recurs throughout his educational writings: ". . . in principle the school has no other educational resources than those which exist outside the school . . . . The sort of material that instructs children or adults outside of school is fundamentally the same sort that has power to instruct within the school . . ." The proper meaning of formal education should be that education in which the resources for learning are organized more consciously and carefully than is possible in the wider life of the community; but the term should not imply that the resources are inherently different.

By the time he wrote *Democracy and Education* this thesis had developed into a powerful critique of the schools: that in isolating subject-matter from active life-experience, the underlying identity of education with "all human association that affects conscious life" is lost sight of; and education is conceived only as "imparting information about remote matters and the conveying of learning through verbal signs: the acquisition of literacy." Not only is such a conception inadequate to the necessities of life, but it is ineffective within its own limited domain. The more varied the range of connections in situations which are educative, the more available is that which we learn from them for later recovery and use in new situations; the more learning is cut off from such connections, the more it is narrowed and formalized, the less it can be used. Having been excluded, the paths of connection are not available when needed. This is Dewey the psychologist speaking, attacking the doctrine of "transfer." The one way of learning is superior to the other not because it facilitates "transfer" to new situations, but because *what* is learned is already more richly coordinated with the rest of experience, more intellectual in quality. There is a place for formalism in education, for abstraction and schematization; but it is a place *within* education, not of the essence.

Dewey's emphasis upon the developmental character of learning has many other consequences for his philosophy of education. In attacking the "preparation for life" view of education, Dewey emphasizes the positive, constitutive characteristics of childhood. Children are said to be dependent and plastic, but these are only the negative aspects of extraordinary powers: their equipment for social intercourse, and their power to profit from experience in the development of dispositions, attitudes and concepts. Put together, these two constitute the power to grow. "We do not have to draw out or educe positive activities from a child, as some educational doctrines would have it. Where there is life, there are already eager and impassioned activities. Growth is not something done to them, it is something they do." Children are engaged in recreating the whole complex apparatus of conscious adult life, which we, in the innocence of our adulthood, take for granted as second nature. Because of the intensity of their involvement with the present, we sometimes speak of children as egotistically self-centered. "To a grown up person who is too absorbed in his own affairs to take an interest in children's affairs, children doubtless seem unreasonably engrossed in *their* own affairs."

It is here we must assess the validity of the Deweyan slogan that we "learn by doing." If learning can be thought of, as it mostly is, as an assimilation of verbally transmitted instruction, the slogan sounds romantically reactionary, as though it repudiated all the guidance of accrued culture. But if learning is thought of as the development and enjoyment of effective tools and dispositions which, among other uses, make *possible* the assimilation of verbally transmitted instruction, the Deweyan slogan has quite a different meaning. Let me make use of a mundane analogy that is actually rather more than an analogy: that of classification, of a filing system. It is the analogy with which philosophers have worked in discussing the nature and origin of the categories, of the essential schemes according to which we group, divide and then organize our experience. A functioning apparatus of this kind is presupposed in inquiring and knowing, and in intelligently saying things or understanding what is said. But unless this apparatus is simply in place and ready for use from the beginning of life, it also is *learned*, developed in the course of experience and as a result of experience. At every stage we must describe the infant or child as having some such apparatus, however primitive, and as willy-nilly engaged in its further evolution through probing and testing his environment. He not only stores information in the files, but he continually modifies and reconstitutes the filing *system* by using it. The filing system is evolved through use, through "doing"—his doing, and no one else's. The young child learns to hear and speak by hearing and speaking, and not, except very little and late, by being told how to speak. He learns to think arithmetically, or causally, by coping in many ways with things that embody arithmetical or causal patterns. It is only *after* the child has begun to think arithmetically, or causally, that he can begin a further stage, which is to think *about* arithmetic or causality. It is an error, a confusion of levels (a widely pervasive one), to suppose that we instill the apparatus of thought in children by talking about it to them or at them.

It is also a mistake, which Dewey never tired of pointing out, to think that active learning, learning by doing, is opposed to the process of acquiring the transmitted culture of society. Rather, it is the most basic mechanism by which that transmission is accomplished. The environment in which a child learns is a natural environment transformed and enriched by human habitation; by tools transferrable to his hands, by other artifacts and by the human inhabitants themselves, who are not only objects of his inquiry, but also associates in it. The doing is never sheer animal activity except in the case of the grossest child-neglect. "It is simply a product of abstraction, of adult reflection when we try to separate experiences into two parts, and distinguish between what the child learns from things and from people . . . . There is no contact with things except through the medium of people. The things themselves are saturated with the particular values which are put into them, not only by what people say about them, but more by what they do about them, and the way they show they feel about them and with them."

Thought and knowledge are inherently social, inherently related to the social evolution of culture. As a philosopher Dewey was not advocating that thought be more social, but attempting to show that it *is* so, even in its most asocial expressions. This ascription of priority to the social nature of man was a consequence, in Dewey's thinking, of his rejection of the metaphor, so long dominant in modern thought, that the mind is a prisoner inside the body and thus inherently in a state of solitary confinement. With this metaphor Dewey also rejected any *metaphysical* distinction between thought and action. For him the one, as the other, gain their characteristic expression in and through the working human community and its culture. But Dewey was an advocate as well as a philosopher, and in his thinking about the practical operation of a school he put great emphasis upon the importance of the school as a human community, through which children would best learn, by participation, the discipline of social life and purpose. This social discipline would affect all their learning, not just their learning about occupations, history, etc. It would provide a framework for all their more particular acquisitions.

The curriculum was conceived, in Dewey's language, "as a movement of life and thought, dramatically and imaginatively re-enacted through the major basic accomplishments of civilization." Thus in the Chicago Laboratory School a major portion of time was devoted, in the early years, to the re-creation of various modes of life and occupations. Since then much of this has ostensibly made its way into the standard curriculum, but little of the essence was in fact retained. From *The Dewey School*, by Mayhew and Edwards, we know that such activities as spinning, weaving, cooking, shop-work, modeling, dramatic plays, story-telling, discussion were the order of the day. Arithmetic, reading, writing, and other special "disciplines" flowed from and back into these activities without formal distinction or programming, as need and opportunity arose. Thus a seven-year-old group (in its fourth year of such work) re-enacted a series of stages in the history of an imaginary people emerging from a savage state to the invention of a settled agricultural existence. They canvassed, discussed, and in their own way settled a wide range of problems from technology to social and political organization. Much of this work had a tangible product climaxing considerable experimentation, for example in their working out of successful techniques for shaping, drying, coloring and firing clay vessels. Later they made a similar investment of research into spinning, dyeing, weaving, and still later, into the working of metals. Along the way there were many representations of life in mapping, painting and story.

It is not easy to define the quality of educational work from the reports of participants and proponents, as Mayhew and Edwards were. One sometimes senses, in their book, some admixture of the hoped-for with the actuality reported. On the other hand there is overwhelming evidence that children lived and worked in a rich and absorbing environment, under teachers of high morale and considerable talent. There was a good teacher-pupil ratio, including several teachers with specialized skills available as consultants. If I knew of such a school in today's America, I would be powerfully moved to go and study its operation.

The curriculum was in no wise "permissive"; the school operated under a rather carefully planned year-to-year sequence, with every major component and transition discussed at length. Within the curriculum, there was freedom for teachers in the working out of their plans of strategy, and within the class, freedom for individual children in their choice of topics and roles. But the embracing fact of social life, both in the treatment of subject-matter and in the organization of work, is everywhere conspicuous.

With this emphasis Dewey consciously parted company with many of the Progressive Schools, which tried to give priority to the development of individual talents without the discipline of social goals expressed in the Deweyan curriculum. Nothing would have been more alien to Dewey's educational philosophy, or to its embodiment in the Laboratory School, than the currently fashionable American image of progressivism. Dewey was much too good a philosopher and moralist to accept the slogans either of "self-expression" or of "social adjustment."

The experiment of the Chicago school is past, but there is much to be learned from its history. Although it was the work of many people, the design and spirit was acknowledged, by all, as Dewey's. The main thing to be learned from it at this date, I think, is something of the real point of Dewey's philosophy. As a model to be followed, it has essential drawbacks. Such models have never been influential except in passing. They are the creations of special individuals under special and very favorable circumstances, and they seemingly lack the power of self-reproduction. The good schools of our future will be evolved out of the main stream of public education, through influences affecting all of its aspects. Nor would Dewey have thought otherwise. The Chicago school was for him what he called it, an experiment, a test of an educational philosophy. It was a good school, but not a prototype. Had we been carrying on, in many school systems, with the same spirit, that one small school would now seen, I am sure, a crude though memorable beginning.

Of such promise, and such non-fulfillment, what should be said? One may belittle the promise, but I for one think the puzzle remains. Dewey was born before his times, but I am not sure when are his times. I see two avenues of critical analysis. The experimental school and the later schools patterned after it were out of the main stream. They and some of the private progressive schools had great periods, but the art and insight thus gained were not effectively transmitted into widening circles of the public schools, and seem in the end mainly to have died on the vine. That is one avenue, exonerating Dewey. The other is Dewey's writing. Dewey's literary influence on the professional educators was large for a time, but is nowadays treated avuncularly, for the most part, as a mark of youthful enthusiasm. This literary influence in public schools was significant here and there, but often attenuated beyond recognition. At least one large school system adopted "Dewey's methods" in the thirties, by vote of its Board!

A tentative judgment would be this: as long as John Dewey and the Laboratory School, Theory and Practice, were together there was progress and a self-justifying optimism of new possibilities in education. Here and there in the next decades similar conditions were re-created, strong enough to establish a minority tradition whose remnants are fortunately still with us. But theory and practice got separated to a large degree and schools of education grew away from any genuinely innovative roles; they were swamped by responsibilities for "training" teachers and by struggles for status in an academic milieu of indifference or hostility. The schools themselves, the vast and growing American public school systems, went their way with little change in any of the fundamentals, looking beyond for a guidance that never came, until they mostly forgot what they were looking for. In speaking thus I do not wish to bury the valiant teachers who have struggled against such tendencies. The faults have been faults of the social system, not merely personal ones.

I implied at the beginning that Dewey's philosophical synthesis was not wholly successful. I have not expanded upon that remark, but have thought it proper instead to emphasize his many strengths. Yet in acknowledging the superficiality of Dewey's influence on American education I am tempted to ascribe some part of the lack to Dewey himself, to his philosophical position. It is a fact acknowledged by Dewey that he never developed his many psychological insights, often acute and powerful, into a coherent general theory. Lacking such a framework, he is sometimes unincisive in his discussion of intelligence, or the scientific method, or in defining the very creativity which he sought to foster. The result is easily taken or mistaken for a serene and dogmatic liberalism that blinks the hard problems. There is in Dewey a blandness of moral tone, a persistency in asserting his confidence in the power of intelligence to guide man's evolution toward a life of greater power, knowledge, and happiness. A generation which knows Martin Luther King and Daniel Berrigan needs more piss in its milk than Dewey will summon for them. It will be a sad day, however, when a philosopher is measured in so volumetric a fashion. Dewey knew alienation, but regarded it as a phase of something he preferred to celebrate, which is the courage to grow. Dewey knew the tensions and conflicts of industrial society, but he preferred to seek out its potentialities for growth rather than to dwell upon the obstacles. Thus although he was an activist and not an arm-chair philosopher, and although he knew many of the miseries and frustrations endemic in our society, he was in a certain sense utopian. That is not a bad word, except to the disillusioned. It simply implies a limitation. I am not sure I could get to the root of this limitation in Dewey's basic philosophy, even if space allowed. Let me only suggest, and illustrate. Dewey is committed to a principle of continuity which justifies a minimizing of all stark contrasts—"dualisms"—and all discontinuous changes. This is a requirement, even a definition, of Dewey's Naturalism: no miracles, no theophanies, and also no evils beyond the reach of intelligent remedy. Such a Naturalism is, I think, too easy. Nature is more complex than *that*.

Another set of contrasts, related to continuity and discontinuity, are those of chance and order, spontaneity and intervention, acceptance and control. Like Hegel and Marx his thought moved frequently between such dialectical poles. But whereas their dialectic operated through a heightening of contrasts to the point of unbearable contradiction, Dewey's dialectic is more nearly that of mediation. In politics this led Dewey to reconstructive democracy rather than revolution. In education it led him to the ideal of school as community, in which teachers could seek out and provide for children's spontaneous interests and curiosities, then finding, and investing with adult authority, those directions of work seen as genuinely educative. This did not by any means imply a sheer acceptance, benignly permissive, of children's spontaneous activity. Nor did it mean ever a close didactic control, geared more to clock and calendar than to the need and promise of individual children.

But as in politics so in education Dewey did not face steadily those societal conditions tending constantly to undermine and frustrate the very organization and style he advocated. The children he saw were not those most damaged by the deprivations and anxieties of poverty. In the main they were of a stable middle-class and professional background. Nor did the schools and teachers he supported face the full range of constraints and frustrations of American education in the main stream.

Dewey's perception of and delight in children's spontaneous capacity for the world around them is far closer to the truth than is the didacticism, the master-slave conception so dominant in our schools. But it is not the whole truth, and it is not the hardest part of the truth. Dewey's eulogistic account of children's capacity for communication and for immersion in fresh subject matter is not exaggerated. But to realize those capacities within the institution of the school requires a far greater marshalling of resources and a far greater cultivation of professional skill than we have so far acknowledged. Children already damaged do not verify Dewey's vision merely by being liberated from the routine and boredom that we criticize. On the contrary. The freedom to learn must itself be re-taught, and to teach it requires all the arts of intervention and withdrawal. I know that Dewey would acknowledge, did acknowledge, all these statements. But he did not relish them or insist upon them when unprovoked.

America has simply not been ready, after the first great wave of support for universal education, to explore the deeper problems which that wave laid bare. Perhaps the readiness is now growing. If it is, we have much to learn by becoming reacquainted with our own lively past—one dominated, for a time, by a good philosopher, perhaps a great one, who, almost uniquely among his kind, really looked at children.

On Living in Trees

To illustrate what I said about the elusive intelligibility of Dewey's writing, and as a sort of background for the essay which follows, I would like to mention one of his more popular writings. It is "The Child and the Curriculum," from which I am sure many education students have in the past been offered sustenance.

After reading this essay several times and discussing it with my students, I finally myself came to see what Dewey was really up to, and was shocked to realize he had somehow let us miss the point. Dewey starts clearly enough with the popular opposition of the child versus *the curriculum, of spontaneity versus discipline, of life's golden tree versus the grayness of all schooling. Having set up the opposition in a plausible and attractive way he then puts us on ample notice that he is going to undercut the opposition, is going to force us to go past it, to take it as a starting point for the enlargement of our own understanding, for seeing that "the facts and truths that enter into the child's present experience, and those contained in the subject-matter of studies, are the initial and final terms of one reality."* I shall not try to summarize the argument, which formulates and then again cuts through several familiar moves of popular argument about education. But what it leads to —as we nod our heads in agreement at each step—is a rather awesome demand. It is nothing less than the demand for a radical expansion and reorganization of academic subject-matter according to a principle which is unprecedented in the annals of knowledge and education. This reorganization is nothing so simple as a rewriting of textbooks or anything of that easy sort. It lies rather in a commitment to redesign and enrich the* environments *in which children live and learn, so that they in their own native style and tempo are directed by* the inducements of that environment—*and thus only indirectly by adult command—to move toward the assimilation and reconstruction of the culture of the race. The curriculum, Dewey says, is not something we should transmit directly to children, spelled out so to speak in syllabus and timetable. It is such*

---

*John Dewey, *The Child and the Curriculum* (Chicago: Phoenix Books, 1956), p. 12.

a view of education which has in reality created the very opposition between the needs and talents of children, and the demands of the curriculum, in the first place. The curriculum, rather, should be what guides teachers *in the art of designing the kinds of environments which induce curiosity and involvement with subject matter, and which lead among other things* toward *the stage in which the logical ordering of subject-matter is prized and valued for its power to extend and enhance experience. But this task is no minor matter.* To understand *mathematics, or physics, or geography well enough to know ways of reconstructing them, of rooting them so to speak in the child's garden, is a major intellectual undertaking for the best minds we have. Only a good and reflective physicist can see the beginnings of his own basic schemes and abstractions nascent in the experience of childhood, and only an inventive teacher, supported by such knowledge and insight, can undertake the reconstructive process which Dewey's analysis reveals as necessary.*

And here I think we sense something of the blandness, the over-easy assumption that the possible is probable, of which Dewey is sometimes guilty. The essay ends, dramatically enough, with a call to wisdom:

"The case is of Child. It is his present powers which are to assert themselves; his present capacities which are to be exercised; his present attitudes which are to be realized. But save as the teacher knows, and knows wisely and thoroughly, the race-expression which is embodied in that thing we call the curriculum, the teacher knows neither what the present power, capacity, or attitude is, nor yet how it is to be asserted, exercised, and realized."*

I suspect that if Dewey had really taken himself seriously here, taken himself with practical seriousness, he would have been appalled at the magnitude of the self-educative task implied, and would have rushed to underline how much help and support we teachers must define and demand for ourselves, poorly educated as we inevitably are, before we can advance very far toward the new land which our philosophical Moses has promised. And that is the demand to get on with.

In the two essays following I was trying to work out some of the consequences, theoretical and practical, of the kind of reconstruction which Dewey —though I only understood his argument later—was calling for. I saw this —and still see it—as an intellectual organization more complex than any kind of textbook order and more difficult, for most of us, to conceptualize

*John Dewey, *op. cit.*, p. 31.

(though not, with a good education, to begin to achieve). It is an organization designed not for maximum efficiency in problem solving by those who have—somehow—already mastered it, but for maximum accessibility to those whose minds are still developing through the many levels of common-sense informal education.

These two essays, like some of my others, have sometimes been read as calling for a kind of anarchy, an abolition of all pre-determined structure. Perhaps I could have struggled harder against this misinterpretation. At any rate let me say it here: we need to find or create a structure of knowledge which is rich enough to allow many ways of entry into it and of assimilation of its discipline. From such a predetermined structure, or curriculum, it is possible to meet the developmental and environmental diversity of childhood, to engage a child at his own level in kinds of learning which will carry him beyond that level. This implies a richness of opportunity and inducement for which the only narrow conventional name is Inefficiency. The truth is the reverse of this conventional view. Conventional curricula, conventionally administered, aim at targets they mostly, and wastefully, miss. The point of these essays is to characterize in some formal way the kind of richness and redundancy—"inefficiency"—which can, in fact, raise the efficiency of present-day formal education from its present mostly low level.

On Living in Trees
(1965)

I took my title from a coincidence of ideas and recollections. One of these was a flashback to a conversation with Karl Muenzinger. Those of us who were privileged to know him can remember, with gratitude, the variety of his involvements with the world, and with the University of Colorado, both faculty and students. I did not in one sense know him well; a dozen hours or two would measure our personal association. But the knowledge was often consequential. In quiet conversations and in some academic battles he was a good friend, as only a good man can be.

Before I tell the story of our conversation, let me say that in choosing the title I was thinking not only of the literal tree, of root, trunk, branch, twig, leaf, and fruit, but also of a more abstractly symbolic tree, a graph or diagram branched like a tree. Instead of this mathematical term "tree" I might have used "maze"; and the conversation with Karl Muenzinger had to do with one of his specialties, the way in which our cousin the rat learns to get through mazes, and what light if any the rat's learning sheds upon the condition of his cousin the man. The conversation had specifically to do with what used to be called latent learning. In teaching rats to get through mazes it was standard practice to starve them up to a point, or get them excited about some other rat goodies, and then put them in the maze with the promised reward at the other end. Some time before, it had occurred to Professor Edward Tolman of Berkeley to put rats in the maze *after* they were fed, and without any of the other standard motivators. If they had any aim it was, as the poet said, not to eat and not to love. So of course the rats just sniffed and wandered and generally made themselves at home. A blind alley was no longer a false choice, a frustration, but rather a nice place for a nap. What was interesting about Mr. Tolman's rats was that after a month or so of being at home in this way, the rats, brought back to the hungry state, turned out to run the maze better than some hard-working fellows who had been going at the maze all month in standard highly motivated fashion. Other laboratories did not seem to get quite the same results, as I recall; I always suspected that their mazes were not as ratty as Tolman's. In the conversation I referred to, at any rate, Karl Muenzinger and I made the obvious analogy and drew the obvious moral: that students are not given nearly enough time to just wander and sniff in the academic maze; they are too much in the position of the control group of rats who were forced to hit the books all month while the experimental group was being pampered. Just substitute dormitory for cage and course of study for maze. Instead of the incentive at the end of the maze, supply the A.B., the wedding bells, and the job, and the analogy is complete.

Another synonym for *tree* or *maze* is *labyrinth* or *baffle*; for both of these words, however, the secondary connotations are evil. A labyrinth is a tree or maze from which *all* relevant clues have been removed as to when you should turn left and when right. You want to get through but you know the odds doom you. The labyrinth is a geometry of bad dreams. You can memorize your way through a labyrinth if it is simple enough and you have time and the urge to escape. But the learning is of no use for the next time when the exit will be differently placed.

The labyrinth comes into the discussion of education as the invention of psychologists who wanted to be very scientific, removing most of the relevant clues from choice-points in the maze, so that the behavioral effect of these clues could be studied one by one. The effect, unfortunately, was to give the hard-working animal very little for his intelligence to work on, so that rat or cat, pigeon or man perform about equally. The motto of the lab psychologists is *confundeo non confundeor*—"I baffle but I am not baffled." Of course the real theoretical baseline is laid down when you remove *all* clues from the maze, and that is the true labyrinth. If you think we do not use this approach in education, let me point to a precise parallel between the pedagogy of rats and that of men. One of the rudimentary precautions that had to be taken in the old rat-labs was to remove from the maze the scent left by successful predecessors, which of course was more pungent along the right paths than the blind alleys. Compare this with the file of A papers on almost any subject reputedly stored in fraternities and sororities in spite of all deodorizing efforts of the university.

So now you see my drift, which has to do with the world of education and which I symbolize by words like tree, maze, labyrinth, or baffle. As you now realize, these structures are supposed to represent, in a serious way, what may be called the geometry, the topology, of learning. The learner finds in the tree, or looks for and fails to find, clues and evidences, fruit or frustration. When he finds the fruit, he may only ponder and enjoy, or he may go forward to some goal thus reinforced, or backward on the hunch of error. Mathematically considered, a tree has direction to it, from roots to growing tip. It represents what is called in mathematics a partial ordering, because things along alternative branches cannot be directly compared as to greater or lesser, better or worse. Its branchings in the forward or upward direction represent choices, and my symbolic use of the tree, the dendritic representation of the learning process, signifies that a learner learns through a process that depends on his own activity. The fruit that is found along the way is not merely consumed or assimilated; it is enjoyed as the fruit of active choice. What is laid down in memory is not merely the enjoyment but the pathway that led to it. There thus begins to emerge a sort of map, a structure of learning which is more than passive recording can ever provide. It is the indispensable source of what we refer to in learning as conceptual or cognitive.

There are two other structures I want to refer to in this discussion besides trees, one simpler, one more complex. If you follow one branching pathway of a tree and lop off all the others, you get another structure commonly known as the ladder. Mathematically speaking everything is now well-ordered. Of course not much fruit is left, and there are no choices. There is no denying, however, that things are now well-ordered. The ladder renders maps unnecessary; all you need is dutifully to follow your nose. Since human language, frozen in text, is necessarily well-ordered, the ladder also represents the formal verbal level of learning, the textbook and lab manual.

A final mathematical structure develops from the tree in another way. To find it in the botany of trees you must look at the veining of a leaf, where paths not only diverge but converge. This is the network, with paths crossing in various directions, meeting at nodal points, few or many to a node. The network cannot represent the pathway of learning, because it cannot incorporate the direction of time. Its ordering is more complex and more partial than that of a tree. But if you look at a network, for example a highway map, you can trace out a route to San Francisco from Boulder, and that is a ladder. You can also trace out a tree. Commit yourself to Nederland, but then you may go south or north; for that matter you can go west, ending in the blind alley of 4th of July Canyon, and have your nap or climb the pass on foot. At each point of junction you have choices. In this way you construct a set of possible *histories* for yourself of paths through space and time as well. This graph will now be seen to be a tree and not a network, for later points of choice will never rejoin earlier ones. Later paths may come back to Nederland, but not to the Nederland of day before yesterday.

In this sense a network will accommodate many trees that can be cut out of it, yours marked in blue crayon and mine in green. The network itself symbolizes in my thinking the real order and connection of the world which each of us explores along the forking paths of his own experience, meeting now and again for conversation, fitting the maps of our separate trees together within that common order.

The tree remains my symbol for the patterns of individual learning and searching while the network, the public map, represents some ultimate order, never fully achieved, of what is there to be learned. The academic world, with its prerequisites and gradations of rank, remains a tree as well, and now I want to come back to it.

In the last three years I have left the part of that tree where I normally live and gone to study an earlier part, the elementary schools. As you will soon see, and I might as well admit it, I am very pleased with myself for having done this. The university world maintains very little connection with the earlier parts of the tree, except what it often regards as a kind of trapdoor in its treehouse, the School of Education. I can claim no moral credit for having disregarded this regrettable bit of academic snobbery. For one thing I have been exposed, for years, to propaganda from those who work happily among the lower branches. For another I belong to the department of philosophy. This department nests among the highest and most fragile branches, but its denizens often scamper down and wander in the rest of the tree, especially where the footing is a bit safer. In spite of a general disapproval of such behavior, the university never quite knows what to do about the department of philosophy though its members are regarded as reasonably harmless.

During the period I speak of, I have been involved in the work of a special group set up in Massachusetts, in what is known as Greater Cambridge, identifiable by the suburb, Boston. It was and is the purpose of this group, called the Elementary Science Study, to work for certain innovations in elementary schools, connected specifically with the teaching of science. Its staff has come from a good many parts of the academic tree, but with a strong representation from the university world. Its major purpose, born of a conviction of need, is to bring to the schools a style of work for children which is more tree-like and less ladder-like, which cultivates in them the spirit of science, the initiation and pursuit of learning through the study of nature's own book, through exploration and observation and, often enough, through individual lab work. When I say lab work, here, a college audience is likely to misunderstand me. The college lab, like that of the high school, is traditionally and still predominantly conceived as a ladder, a kind of textbook with blanks in it that a good and obliging student will fill in from reading and measurements from the apparatus before him. Because of various hints and redundancies available to the clever, they are often able to invent better data than captive nature can supply them with, and with less fuss. Chemistry students have traditionally, and with characteristic humor, called this sort of lab "dry." And it is.

Our concern, in contrast, has been to use the lab as a way, not of answering questions, but of generating them, as forks in a tree, not signposts. Even more fundamentally, we have seen the lab—which means the tin cans and soda straws, the aquarium, the magnifier and the compound microscope, the mirror and the pinhole image, the paramecium, the butterfly, the corn plant and the aspergillus, the gerbil, the test-tube and the pneumatic trough—we have seen the lab as a way of lightening and enlivening, and in large part of replacing, the ritualism of symbols which pervades our classrooms, unrelated to that which, by intention, the symbols symbolize. One of our slogans, nailed over the door as it were, is from that great figure Alfred North Whitehead: "In the Garden of Eden, Adam and Eve first *saw* the animals, before they *named* them."

What we have been working for, in short, is rather radical innovation in the American classroom. In undertaking such innovative work we knew at the outset, or soon learned, that we were faced with a full range of human problems, and not only the scientific and pedagogical ones. As always happens when there is an institutional hierarchy, a pecking order, those seen as pecking first do not go unresented; and often enough they justify the resentment against them by easy assumptions of omniscience. Many teachers, principals and supervisors, many teacher teachers have labored long and hard to improve the quality of education as they saw possible. There have been dry years, and indeed dry decades, in American education, when public attention and public budgets were directed elsewhere: to war; then to the preoccupations, militaristic and otherwise, of the cold war; then to the era of space technology, born of romance out of military hardware. Indeed education itself has come back to some place in the public attention in part through the demands on vocational training for an ever-increasing supply of scientific and technical manpower.

Those who created the parent organization of ESS, Educational Services, have been proud of the fact that their efforts well-antedated the hue and cry raised by the first Russian satellite. It is obvious, however, that funds for educational innovation became possible, in part, because of the attention focused on scientific technological manpower needs. Another source of concern, more recent and now in a sense more pressing, is the recognition that a large fraction of our population is not being equipped, educationally, to fill any of the jobs which our economy increasingly requires. To put it positively, some 30 percent of our population is being educated for what is euphemistically called leisure: for the enforced leisure of slum living, relief roles, and human dehumanization. This is education—negative education; it is the schooling we provide for a large percentage of our children: education in fear, frustration, and futility. The drop-out is as true an alumnus of the school as any, and he returns to test its conscience.

We are, at any rate, in a new period of educational reform and innovation, and the dry years have been dry enough and long enough to discourage the faithful and alarmingly to deplete the numbers of those of high professional competence, who know the paths to be taken, without making the merely foolish or futile errors. We might, I suppose, continue in our past contentment and ignore the widespread failures. For does not every country have them? And do we not provide equal opportunity for all to go to school until, as Anatole France might have put it, they exercise their equal opportunity to fail? Fortunately the Negro revolution will not allow this way out; nor will, I think, the commitments of the American political community. So there must be an increase in efforts devoted to education, and this must include the labor of many amateurs, inspired or otherwise. There must also be a marked shift in vocational aspirations; many who would once have scorned to work in the lower branches of my tree will now aspire to do so, moved by the challenge of a career so fraught with excitement and novelty.

Do you think I am talking about education on Mars? Perhaps. But then, perhaps, we will rename our planet! Let us at any rate try. The old pro's will accept us when we have been a little humbled by our failures, and, grudgingly or not, their own morale will rise. But now I must turn to another aspect of the problem of contemporary education, intensified by the neglect of decades.

When you look over the range of those who call for an improvement of education you do not find a unanimous viewpoint; not among the amateurs, certainly, but not even among those who, by a sort of institutionalized truce, accept each other as fellow-professionals. In talking about elementary education I am speaking, perforce, not only as an amateur but also as a partisan. There is no other way of speaking. In order to state my case, I come back to the geometry of trees and mazes, ladders and networks.

Lest I seem to have disparaged the laboratory psychologists and their contribution to the theory of education, let me now deny this. The problems of education are very complex and thorny. Laboratory psychology, for better or worse, has been wedded to the proposition that science must master simple problems before it can tackle difficult ones. Still, one may hope that generalizations from the simpler phenomena, from rat, cat, and pigeon psychology, will have some relevance to human education above the level of rote learning.

One of these relevant generalizations concerns the relation of reward and punishment, the carrot and the stick. Learning is better reinforced by the rewarding of success than the punishment of failure. This implies, by obvious logic, that there must be successes to reward, the more, in fact, the better. But that would seem to imply, in turn, that the problems of successful teaching have already been solved. Not at all, but there is a way out. Make the individual steps so small that the learner can hardly fail in them, one by one. Cut off the side branches in the maze, in effect, by careful and explicit signposts at every turning, and leave a piece of candy on the tip of every pointing arrow. The result is something now widely heralded under the slogans of programmed learning. In effect, we have now replaced the tree by a ladder, with goodies at every rung. And why not? Every step will be a rewarded success. Progress will be slow, to be sure, but every step will count more efficiently, in the end, than from wandering, forlorn, in the great maze of wrong turnings and blind alleys.

I shall criticize this movement on two grounds and then defend it for a minor role. The first ground of attack is that the movement toward programmed learning is almost entirely aimed to build ladders of words. The movement did not invent this emphasis but merely took it over uncritically from the prevailing practice of the schools. I do not mean, of course, that programmed texts do not teach performance. They will teach manipulatory skills, but the skills are only skills of symbol manipulation. They will not merely exploit the already-learned skills of notation, but create new ones: vocabulary building, mathematical definitions, reading; all will come by sure short steps, which catch error in the bud and reward successes promptly and often. Or so it is claimed.

Not all programmed learning need be symbolic, of course. I do not know how far most proponents would go, but one hardy defender of the faith was prepared, in debate, to argue the virtue of programmed courses in oil painting, bicycle riding, music appreciation, and creative writing. Indeed the movement is not really new. Thanks to the classic research of Professor Harold Benjamin, former head of the Department of Education at Colorado, we know that programmed learning goes back to the dawn of human culture. Our ancestors survived the great glacial period of Europe by learning the three great and fundamental arts of fish-grabbing, little-wooly-horse-clubbing, and sabre-tooth-tiger-scaring. When the glacier began to retreat, the streams got too muddy for fish while the horse and his companion the tiger went north with the ice. So the three fundamental arts were perforce taught in a merely symbolic, programmed form.

A great reform in education took place in later neolithic times, however, and ritual performances were replaced, once more, by real ones. At considerable financial sacrifice the community cleared a stream and stocked it with grabbable fish, herded south a few clubbable wooly horses, and trapped and caged a real if mangy, but scarable, tiger. More recent research, supplementing Professor Benjamin's, shows that the teaching of each fundamental art was eventually refined into a large number of easily learned steps, namely twenty-seven for fish grabbing, sixty-three for little wooly horse clubbing, and one hundred thirty-seven for tiger scaring.[1] This result has hardly been excelled, even in our own century.

Returning now to sobriety: what is wrong with the programmer's art is that it puts the most essential motivation of learning, the exploratory, in a strait-jacket and robs the learner of that autonomy which is his chief means of self-education, reducing him to a state of passive obedience—or active rebellion. It purports to teach by a pattern in which nothing taught could *ever* have been discovered in the first place, and it reduces human differences, qualitative and many-dimensional, to differences in the rate of climbing ladders. Programmed instruction does not invent these shortcomings; they are already inherent in much of our educational practice. But it intensifies them and reinforces the already powerful image of the merely passive learner. I hasten to add that there is surely a place for passive learning and its automated guidance—a much smaller place than it now holds. When essential ideas are already developed and we wish to put things in a kind of stepwise order, then we readily accept, and even seek, the programmed order. But not before!

Let me now come back to the affirmative. Laboratory psychology lends theoretical support to programmed instruction, with its ladder-like sequencing of materials, but it does so only on the basis of an unexamined commitment. It is a commitment which I wish to examine and thus to state my own view in opposition. And make no mistake about it, this opposition is not only to the special fashion of programmed instruction but to the overwhelmingly predominant pattern of instruction in American schools, which programmed insruction only raises to a higher level. You will tell me that there are exceptions to that predominant pattern, and I know there are—very few exceptions.

The unexamined commitment is that we somehow must set all learners the same goals, day by day and week by week and month by month and year by dreary year. If we must do that, then the programmers' approach simply carries to a high pitch of organization what goes on anyway, less carefully organized. It allows children to go at somewhat different rates, and it gets teacher out of Johnny's hair a little more of the time. But it carries them all along the same prefabricated ladder, and transforms them and their motivations, builds maps, equally little in the process. It allows for individual differences, but only as those differences show up on one dimension, a rate of progression along this ladder. So to represent individual difference is to trivialize the profound importance of those differences.

My counter-commitment is that we should emphasize individual differences, in *all* their qualitative richness. This means that education should provide always for differences of interest and of momentary capacity or readiness and should do this by not merely permitting, but encouraging, diversity in the way children spend their time in school. It means to give them significant choices, to let them become responsible, in every way possible, for the regulation of their own learning. Let me repeat a little, in order to show that we must abandon the image of the ladder of progress and go back to that of the tree. On a ladder there is only one way to go; you have no significant choices, except to get off—as many do. But the tree we must go back to is not the deodorized maze of the rat lab; it is more like the maze of Professor Tolman's experiment. For those contented rats there were no right or wrong turnings in the maze. Their educational careers were not blighted by failure nor rewarded by extraneous reward. There was prompt and positive reward or reinforcement, in another sense, *whichever* turn they took. For it was their motive to explore, and it was their reward that every new turning brought novelty. Of course a maze in a rat-lab is not much of a world to explore, not nearly as exciting as the attic corridors into which such rats sometimes escape. But it will do as a model.

What I believe is true for the rat, and am sure of in the case of man, is that the most powerful learning mechanisms available to us are built in, biologically rooted mechanisms of search and exploration, relatively separate from the primary biological drives of hunger, sex, and the like. These learning mechanisms have a lower priority in the short run than drives relating to hunger, sex, pain, and fear, so that exploratory behavior dominates only in the absence of other more urgent need. The exploratory, map-building tendencies of rats and men are in the long run just as important for survival as hunger, sex, and fear, but this value depends upon the fact that they are *not* exercised *for the sake of* survival.

John Dewey, a powerful and positive influence in American education of his day, made a serious error, I think, in asserting that the activity of the human intellect is primarily motivated by the need to solve problems which arise in the course of practical activity. The rat who pokes around in his world, who learns its highways and byways just because he is well-fed and curious, will have a better chance of escaping enemies than one who does not; but he does not explore well *in the presence* of enemies, and when he explores well it is not out of anxiety *about* those enemies. The map-building propensities of men are vastly larger, and education confines at its peril. For the only motivation of learning that is really important is the motivation intrinsic to learning itself. And the only satisfaction, the only reinforcement that counts importantly is that which accrues from discovery, from finding structure and order in our own individual and unique experience.

If you grant the desirability of providing for an essentially greater diversity and choice in children's school work, there are practical problems of school organization and teaching that must then be faced. But many will indeed question the desirability of doing as I urge. A familiar counter-argument puts what I am urging in a bad light as follows: "It is all very well to let children discover things for themselves; but it took a million years of that sort of method to get where we are, and a child must be educated in only a few." Another variant I have gotten repeatedly is this: "It's all very well to spend six weeks studying the pendulum, but how can you justify that when there are so many other subjects to cover?" These are the protests of the ladder lovers! What the objectors meant was that I could have told the kiddies all about the pendulum in half an hour; and what they did not add was that it would have made no sense and the kids would have been thoroughly bored and learned nothing.

I must say that I find this sort of objection discouraging. To learn well, to make the pendulum his own in a very real sense, the school child who gets excited about it does not have to relive the history of science from the time of Galileo. He does his exploration *in* the twentieth century, with access to books and conversations, with traps laid for him, to catch his imagination and evoke his understanding. He takes giant strides by the measure of history. But he takes them in the manner that history took them. As new components of his learning fit into place, he becomes the inheritor, but a critical and imaginative inheritor, of a powerful body of ideas and techniques. He does not create them; he re-creates them, he makes them his own. Give a child six weeks for each topic in science which is now compressed into a half hour, and reduce the set of topics in the same ratio, one to three hundred. I say that at the end of eight years the learner will be far ahead. But he does it in his own way and at a tempo which *can* be set for him *only* by the pace of his own development.

What this sort of objection also overlooks is related to the other question, the question of how to reorganize schools. It overlooks the fact that what we normally call teaching has very little to do with learning. This seems like a hard saying, but we all know it is a true one. The stereotype of the teacher is that of a person who composes and transmits verbal structures. The stereotype of the learner is that of a person who receives these verbal structures intact and records them in a form ready for retransmission during what are known as examination periods. The implication, clearly, is that nothing of any importance happens at either end except a kind of phonography.

The Swiss psychologist Piaget, whose work is more relevant to education than the work of others that I know of, has long emphasized the psychological importance in learning of what he calls the "structure" inherent in any situation or subject matter with which a learner is involved. It is what I called the map, or tree or network. I shall come back to this matter of structure, but let me for the moment just take it to mean the order, coherence, unity which relate phenomena to each other in our understanding.

In a recent discussion of education Piaget commented on the efforts of some of his own followers to lay out programs for "teaching the structure" of a subject. What this means I do not really know, but I shall make a guess. It means squeezing a network into a ladder. It means what is meant by the following advice: "Don't tell 'em a lot of unrelated little facts; tell 'em the big facts, the ways in which all the little facts are related to each other."

Now this is, indeed, a step in the right direction. To say how all of the little facts about a subject are related is just what a good lecture, or a good textbook, does. It used to be advised, for example, that in teaching science one rehearsed with the children enormous numbers of little "science facts" such as, "Water boils." "When water boils it turns into steam." "Steam condenses into water." "The sun is ninety-three million miles away." "In the presence of sunlight some plants turn carbon dioxide and water into sugar." More recently emphasis has shifted from "teaching facts" to "teaching concepts": of velocity, or force, or atmospheric circulation, or natural selection.

We begin to see what Piaget calls the "structure" of a subject when we begin to grasp the essential concepts evolved through past investigations of that subject. But the main point is still missing: *Whose* investigations? It was at this point that Piaget was aiming:

> The question comes up whether to teach the structure, or to present the child with situations where he is active and creates the structure himself. The goal in education is not to increase the amount of knowledge, but to create the possibilities for a child to invent and discover. When we teach too fast, we keep the child from himself inventing and discovering. *Teaching* [my emphasis] means creating situations where structures can be discovered; it does not mean transmitting structures which may be assimilated at nothing other than a verbal level.[2]

Since the teacher who thus creates does not have to be with each child all of the time, diversification is not as difficult as it sounds. Piaget added, later,

> Words are probably not a short-cut to a better understanding. The level of understanding seems to modify the language that is used, rather than vice versa. Mainly, language serves to translate what is already understood; or else language may even present a danger if it is used to present an idea which is not yet accessible.

I think that Piaget has said for me, very simply, what is my main point in this essay: That the understanding of a subject, the grasp of its structure, comes—in short, *learning* comes—through a self-directed activity of the child, an activity of inventing and discovering. To teach means to *facilitate* learning by surrounding the child with, and helping him into, situations where learning can take place. When a child has begun to explore, is on the track of structure, then language begins to be important. The child wants to communicate about what he is doing and what he has seen (to see the animals first —*then* name them). Others want to join in. They have not all been doing the same thing; they have spread out in the network. So each child's remarks have a place. As work continues, communication around it gets established. There is a widespread opinion to the effect that young children do not listen to each other, but only to the teacher. The reason is generally a good one; they do not get much chance. In one of Piaget's remarks he suggested it would be a good thing to have two rooms for each class: one where the teacher was and one where the teacher wasn't!

But I do not want to belittle the role of the teacher here. The evolution of class discussion, *among children*, requires several conditions, and one is an artful teacher. First, they must have significant experience to tell. Their involvements must overlap or be related in ways meaningful to them; yet each must have something, in the telling, not identical with what others have focused upon. They have all been in the same network of phenomena, spread out but connected, but not all climbing the same prefabricated ladder. And finally the teacher must moderate with some human skill: to amplify, to pick up the shy and confront the bold; yes, and to make direct contribution, but not to dominate, and not to become a teaching machine, or an animated work book, with blanks to be filled in.

Of course I do not want to forbid teachers their joy—and mine—of lecturing. There is a place for lecturing, for "teaching" in that all-too-standard meaning of the term. It is a very special place, like that of the discussion, the colloquium. Indeed the two merge easily together. The place for talk about the subject, for verbal discrimination and communication, is late in the phases of learning; not at the beginning, and not all the time; here and there, gathering momentum as interest mounts. But never too much. As I know to my own embarrassment and sorrow, a teacher can kill a subject by his own eagerness—egoness—to show himself its master. Interest mounts with active learning, with self-directed work; it declines when the halter and the feed bag are put on, *except* when the right conditions are met.

The real virtue of the lecture and its pale but better-ordered imitation—the programmed text—is that they bring things together in synopsis. A structure, a meaningful pattern, has been traced out slowly, with many twistings and turnings, and a child has become familiar with his subject, by a route that only he, if anyone, can trace. His understanding is spotty, partial, and easily confused. He has had exciting moments of insight, but lost them again. Nevertheless there is a time, a late time, when he will sit absorbed, passive in posture but not in mind, and listen to the coherent and sequenced formulation. He can now exercise a remarkable talent and, as education goes, a rare one: he can *follow* a discourse, as water follows the farmer's trench, crowding the spade that digs it. Before I finally oppose the lecture *method*, moreover, let me praise the well-timed lecture even more. I know of no way equal to it, in which doors can be opened and new vistas seen. In the act of bringing precision and coherence to a subject already partly grasped, it transforms the private wanderings of thought into a public order, into what we know and prize *as* knowledge.

The trouble with our educational system—profound and not superficial, difficult to remedy but as inescapable as failure—is that, in its ways of thought and in its institutional habits, it wrongly represents the nature of the human capacity to learn, and in so doing it creates an often unbridgeable gap between the child's own active intellect and that which it would have him assimilate or to which it would have him accommodate in knowledge, insight, skill, and enjoyment. Having created this gap, it fails to see the gap for what it is. Indeed our system constantly measures the gap; the measure is, I think, the inverse of the I.Q. and other such performance measures. What we take to be a measure of ability, and almost unconsciously accept as an independent constant of education rather than a variable dependent on it, measures the extent to which, with children in all their constitutional and acquired differences, we have systematically failed to enlist their capacities for active inquiry. Our remedies are superficial, and often reinforce what they would cure. Instead of diversifying, of preparing the good rich tree for children's delight in exploration, we homogenize. We resort to streaming, to so-called ability groupings, ignoring the uniquely important difference *within* any such group. For each group we fabricate its ladder, varying only the speed and spacing of the rungs. We equate planning with routinizing and invent schemes of team teaching which forbid improvisation rather than encourage it. We budget time, rather as though it came minted always in nickels and dimes. We no longer bolt down the desks and chairs, but they always face the teacher. And we are charmed by the great innovation which builds classrooms without the distraction of windows, an *ultimate denial* of a child's right to be bored. We speak to each *other* about the child-centered program, but of children we demand the quiet classroom. We discipline teachers by a routine of lesson plans and curricular supervision that typically makes them shrink from spontaneity or innovation; we adopt new reading programs or new mathematics programs, new textbooks and all the rest, as though the teacher were a dutiful automaton; and human clay being what it is, this can easily become a self-fulfilling description. In short, there is no health in us—or not much.

But in case you think this essay is turning into a Jeremiad, let me now close with what I regard, at least, as a fair and optimistic statement of the case. The truth is that institutionalized education in the full sense is very new in this world, and what we should but do not yet know how to practice, we have only recently begun to understand. The idea of universal public education is only three or four generations old, and the institutions that serve it are even younger. The academies, the secondary schools (for some), are older, and the universities the oldest. Institutionalized education has grown *downward* in the age-range it spans. It has, at the same time, grown *outward* in the range of population it embraces. Obviously, then, the early and most fundamental learning has only recently commanded any real attention.

Where the fraction of the population to receive formal schooling was small, the universities, the academies, and the first elementary schools did not face the problem of early or preparatory education; they solved it by selection, mistaking the fruit of early learning for innate ability, tailoring their curriculum and their style of teaching to the already considerable attainments of those selected. The intensity of the problem has increased, moreover, because in greater and greater sections of the population the family has become less effective as the institution of early education: partly because of the separation of family life from work, and partly because of growing instabilities in the family institution itself.

Whatever the reasons, it is true, I think, that until recently the function of education as a public concern was performed in a way that gave but slight support to any searching beneath the surface layers of the process. Children were assumed to come to school readymade, with the linguistic and conceptual equipment that allowed them to welcome, or at least to comprehend, the disciplines to which they were then subjected. My father, born in the Civil War to a rural professional family, went to school at ten or so to polish his spelling, acquire a proper orthography, and master arithmetic up to the double rule of three. After a short span he became himself the teacher in that school. The drill he received, and the drill he meted out made sense to him; they prepared him, evidently, for the next step, a university course in law. But I know, I think, where his essential education came from. It was not from the school, that was only the last ten, or the last five, percent, and it was acceptable, indeed useful, because of that fact.

Our schools have evolved beyond that point, in resources and in complexity. But the need for them has evolved faster, and the gap which I have described has widened rather than narrowed. The most conspicuous case, which now catches our attention and demands at last a major effort of discovery and innovation, is the plight of children from the midst of urban poverty and family demoralization. In spite of many potential human strengths these children are very often essentially lacking in the specific preschool attainments: in language, in conceptualization, but above all in any acquaintance with a world which values that which the school purports, as the birthright of Americans, to give them. They lack this acquaintance before they come to school, and the school effectively maintains the lack. It gives them custodial care, harsh or gentle as the case may be, until they disappear. They are typed and measured, and the prediction of their failure is self-confirmed.

At the other end of the social scale we see another phenomenon, Harvarditis—the mounting pressures for scholastic attainment as a means of personal success, of what the sociologists pleasantly call "vertical mobility" upward. One must go to the best and most prestigious college, and to do that one must seek the secondary program which best insures college acceptance, by the criteria dominant at the moment. These pressures telegraph down the line, and finally the nervous parent is looking for a kindergarten or even preschool which seeks prestige because of its new reading program, new math program, new ladders for little ones; thus the general tone of getting 'em ready sooner, and better, toward an ultimate goal that no one dares defy—except that not too infrequent casualty, the child or youth who does avoid the insult in the only way he knows, and ceases to perform.

In both cases, at the extremes of apparent economic welfare, the pressures of our society work against what will, I am profoundly convinced, be its only educational hope: that if we can but abolish the predominance of ladders and relax the pressures toward pleasing adults by dutiful performance, *and at the same time* invest major efforts in the artful enrichment of the world that children will encounter at school, we will begin to see gross transformations of their characters and capacities. The investment must be major and must enlist the enthusiasm and imagination of many talented persons.

I said I would end in optimism, and I shall. I believe that the worst of the dry years are past and that our society is ready, as never before, to face the obligations and implications of its educational commitment. In the midst of unresolved controversy over federal aid to education, we are in fact spending increasing amounts in educational research and innovation. The sense grows that the deeper problems of education are there to be faced and that in facing them we must transform our conceptions of learning and of the massed potentialities of men—and children. We start this innovative push with pitifully meager resources, but we can multiply them rapidly. Our present educational budget is about thirty billion dollars. This is to be compared with NASA, the space agency, which already competes at five billion.

What I would propose, as a start, is that from whatever sources—local, state, federal, private—we build a *special* budget for educational innovation over and above the regular one, that would *begin* to compete, in turn, with NASA. There is a romance about exploring the solar system, and surely we will find many wonders in it. But there is a greater romance, and a more enduring one, in the optimistic exploration of education. To misquote Alexander Pope, "The proper study of mankind is children!"

But this is the optimism of possibility. Whether we *will* do what such optimism says we *can*, I do not predict. What is needed is the active mood, not the predictive mood. What is true of the child or the adult in his learning is true likewise of the massive searching of a whole society: Its pathway into the future is not a ladder or a highway, but a world of choices. Its choices are now predetermined or predictable, but will be fixed only by the discoveries it has made, and will yet make, along the way or the lack of them. As we must learn, so we ought to teach; only so can our kind live well in the multiplicity of its trees, a garden of forking paths.

REFERENCES

[1]Harold Benjamin, *The Sabre Tooth Curriculum* (New York, 1939). My supplementary information comes from the eminent Spanish archeologist, Jaime de la Cueva, "Notas sobre la pedagogia neolitica Altamirense," *Revista española de educación,* XXIX, pp. 100-107.

[2]Quoted by Eleanor Duckworth from unpublished remarks of Piaget at recent conferences at Cornell University and University of California, *ESS Newsletter* (June 1964).

On Understanding the Understanding of Children

In "On Living in Trees" I tried to keep a light touch; I was exploring the potentialities of a metaphor. The metaphor of the tree dweller has, or implies, a certain formal structure, and in this structure I saw the pattern of a certain line of theoretical development. So the play was serious.

I trust this spirit is still visible in "On Understanding the Understanding of Children." Here the audience was a rather special one of persons involved in pediatric research, and I was trying to tie down the image of the tree, and that of the network. These were people who knew the literature on child development, some of them being contributors to it. While it would have been pretentious to offer such a group any serious and literal-minded "theory" to embrace their many-sided concerns, it seemed right to try to be more detailed and technical in disciplining such theoretical trials as I am committed to.

It is serious play again, of a kind we advocate for children's growth, but tend to disparage for adult concerns. I do indeed believe that the general characteristics of the nervous system I describe, and the general style of learning behavior associated with this, will turn out literally to be a fair fit to the truth. If so and when so, we will be freed once and for all from the narrowing dominance of single-track, mechanical conceptions of learning, and will be able to see how it is that the best of practical human insight is matched by the sober conclusions of "hard" science.

On Understanding the Understanding of Children

(1967)

In what I have to say today I shall be both reporting and theorizing; reporting on some recent innovative work in education, and theorizing to explicate the presuppositions of the work and the implications of its findings. The scientific study of childhood intellectual development is, of course, a very complicated and manysided affair which I cannot even summarize, characterized as it is by many different and even disparate approaches, as well as by large areas where there has been no approach at all.

The study of infancy and childhood belongs, in one very important phase, to that puzzling class of topics for which empirical information is an embarrassment rather than an asset. Probably most of the essential behavioral phenomena in this field have long been known to adults, and some of them passed on in disguise without benefit of texts and treatises in the common culture. Mothers often, teachers sometimes, and sometimes perhaps pediatricians, have seen and recorded phenomena that would, if suitably trimmed and ordered, lead far beyond the present state of learned understanding. What matter are the criteria of selection and ordering, and that is why the need for theory is so pressing.

I should like to begin by alluding to the old and sterile heredity-environment controversy, which in the present context takes the form of a contrast between the developmental and the experiential. This sterility derives from an assumption shared by straw man developmentalists and straw man environmentalists which is almost certainly false—namely, that the relationship between the two sets of variables is linear. But without this assumption no significance can be attached to the notion that one of these variables is more important than the other except in very extreme or in very carefully limited cases. The true relation between the variables is one of complementarity or covariance, in which a change in one set of variables can be defined in its effects only for specific values of the other variables.

What we should recognize, instead, is that the viewpoints in question are literally just that; they are viewpoints, corresponding to the demands of specific methodologies. The developmentalist has typically been an observer who, with notebook and calipers in hand, has sampled infant and child behavior at periodic intervals and recorded vast amounts of data. The data are then reduced to statistical norms, to ideal types; thus, for example, Gesell or, with quite different intent, Piaget. The environmentalist, on the other hand, has typically been one with the interests and working viewpoint of a teacher, who hopes to record differential changes in development in response to changes in environment. A classic example of this controversy was waged in the thirties, when Stoddard and others at Iowa found themselves in a position to induce radical changes in the environments of young children, and accumulated evidence of large changes in what was then the academically sacred intelligence quotient, the interindividual variance of which had been dogmatically set forth as genetic.[1]

The theory of childhood intellectual evolution should not depend, obviously, upon a prior choice of methodology; it ought, as far as possible, to relate usefully to any method of study, even to suggest new ones. But I believe there is one very important feature of the developmentalist view that we ought to take seriously. We know enough about biological development to reject some versions of environmental influence as implausible, except in special cases when substantiated by very powerful evidence. One example of such a claim is the Freudian hypothesis of the unique trauma, as contrasted with those more constant and furrowing environmental influences within which traumata are likely points of consolidation. Another example is the prevalent belief that a thin stream of verbal flow directed at a child, and identified as instruction, will significantly alter his intellectual evolution.

I want to make a careful and plausible argument here, and not overstate it; for even an understatement, I think, will accomplish my purpose. Let me look at the role of experience from two different viewpoints; one is the neurophysiological view, the other the more humane view of a child's characteristic styles of learning. I shall try to show that these two accounts mesh together in certain important respects to give a plausible, coherent picture, a picture which suggests the gross inadequacy of certain highly simplified representations of the learning process, for example, those of classical or operant conditioning. I do not want to say that these are incorrect as representations of the particular phenomena studied, but that their use as representations of the major phenomena of human intellectual development touches only one generic aspect of the process which, although essential, gives us no key to understanding the rest. No theory of brain function in learning can escape critical scrutiny without some hypothesis of reinforcement: pathways, or sets of pathways, are affected by use in such a way as to be more available for future use. The nervous system is inherently and essentially "memorious." As far as one can see there is no reason to believe in any one unique mechanism of reinforcement, applicable to all parts of the system, or to the same parts at different times.

There is one general characteristic of brain function, summarized by Lashley in his so-called laws of equipotentiality and mass action, which implies that any function of the brain is widely distributed among its structures.[2] Another way of stating this implication, supported by familiar facts of anatomy, is that the brain organization has the style of an elaborate network of essentially complex neuron modules, with hundreds of end-feet of other neurons impinging on a given neuron. I mention this because it fits in a very interesting way with certain theorems in the mathematical theory of computation, namely, that any very big network capable of functioning reliably as a computer must *of necessity* distribute each functional unit of computation among many physical modules of the network. Such theorems assume that in a very large computing network the probability of failure of components, even though small per component, is nevertheless large for the system as a whole. Thus the system will fail if its successful operation depends on error-free functioning of all components. Moreover, there are almost certainly random effects in the organization of the network. A "wiring diagram" of the human brain must specify some 10^{13} connections, and any but a statistical specification of these in genetic terms seems impossible. The theorems in question state that efficient computation in such a system is possible *only* for networks which provide complexly interconnected modules functioning collectively in such a way that each computation is spread among many modules, and each module is doing parts of many computations at the same time.[3] Such mathematical models give, in fact, a very clear meaning to the old idea of organic wholeness. Nets of this wholistic type have been called "anastomotic," a word first used to describe the interconnectedness of veins in a leaf, and later the pattern of neuron organization itself.

In this report I want to avoid the technical language of neural nets, physiological or mathematical, partly because a simpler language is possible, and partly because of the application I want to make. For a first move in this direction, let me equate the verb "compute" with the verb "classify." When we compute a function Y of some variable X, we are in general dealing with a situation in which several sets of values of the variable X correspond to a single value of Y. Thus, if we compute a sum of two variables and find it is 12, there are several pairs of natural numbers which could give us that sum. The output of a computation characteristically gives us only incomplete information about the input, or again, the computation maps input into output in a many-to-one mapping. Still another way of talking, and this is the one I prefer, is that we may group together all those inputs, which have the same output, as belonging to the same class; they are indistinguishable or equivalent with respect to the computed output. In this sense six and six are indistinguishable, with respect to addition, from five and seven or three and nine. Now just as any computation may be regarded as a classification, so any classification may be regarded as a computation.

This equivalence of computation and classification is illustrated in matters of organization, as well as in the end-result. In a formal computing network the modules are organized by *ranks*; that is, there are modules of the first rank which compute certain intermediate functions of the input variables. The output of these modules then go as input to modules of the second rank, the output of which is input to those of the third rank, and so on. Nets may, of course, be cyclic, so that output is fed back from later ranks to earlier ones. A characteristic feature is that the number of computing modules tends to decrease in later ranks, since each computational step tends to simplify, to have less variety in its output than its input.

If you think now of any familiar classification system, it operates in the same manner. To begin, we have something given for classification with many properties, i.e., many input variables. These are divided into two or more genera, each with a smaller internal variance than the universe from which the sample was taken. In the next step we find directions for subdivision appropriate to each genus, and thus arrive at lower genera, and this process continues until some stop-rule or decision terminates it. The terminal species thus defined carve up the original universe in the same way that the set of possible outputs of a computation carves up, into equivalent subsets, the set of possible inputs.

There is an interesting point of apparent dissimilarity between these two ways of talking. I have said that in general there will be many computational modules in the first rank of a computing network, the number progressively decreasing in later ranks. Thus a diagram with input at the top and output at the bottom will look like an inverted pyramid. A classification system, on the other hand, looks like a normal pyramid, with undifferentiated input at the top, a few genera in the next rank, more in the next, etc. But notice that the *variety* within the successive categories is greatest at the top and decreases steadily along any pathway of classification. This means that the *first* division of the universe into genera must find the differentiating characteristic of a sample against a very wide background variety. If we think of classification in terms of the *extension* of classes rather than *intension*, its representation is the same as for computation. The most fundamental differentiations we make are often the most complexly mediated, even though we may think of them subjectively as the easiest. A child working with a compound pendulum, apparently finding that it was not working the way he wanted it to, was observed holding the bob in his hand and moving it repeatedly in a desired path. When the teacher made some polite inquiry, he said, "I'm trying to train it." Now a pendulum is at the very opposite pole from an animal, it is totally *un*memorious. But this was a new situation, and the child was very clearly *not* making this "obvious" computation or discrimination. Why not?

A good theory points, sometimes, toward the nonobvious. The theory of computation requires that the distinction between the two wide genera of mechanical vs. vital phenomena be computationally a very complex one, even though it may be partially and incompletely acquired at a relatively early age. If you try to design an automaton that will discriminate such categories across the wide range of individual instances, you will find that you are, in fact, committed to a very complex computational design; so complex that the meaning of the distinction is still being argued, after 2,000 years! Yet very much of our educational system is based on the assumption that broad divisions of this kind are obvious and need only be properly verbalized. Aristotle said that what comes first in the order of understanding often comes last in the order of experience, and in this he is at one with present-day analysis.

The example of training the pendulum, which can be multiplied many times over, brings up another point. The ways of classifying things and situations, so indispensable to any intellectual grasp, are products of experiential evolution, interacting no doubt with postnatal embryological development; this means that our patterns of discrimination and classification are inherently adaptive. If we now go back to the language of computation and computational networks, this means that we have a new criterion to impose.

This mathematical model of the anastomotic net has been elaborated in relation to the postulate that any module, any computing element, is inherently unreliable, inherently subject to failure with some small but not negligible probability. In engineering language, its signals must be processed in the presence of noise which may corrupt those signals. But this is an unstable distinction between signal and noise, because we can give it a *sharp* meaning only with reference to a functional definition of the module, to an implied knowledge of a fixed and reproducible operation. In communication we can *define* the noise which corrupts a message only when we can compare the received message with that transmitted; in computation we can *define* an error only when we know the function to be computed. In learning we can *define* similarities only against a background of differences, and differences against a background of similarity.

If, on the contrary, we demand that neural modules and the system composed of them be inherently *adaptive,* then their description as nonconstant and spontaneously variable in operation is as essential to their nature as spontaneous variation, or mutation, to the efficacy of Darwinian evolution. The concept of reinforcement essential to any theory of learning *requires* noise and spontaneous variation just as surely as natural selection does. If there were no

noise in such a system and no cushion of redundancy, or anastomosis, in its design, then we would be dealing, I claim, with a
nonadaptive system. I cannot prove this statement, but I think I can
make it plausible.[4]

In the first place, let us examine the inductive behavior of young
children. The other day we had a visit in our laboratory from a
group of 3- and 4-year-old children, who immediately spread out
among the variety of manipulatable goodies which it provides. One
child found a scoop, a large tray of peas and beans, and a sizable
equal-arm balance composed of two paper pie plates hung from a
cross-arm. She put a scoopful in one pan, and it went down. She put
a scoopful in the other pan, which slightly overbalanced it the other
way. This process was then repeated some 18 times, with the child
being completely engrossed. Of course the amounts were never
quite equal, but the balance was insensitive enough to give a sort of
tippy equilibrium two or three times. It was interesting that she
obviously seemed to adopt a rule early in the game, i.e., put the next
scoopful in the upper pan; but what was more interesting was that
she *later* mixed her strategy and put the next scoopful in the *lower*
pan, whether it had gone down the time before or failed to rise. Each
time she watched to see the result of her manipulation. Now anyone
familiar with modern psychology would be likely to look at such a
phenomenon in terms of operant conditioning, and think of producing a learning curve. But this is entirely inappropriate, for the
following reasons. First, the circumstances are such that no well-
defined task is involved; from the adults there were no "kindly, but
firm" instructions, and the child adopted this collection of equipment on her own. Second, the circumstances were such that the
phenomena were essentially multivariate and nonreproducible.
The standard learning curve, if you were misdirected enough to
draw one, would be rather flat, negative-sloping, or erratic, and
would represent the gap between a research stereotype guaranteed
to teach nothing, and a more interesting analysis. Substitute a set of
carefully defined weights, a clinical ambient in which the child has
no significant choices, and an adult who instructs the child to add
weights to change the balance. Then, if the child adopted, or was
pushed into, an obedient attitude, the standard curve would certainly eventuate. Of course, with a sturdier ego the child might still

think of several other things to do, and thus frustrate the curve-fitting.

For my first example I have deliberately chosen a rather highly constrained situation, that of the equal-arm balance. If you substitute for this an unequal-arm balance, with a variety of sizes and densities of things to place or hang on it, the above result is guaranteed: you will not be likely soon to see a child discovering the textbook properties summarized in the law of moments. But what you *can* see is even greater absorption, an attention-span many times longer than what some psychometricians have said is characteristic of children of that age, and much more invention, evidently connected with other sorts of experience already laid down or mapped: of levers, for example, or catapults, or the school-yard seesaw; of weights and densities and volumes. One is tempted to say that any one conceptual topic is touched on in many episodes, and that each episode involves many conceptual topics; and that, in its own way, it is a kind of anastomosis characteristic of the child's native style of learning. The child in my example was not studying the equal-arm balance, or the principle of symmetry, or the additivity of mass, or the uniformity of the gravitational field, or any one of a dozen other conditions which are, in fact, relevant to the operation of the equal-arm balance. A learning curve which assumed that any *one* of these was her goal would be flat or fluctuating, except accidentally. If we can impute any purpose to her, it is one which she would or could not synthesize or verbalize; it is that of exploring connections between a newly encountered situation and her own partially organized schemes for classifying and sorting experience, in this case inanimate environment. If we had the wit to define this goal in terms specific enough to match the particularities of her preoccupation, we could, I am sure, emerge with a standard learning curve, and be none the wiser for it. Lacking that definition, which even a skillful and watchful teacher keeping track of her development over months might only crudely approximate, we note instead the intensity of her involvement and the watchful style of her operations, and conclude that she has found what is, for the moment, a satisfying match for her insight and capacity.

Let me generalize the description, asking you to imagine a hundred mornings, densely marked with attentive encounters over significant areas of experience as they might be made accessible to this child in a good school. Include in your account, as you well might, the return engagements with any one aspect, for example, the one of balance I have singled out for the sake of vividness. Notice the change in her style of work amid the shifts and recurrences of interest; notice the way in which this pattern of work is coupled to an evolving pattern of peer- and teacher-association both stabilized and enriched by the common bonds that develop among fellow-enquirers. But especially, notice two pervasive characteristics of the entire environment which the particular child has contributed to only slightly and indirectly. One is the physical organization of space and materials which permits this pattern of work to develop quickly within a new group, to proceed harmoniously over time, and to provide attentive encounters between children and things—samples of the wild environment or man-made artifacts—which embody what we know to be potent ideas in such a way as to be useful in many situations and for many purposes. The other thing to notice is the style or organization in the hands of a skillful teacher after a day, a month, and a year of school. What you see here is an evolution from early and excited sampling—what Frances Hawkins calls the Christmas Morning Syndrome—to more quiet and steady work. On the average, the variance among activities will remain high and stability will remain relative. A power shovel across the street, a spider found in the corner, a collection of rocks and seed pods, and a rusted horseshoe brought back from a field trip—all these will generate new involvements, new investigations, and create new opportunities for teachers' diagnoses and interventions. Watch for the unusual associations that develop, the cross-category analogies and associations that lead from the study of the pine tree to the geometry of tessellations, from the pendulum to the planets, from a study of seeds and cuttings to new experiments with color in optics and painting.

I give these examples rather breathlessly, but it is no longer Christmas morning; each transition is the cumulative expression of much work by one or a few children. Watch also for the more reflective and synoptic phases: a classwide discussion, a short lecture by the teacher, a growing commitment to communication in all its forms, including writing and reading, but also talk—endless talk—painting, and clay. Notice how the three R's are woven into all the work, with occasional but not obtrusive formality. The study of figurate numbers leads back to the geometry of tessellations, and on to the construction of a pegboard graph which embodies the algorithms of computational arithmetic.

I will not try to carry the description further in depth, nor beyond the first years of preschool and school, from 4 to 12 in terms of age. I have not often seen such practice in secondary school or college, though I have seen it occasionally in graduate school, and more often in the secret lives of some college students who have learned how to get by the formalities with minimum effort. I see no block to an interpolation across the whole range. And, of course, nothing in my description cuts out the formalities, the tight, nonredundant organization of the physics text, the term-long concentration on the Iliad, or the structure of "p-adic" number fields. It demotes them, though, because usually they are seen, somehow, as the whole end and aim of education.

I have said that the pattern of the anastomotic net, anatomically present in the brain, is required by the theory of efficient computation or classification in the presence of noise. I have suggested that an adaptive net must *eo ipso* function in the presence of noise, of spontaneous variety, as a condition of its adaptability. I have tried to illustrate the native style of such a process by examples from the work of children coping in essentially multivariate situations, where each episode implicitly involves many conceptual topics and each such topic is returned to many times. I have then tried to suggest the evolution, usually gradual, by which children can begin to sort out the multiplicities of variables, begin to develop the abstractions, and later accept the formalities, the tightly constrained, nonredundant organization which is essential to adult understanding, visible above the surface of public discourse as codified knowledge, and often mistaken for understanding. What is under the surface is the far richer preanalytic network of associative connections, for which the human brain is especially apt, established through the adaptive filtering of many megabits of motor-sensory information.

I have also, I hope, made some hints of propaganda against the overwhelmingly dominant style of our schools, which mimics the child who tried to train the pendulum, but with the opposite error; I have suggested, at least, one way of understanding the fact that the schools are filled with bored and disoriented children.

But my main intent is really to suggest a theoretical framework for the comprehension of human learning, to coax psychology into a frame of thought consonant with what skillful teachers, in their often more "anastomotic" intuitive fashion, already know.

I fear, of course, that I have in the process offended all the puritans among you, who I trust are an empty subclass of this audience: both the moral puritans, who want to prepare children for a hard life by making it hard for them to learn, and the scientific puritans, who cannot imagine that a do-it-yourself curriculum, woven together by the art of advisers and teachers and children, can possibly be efficient in comparison with the handy-package approach that has been the principle product of our recent efforts at curriculum reform. The handy packages we need, of course, those that can be used for many purposes, include many not intended by the designers. (In fact , it would be a nice figure of merit to use the ratio of unintended to intended uses, classing among the former those which do not follow the neat postanalytic structures of the designer, which do not minimize the large redundancy unnecessary in the formal product, but essential to its evolution; such redundancy is mostly absent in the textbook, but present in every educated mind.) From this point of view, indeed, an educated mind could be defined as one that can make its way around in the network of its own resources. It no longer needs to be in school, it has become its own teacher.

REFERENCES

1. G. M. Whipple (ed.): *Intelligence—Its Nature and Nurture: Part I: Comparative and Critical Exposition, 39th Yearbook of the National Society for the Study of Education* (Bloomington, Ill: Public School Publishing Company, 1940).

2. K. L. Spencer: *Brain Mechanisms and Intelligence: A Quantitative Study of Injuries to the Brain* (Chicago: University of Chicago Press, 1929).

3. S. Winograd and J. D. Cowan: *Reliable Computation in the Presence of Noise* (Cambridge, Mass.: Massachusetts Institute of Technology Press, 1963).

4. H. D. Block: *Adaptive Neural Networks as Brain Models: Proceedings of Symposia in Applied Mathematics* (New York: American Mathematics Society, 1963).

Human Nature and the Scope of Education

The essay which follows, last and longest of the present volume, is in turn a sort of preface, an outline of a general theory of education. In it I have tried, along the way, to suggest some of the kinds of more detailed questions, needing further investigation, which a general theory can underline, can help clarify and formulate.

Unlike most essays in this volume it was constructed without improvisation, was written to be read by others rather than to them, and is unabashedly "philosophical." It treats some topics discussed in earlier essays, "saying the same about the same." I hope it is more explicit in setting forth the underpinnings, and thus more open to systematic discussion, than more informal essays are likely to be.

Human Nature and the Scope of Education
(1972)

I shall be concerned in this paper with three postulates or conditioning hypotheses which have underlain the classical theory of human nature. My particular focus is the central place of human educability in the theory of human nature. In each case the postulates in question are relevant to education and in each case their significance has been blurred. For there is a wide array of plausible belief which appears to contradict them, and in any event they have never been consistently applied to the estate of childhood. On the other hand, there are serious difficulties and misfortunes connected with their overt denial. I propose to examine some of the fruitful consequences of these postulates, properly formulated, for a theory of human nature which gives place (as the classics do not) to education and development.

What is true of scientific theory generally is conspicuously true of the subject matter we deal with here. In the short run only a part of scientific theory is determined by empirical evidence supporting specific, testable generalizations; a part consists of some framework of categories and beliefs *brought to* the gathering of evidence and linked by boundary assumptions which suggest the kinds of generalizations to be sought and tested and the sorts of inferences these generalizations will sustain. In the long run it is not possible to justify a sharp and unchanging boundary between such relatively *a posteriori* and *a priori* components of knowledge. Research not guided by general theoretical formulations and arguments is likely to be inconsequential. Theory which is not linked to empirical research, to some form of practical experience and discrimination, is empty and cannot progress. The second of these propositions is widely recognized but the first is less so. In the "developed" sciences, like physics, theory is acknowledged to have sway. But in "undeveloped" fields like ours, it is often believed that theory is a sort of idle luxury or even a fraud, purporting to lay down encompassing generalizations which in fact have not been "empirically established."

On the contrary, it is in just such fields as ours that theory is of the greatest importance, though much neglected. For we do in fact already know a great deal about education and development; the problem is rather to marshall that knowledge in a coherent usable form. Empirical investigations conceived within such a framework of theory can react upon, can modify or extend knowledge. They cannot amount to much without it.

These remarks are by now only slightly controversial in the philosophy of science and may be illustrated by numerous passages from the history of astronomy or physics or biology. But let me come back to the particular categories and postulates I wish to discuss for the theory of education, picking up historical analogies as they seem helpful. For the sake of the orientation and controversy they suggest, let me use traditional labels. The postulated character of human nature is implied by three sweeping propositions: men are equal, men are free, and men are rational. These propositions have been often reasserted and argued over. They are the logical backbone of modern political theory as formulated in Hobbes's *Leviathan*, Rousseau's *Social Contract*, and Hegel's *Philosophy of Right*. The major consequences, common to this tradition, are the following: Without equality among men there is no profound *problem* of politics; the obviously superior will rule. Without freedom there is no deep *problem* of how the rulers can rule; they will rule by force or by psychological manipulation. Without rationality there is no alternative to force or manipulation, no meaningful debate over ends, no *problem* of consent or consensus. I mention these consequences because my own use of the postulates parallels them. Without them I cannot even define what seem to me to be quite central problems of educational theory and research.

In this specific context, however, my general remarks *are* somewhat controversial. It is usually believed that the classical theory (which, with emendations, I follow) is not descriptive but normative—that is, *morally* normative. For men are, often and profoundly, unequal, unfree, and irrational. The classical theory is taken, therefore, as only a hoped-for view of a case which, it has often been held, has been shattered by new discoveries about man and his career—discoveries in psychology, anthropology, literature, history—and so by a new and more sober enlightenment which penetrates through the optimistic superficiality of the eighteenth-century Enlightenment.

But the contrast between the normative and the descriptive is changed if we take account of the requirements of *descriptive theory*. For theorizing has its own norms—of self-consistency, of completeness, of definition and organization, of adequacy to subject matter, of fruitfulness. Because of these requirements a *good* theory outruns the "hard" evidence available to support it and if it does not, it is not a good theory.[1] But the basic postulates of a theory are not therefore to be taken as *mere* assumptions. They are supported by the kind and degree of organization they induce, by the new phenomena they lead to or highlight. They may be put forward wishfully—if so, the wishes that lead to a good theory are well rewarded!

I believe that a careful reading of the classical writers will show that their "normativeness" was primarily of this kind. The founding

spirit, Hobbes, was first and foremost a theoretical physicist who
sought to give the study of human affairs the same kind of logical
organization which he and his scientific contemporaries saw developing from the work of Galileo and which reached its first great
culmination in the work of Hobbes's much younger contemporary,
Isaac Newton. I believe also that extensions of the classical viewpoint
will prove their vitality for today and are sorely needed. So I wish to
be judged on my position by the criteria of theory. But I do not wish
thereby to conceal any of my own value judgments along the way. If
the theoretical framework being developed is any good, it supports
these judgments—and if it is not, then not.

The Educational Cycle and Its Closure

I begin by noticing a formal constraint upon educational theory
which derives from the purposes it serves and which therefore
determines its range or scope. A theoretical structure which fails to
meet this demand is not thereby incorrect; it is simply inadequate to
meet certain sorts of demands either correctly *or* incorrectly. In the
classical writings this constraint is satisfied, but with equivocation
and perhaps some embarrassment: *Adults* are equal, free, and rational; infants and children are, so to say, noticed in passing, but that
is about all.

At its simplest, the demand is for a recognition of the full cycle of
cultural self-reproduction. Thus persons must be describable both
as learners and as teachers, as both subjects and agents of education.
Childhood is no more transient than adulthood, they are both here
to stay. In the cycle, childhood is an end as well as a means or, in
other language, a sufficient condition of adulthood as well as a
necessary one. In order to have a theory which is relevant over the
whole cycle, its basic postulates must be formulated so as to obtain
over the range from infancy to adulthood. In their ordinary usage
the concepts of equality, freedom, and rationality are explained by
reference to supposed characteristics of *adult* behavior. And among
many of us, as among some of the classical writers, these characteristics are denied infants or children, or affirmed of them only in
minute degree. But human development is not simply quantitative,

and measures of it (such as the mental age of intelligence tests) are averages over many sampled dimensions of behavioral development. I do not claim to have found that formulation of the postulates which is invariant with respect to human age. Here, I am only concerned to state that this sort of formulation is a logical necessity for an adequate theory based upon such postulates. Without such a formulation childhood is left in a theoretical limbo, as it was, for example, by Locke or Hobbes. With such a formulation in hand we can then begin to trace those qualitative features of human development which will show completely what the postulates imply for each developmental phase. I shall later examine one attempt at invariant formulation, that of Jean Piaget. One obvious implication of an invariant formulation might be that children are sometimes teachers, curriculum specialists, and instructional consultants—with adults as their pupils.

The formal condition of the cycle is an obvious one to impose, but it is not trivial or always obvious in its logical consequences. Economic theory, in a sense, began with François Quesnay and Adam Smith because they imposed the condition of circular flow and were loyal to its consequences. Once seen, it was an "obvious" condition and (at least in a strong first approximation) factually indubitable. But it led to unfamiliar conclusions about the health and wealth of nations. It widened the geographical and temporal scope of economics and through the circular linkage of production, distribution, and consumption gave rise to a kind of logical closure, so that inputs to consumption reappeared as outputs of production governed by a law of value—in effect, a conservation law analogous to those laws that were to appear later in nineteenth-century physics.[2]

The requirement that a general theory must apply over the whole cycle of the processes it studies is obvious in the case of biology. First, there is the cycle of interactions between an organism and its ecological niche. Second, there is the specific cycle of reproduction, necessary also to the study of evolution. As in economics, some implications of this requirement were realized only belatedly—in the time of Darwin; and that does not end the story. Faced with the problem of the origins of terrestrial life, biologists have only very recently realized that self-reproduction must have appeared before life itself, in the molecular milieu of the primitive earth. For no living thing without that capacity could have lasted long enough to acquire such a central and complex system of processes. Indeed, human biology implies in the same way that the basic processes of education must have evolved among our prehuman ancestors. For on a purely biological level our species is already apt for education and cannot survive without it. We are in a sense invented by education, not education by us.

The self-reproduction of a culture, like that of life or human economy, implies an essential continuity. As the caterpillar becomes the moth, children grow up and replace us who argue about schools, plan curricula, and teach. Such conditions are met in the real world, but some theories fail to meet them. Embryology has not always acknowledged the womb, or the womb within the foetus. So neobehavioristic theories with their S-R schemata have no language for the conditioners qua persons with methodologies, arguments, and truth-claims. Conditioners are *agents* (of a sort) for which the descriptive metaphysics of behaviorism has no place and which it can neither acknowledge nor deny, but can only exclude from consideration. In its methodological aspect behaviorism makes the cut between investigator and subject in such a way that the former is only present by implication. He talks about himself and his peers in a language of agency and choice which cannot be mapped into his own official theoretical language. This state of affairs violates the condition of cyclicity.

To accept the continuity of the cycle, one must impute to infants and children, with such transformations as development may explain, *their* methodologies, arguments, and truth-claims. Such a failure is no criticism of a theory within a more limited scope, though it does suggest criticism. Mercantilist economic theory had its range of validity also. But such a failure demonstrates theoretical inadequacy—in our case to the function of education. Nor does the recognition of failure lead automatically to a better theory, though it may again be suggestive. Solids and gases are pretty well understood today, but liquids are still a mess. So, for example, the large change in viscosity as gases condense to liquids is still a mystery—but the demand which makes it appear a mystery requires a theoretical framework which will itself weather the change of state.

The adequacy of a theory to such demands is, of course, a relative matter. The closure which education requires is different from that in biology. The continuous change from egg to human infant marks a conceptual discontinuity; this gap is of real but peripheral concern for education, the continuity of which is social rather than biological. Genuinely biological variables are important as boundary conditions for education but it is not defined in terms of them.

Equality

The ground level of educational theory takes account of persons, of integral human beings as children and as adults. A postulate of equality in this context has a logical function similar to that which it has in our classical political theory. That is, it requires that certain kinds of de facto *inequalities* be explained as lying *within* the scope of the theory and not as biological boundary conditions. In discussing the meaning and validity of this concept I am not concerned to make moral judgments or to "argue for" equality (or freedom or rationality). In a scientific theory (as distinct from a hypothesis within a theory) a postulate is a proposition set forth as true. On the other hand, the import of a postulate, what it does to or for a theory, is of great importance in determining how to formulate it and how to exclude irrelevant connotations. Morality does imply certain factual egalitarian presuppositions, of course. There is a widespread weak-kneed concession that one should believe *in* equality and treat persons as equal, though of course one is not supposed to dream of believing there is any truth in it. Here, surely, where good theory is at stake, one wants to get the horse back in front of the cart.

The postulate of equality has the logical function of a symmetry condition. How such principles function in science is different in different cases but the logic is the same. To assert that entities of some class are identical or indistinguishable or equivalent in certain respects is to block certain sorts of explanation and to invite others. Elementary particles group in the same few identity-classes everywhere and they therefore do not per se explain the rich variety of nature, which is structure and history—not mere building blocks. The statistical equipartition of energy both blocks and redirects an enormous range of explanations in physics, starting with specific heats and Brownian motions.

Thomas Hobbes' political theory shows very clearly the logical import of the postulate of equality. His famous "State of Nature" is a thought-experiment based on this postulate. In the presence of limited resources for life and in the absence of government, men are inevitably competitive. Because they are so, they are dangerous to each other. In fearing this danger and wishing to forestall it, each man becomes more dangerous to his neighbor, and the situation must degenerate into "the war of each against all." Men are not so unequal in power or ability as to give anyone a natural dominance over others; and if one be for the moment more powerful, a coalition of others will have the ability to destroy him. Equality need not be absolute; the postulate need only be close enough to the truth to invalidate any argument which says that the natural superiority of some men is sufficient, in the "state of nature," to create a stable order based on dominance. In the absence of government, of civil society, men are not good or evil; they are simply determined by self-preservation to be enemies. Nor are they irrational; on the contrary, their very rationality, under these conditions, is what makes them mutually dangerous. If you were put down in such a world, its constraints would soon bring you to be an enemy of others, and like theirs your life would be "poor, nasty, brutish and short." Hobbes has often been criticized on the ground that such a state of nature has never existed, but this misses the whole style of his argument. Hobbes's theory is a mathematical model which in fact and even in some detail anticipates the von Neumann theory of games. The state of nature is a many-person, non-zero-sum game, but a game of life and death. Coalitions may form but they will be essentially unstable, for every power group which forms will be threatened by others which transiently form against it and by offers of new coalitions which divide it. As a result, all genuine possibilities of cooperation are stultified and men realize, on the average, a far less measure of security and livelihood than nature would allow them otherwise.

The "Social Contract," by contrast, is an alternative model. In this model all men, being equal and rational, realize the source of their misery and create by rational consent a sovereign person or group to whom they surrender their power as far as possible. This sovereign (preferably an absolute monarch) is not party to the contract but remains in the "state of nature." Self-interest, not an agreement, guides him to enforce civil tranquility, the rights of property, and the rules of contract. Under these conditions his subjects will be without fear of each other and in self-interest will cooperate with each other and will secure from nature their maximum welfare. Individuals may deviate and be punished, but large groups will not unite to violate the contract unless the sovereign fails to rule well and thus jeopardizes his own security.

There are many weaknesses in Hobbes' theory from the point of view of realism and adequacy, but it is a coherent theory and a sort of first (or, better, zero-th) approximation to the truth. I might mention that at the formal level of proof they sought, von Neumann and Morgenstern[3] were forced to stop far short of the general n-person game and its many alternative "solutions"; and needless to say, Hobbes' arguments are plausibility-arguments, not proofs. It is worth noticing that the later authors also adopt the egalitarian postulate; they do so precisely in order to show how social inequality can then arise *without* appeal to innate differences. Without the postulate their theory would be useless. And so it is with Hobbes. In the postulate of equality he blocked any theory of aristocracy based on the belief that we breed *natural* rulers; the postulate then leads to an alternative explanation of transient inequality in the chaos of the state of nature and also to the possibility of civil society having its investment of coercive power in a governing individual or body. The contract is only possible as an agreement of equals and only stable when governing a society of equals. (For the same reason the choice of rulers is theoretically arbitrary.) Others of the classical political philosophers used the postulate differently, but the logic—simplest and most daring in Hobbes—is always one which brings the origins of inequality *within* the sphere of human control or at least (as with Rousseau, Hegel, and Marx) within the realm of historical-political development.

In education the postulate has sometimes been so formulated as simply to deny educationally significant congenital differences. I do not know any strict formulations postulating absolute equality, but many of us are disposed to believe, in the spirit of Hobbes, that individual or intergroup congenital differences with respect to education capacity are minor compared to those induced within society. From this point of view, unequal results of educational effort cannot be explained by differences of natural endowment, except perhaps for a necessarily small fraction of the population suffering gross constitutional defects. Such differences are therefore subject, actually or potentially, to educational control.

But rather clearly that version of the postulate is wrong. The cells of a single animal (disregarding occasional polymorphism) acquire their morphological and functional diversity as a result of embryological differentiation; my nerve, bone, and liver cells are identical genetically, but they differ by "education." But whereas cells of the same organism have the same heredity, congenital differences between organisms of a species are real and of great multiplicity. A large part of this intraspecific multiplicity (and conceivably, with the exceptions noted, all of it) may be of no great educational consequence. At some level of approximation this is certainly true. Hobbes spelled this out very crisply, as did Descartes.[4]

The purpose of scientific theory is not to *deny* differences but to describe them correctly. Human congenital differences, negligible at the level of a zero-th approximation theory like Hobbes's or Descartes's, have a positive importance for the concerns of education, and I therefore propose a different interpretation of the postulate of equality. If the purpose of the postulate is to place differences where they are relevant, then it seems clear one would do well to emphasize that persons of one very distinct species biologically differ constitutionally in many respects that are potentially important for education. On the other hand, there are no genes for algebra, for painting in oils, for operating linotype machines, or for Chinese calligraphy. Our glory and trouble is not specialized adaptation but generalized adaptability, and this is a universal characteristic of our species, common to almost all of our gene combinations. The niche of algebra and the niche of calligraphy are inhabited equally by many genetically different sorts of persons—if not, these niches would not exist. Nativistically conceived, human "abilities" are not Mendelian traits or simple functions of such traits. They are, in all likelihood, redundant complexes of such traits. Coupled thus to genetic variety is the species-characteristic of generalized adaptability, a certain kind of functional redundancy which characterized our capacities for learning. Put otherwise, the condition of cyclicity in the transmission and evolution of culture implies at most a very weak relationship between individual genetic variety on the one hand and cultural endowments on the other. This is part of the *meaning* of generalized adaptability.[5] To be a human being at all is to be biologically within the reach of many genera and species of human careers.

Let me use and sharpen an analogy. Most of our machines are the very antithesis of our own adaptability. They are inflexibly specialized beyond anything in the biological domain, and even our great ingenuity can readapt them, for the most part, only at the slow rate of capital obsolescence. We may, therefore, seize upon the computer as the first machine having generalized adaptability within a domain—even though that domain is still a very artificial one. The theorem is a theorem of closure.[6] Any machine which satisfies certain simply stated formal conditions of operation can thereby do *anything* that *any* other such machine can do. Regardless of component-entry and mode of operation, any computer can be programmed to operate as a replica of the operation of any other computer. If A has whatever specialized components and style of computation B lacks, then a suitable *description* of the former supplied to B in its program causes B to function in a way that "empathetically" duplicates A's operation. In this basic qualitative sense, all computers are equal. Of course the theorem says nothing about time or energy or cost, and it says nothing about what these universal computers as a class cannot do. Nevertheless, it establishes a sharp, if limited, definition of generalized adaptability, a domain of equivalence among machines across a very wide range of "constitutional" differences.

In our case the equivalence is of a different kind, of which "computing" is only one rather special component, and we do not have the sort of theory to formulate a formal proof. The proof lies in the historical fact that we *are* the matrix of cultural evolution, that cultures are transmitted and evolved with no close dependence on our internal biological variety. Among other manifestations of our generalized adaptability we can, within wide limits, organize ourselves, each constitutionally in his own way, to perceive, to plan, to understand, and to enjoy, *each like each other*. Such an "empathetic" equivalence is a presupposition[7] of communication and of society.

But this is only the negative side. The old egalitarianism leads to one correct conclusion. Differences in educability are not part of the ground plan of our species. Differences are minor, though open, as we well know, to narcissistic elaboration. But there is a stronger objection to this viewpoint. One remembers the French joke about the difference between men and women. About individuality one wants also to say, "Vive la différence!" And this for theoretical reasons first, not moral or ideological or aesthetic reasons.

First, we well know that if any group of individuals are constrained to follow an identical pedagogical track, they will learn unequally, with a large variance in the particular learning rates which can be defined for just that track. The pure egalitarian assumption that children are indistinguishable at birth requires that this difference be explained as a difference in "readiness" associated with earlier experience. The single track remains unquestioned, even by most of those armed with slogans of "individualized instruction," which puts children to the book, or the machine, as though it were more adaptive than they.

But congenital variety among persons, modified by early experience, is not single-track; like biological variety in general, it is many-dimensional, its graph is a profile. And whereas a single well-defined curricular track will spread children out in a long line of march, there is also a variance in the learning abilities of a single child along alternative tracks, assuming for a moment that these are made commensurable by leading toward a common goal. Thus, by a proper assignment of tracks in a way which complements congenital variety, the variance of learning rates can be reduced and with no decrease of any individual rates.

An interesting modification of the postulate of equality which idealizes this fact and is not inconsistent with experience (yet is unconfirmed enough to be challenging) is that for each child there exists *in principle* some unique optimal curricular track, of such a kind that in a group where learning is thus individually optimized the variance of attainment will be negligible (except again for gross congenital disabilities). I hope it is clear here that I am not speaking of tracks as prefabricated, as though they could be defined in a textbook on "alternative tracks." Mathematicians will recognize that I am speaking abstractly of education as a function (or as a functional) over *two* domains of variables which are essentially nonlinear in their relations to each other. We cannot speak of an optimal track in general, except with reference to a particular learner, or of an optimal learner except with reference to a particular track. Of course, there are some universally bad tracks.

Such a postulate is not all that I am after, but it is a way station and it sustains the egalitarian theorem that human "inequalities" are only by way of exception *derivable* from congenital differences. For, although not widely practiced, appropriate provision for qualitative variety in learning styles *is* within the domain of potential educational control. [8] Moreover, the postulate has already the right logical form: human beings qua human are never indistinguishable, never identical to each other, even in respects important for learning and education. They are, rather, *incommensurable* in their differences. For the new postulate as stated leads immediately to a further theorem, which is that by a suitable choice of learning tracks (nonoptimal for some) it is possible to rank n learners in all $n!$ possible permutations of "ability." It moreover suggests a stronger theorem (depending on some plausible side conditions) that for each such permutation there exists some *single* track that would realize that very permutation of the $n!$ individuals. It would take $n!$ no-option schools to do it, in theory: to assign an arbitrary rank order to n children and then pick or design a school which would realize that order, as determined by some antecedently prepared final examination. [9]

Thus, incommensurability excludes marketplace or IQ-dominated notions of unalterable inequality implicit in "the superior student," "ability grouping," and so forth. For these imply commensurability, the belief that "the more able" excel "the less able" along all possible tracks. In this connection it should be emphasized that incommensurability implies that individuals *can* be compared and ranked in many sorts of ways. It means that such comparisons are vector rather than scalar in type. It implies that in general one individual does not excel another in all relevant dimensions, does not, in mathematical language, dominate him. Acceptance of the postulate would have the salutary initial effect of raising an eyebrow at *any* course of study or program directed to "the superior," "the gifted," and the like. There is no doubt that along the small variety of curricular tracks available in our schools conspicuous dominance is unavoidable; indeed, it is sought after in the uniform sequencing of curricular items and lesson plans—self-confirmingly so in the case of many sorts of "ability grouping."[10]

Since the postulate of pure equality or educational identity allows an explanation of variance in learning only as a function of previous learning, it is therefore likely to lead to an emphasis on "remedial" education conceived in terms of slowing down and catching up, e.g., of giving the "retarded" a "head start." Much of the recent effort to redeem the school education of the disadvantaged has taken for granted a particular school language track along which many children are disadvantaged, and concluded from this the need for a remedial priority upon spoken and written English, an emphasis which in many cases guarantees the very alienation which it is intended to remedy. But however much one would welcome in schools (not least for children of the ethnic majority) the addition and enjoyment of black dialect, or Spanish, or the Indian languages—all previously unused and characteristically forbidden—the translation of existing contents into differently colored capsules is a limited innovation, to say the most. The Andersen fairy tale could easily tell in three languages how the king's new clothes were described.

The postulate of incommensurability, on the other hand, takes children as congenitally varied rather than "unequal," and raises questions about the *differential* effect of earlier environment in relation to the kinds of learning it has supported or inhibited. It underlines the importance of local and dependent curricular and instructional choices, to make the curricular spiral tangent at many points to the individual lives of children, to the educative resources of *their* total environment which *they* know or can be helped to discover. (It underlines also the importance of teachers as professional persons who diagnose and plan, not as conveyors of preorganized material to the young and who only when worn need "retooling.") This proposition is no less important for the education of "advantaged" children; it is only at present less in the political focus.

A postulate of sheer inequality, of the natural dominance in abilities of some children over others (racially correlated or not), leads to a quite different emphasis, namely, to the existence of tracks or streams running more or less parallel in the early years and then diverging to appropriate terminals from which each child is to be emitted into his appropriate station in life. Such sortings are strongly self-confirming, a fact visible even to those who embrace dominance as a "hard fact" of life. Such persons are directed by their assumptions to a search for better sorting mechanisms, not to a questioning of their own presuppositions. Some political egalitarians are suspicious, on the other hand, of all proposals for greater internal diversity, of "pious talk" about the educational importance of choice and self-direction of children. The stereotyped image of the curriculum as a sort of "progressive" self-help cafeteria administered in the spirit of laissez-faire in which each child is somehow busy "fulfilling his own potentialities" may indeed properly be condemned as the benign work of an educational system geared to the preservation of social inequality—the malign one being a system of meritocratic groupings or streamings. A rigidly single-track system at least—so it is argued—guarantees "equality of opportunity," however unequally and ineffectively the opportunity in question impinges on the lives of diverse human beings.

But the meaning of incommensurability is that diverse children *can* attain to a common culture—a common world of meanings and skills, of intellectual tools, moral commitments, and aesthetic involvements. Individual development *can* complement individual differences, but only through a matching diversity of learning styles and strategies. Children can learn equally, in general, only as they learn differently. The more constraints there are toward single-track preprogrammed instruction, the more predictably will the many dimensions of individual variety—congenitally and individually evolved—express themselves as a large rank-order variance in learning.

But I described this statement of the postulate as a half-step only. For there is no necessary implication that the goals of education be concretely the same for all groups or all individuals. The idea of multiple tracks toward a common proximate goal is one way of expressing our postulate, but not one which exhausts its meaning.

Experience and learning are many-faceted. Though two tracks lead to algebra (or calligraphy) for two children, the fact that one is optimal for one child and not for another implies that neither track is relevant *only* to calligraphy or algebra, that neither is relevant *merely* to one goal. A track is efficient toward one goal because it is linked to a child's existing interests, knowledge, and skills; being so linked it relates to and supports other goals as well. Algebra is valued *for* the curriculum only because it can be richly cross-referenced to many other domains of experience of form and analysis. Indeed, one can hardly defend its central place in the curriculum without such reference, or therefore defend the teaching of it, as is mainly the case, along a path which does not gain support from and give support to quite other kinds of interests and activities. No track toward algebra can be efficient which is a track to nothing other than algebra and from nothing other than text and teacher. The graph of the domain is not of a collection of mutually isolated tracks but a network of richly interconnected nodal regions, each of which *can* be strategically isolated at some times and for some purposes. But the mind can only isolate or block off connections when it can grasp them. Otherwise, isolation is busywork and we have that in abundance.

For those who would seek to predesign a curriculum by little programmed steps, implications of the network are onerous indeed. If a branching "program" allowed one binary choice per month and every monthly "package" or "unit" were designed to fit all previous choices, about a thousand tracks would be required by the end of the year, and by the end of twelve years, more than there are grains of sand on the planet. Fortunately, the world beyond the symbol is self-programmed, and so, in a sense I shall try to define, are learners when their capacity is not deadened but given active support.

Diversity of pathway in learning implies the network rather than the little racetrack (*curriculum*) and underlines the necessity in learning of constant choice and invention. Human beings are valued within a community for their useful differences moreover—as sources or resources of skill, of aesthetic expression, or moral or intellectual authority. It is not difference as such which we value, but individuality—the unique personal style and synthesis which interests us in each other as subjects of scrutiny, of testing, of emulation, or repudiation. Recognition of individuality completes what I mean by the postulate of incommensurability. The character which members of our own species possess—what we term individuality—implies neither dominance nor identity, but equivalence within a domain of relations sustained by individual diversity. If the old word *equality* should be used in this sense, it is the equality of crafts-men working at different tasks and with different skills, but with plans and tools congruent enough to provide endless analogies and endless diversions. Or, it is the equality of authors who read other authors' books but must each, in the end, write his own.

Educational traditions in their practice or their rhetoric may support or oppose such notions of individuality. I urge them as simply correct notions, receiving support by the same logic that combines diversity of endowments and histories with a complementary redundancy in these endowments—generalized human adaptability. In this way one allows that a common cultural flux is transmitted diversely, yet provides a currency of skill and knowledge accessible to all. Such incommensurability is no weak postulate. In allowing only relational or vectorial differences—differences of "profile" across many entries—this logic denies dominance, denies any single axis of inferiority-superiority. And if we are to urge or claim that we provide "equal opportunity," the postulate requires a providing of great diversity in that opportunity. By this test we have not gotten very far. Along that one narrow track which we do mostly provide, dominance must prove the order of the day.

Discussion of the first postulate has partly anticipated that of the second and third and must partly follow. The implication is clear, I hope, that in discussing match and mismatch between native endowment and learning-career we are talking about learning which is of educationally significant dimensions, irreversible, and, in any detail, nonreplicable, which has a time-scale that spans years or decades. Learning theories trimmed to the laboratory scale *may* have some relevance, just as the clinic may have. But extrapolations from the ambient of laboratory or clinic to education are almost unbounded, as is the shift in subject matter. To assess relevance here we must be independently acquainted *in* the education domain and not just extrapolate to it. To judge well of such matters we must be widely acquainted across the domain of children *and* of the variety of possible teaching situations. Professionalism in educational research ought to interpenetrate, far more deeply than it now does, the professionalism of teaching.

Freedom

The discussion of human freedom—"freedom of the will"—is familiar to most of us in the form of a debate that goes on, starting nowhere and ending nowhere. The focus of the debate is whether "it" does or does not exist, is or is not a meaningless concept, is required by religious faith or excluded by science, and so on. People seem in this connection to know what the word means, although this is usually rather doubtful. What I have in mind to discuss here is much more limited, fortunately. I wish to explicate how a postulate of freedom functions or can function *in a theory* of human nature in which the meaning of the postulate can be explicated by the logical uses made of it. As soon as the term *freedom* is looked at in this way, it loses some of its blank metaphysical debatability and becomes, instead, rather more consequential and interesting. In particular, the word *freedom* is not at stake. Or, rather, what is at stake is not *the* meaning of the word, but a particular meaning which is tied to some very central propositions about human nature—tied by these propositions both to learning and knowing on the one hand and to choosing on the other.

In the classical theories the postulate of freedom, as I call it, functioned in the same way as that of equality—as a preliminary blocking move which limited certain kinds of explanation of human behavior in order to make way for others. In blocking some explanations and allowing others the postulate lays the ground plan for a special *kind* of causality; it does not deny causality in general (as though "free" meant "uncaused"). It asserts the efficacy in human affairs of action with knowledge, of action guided by knowledge, including the special kind of action involved in making decisions and in seeking more knowledge. And on the negative side the postulate denies that explanations in such terms are universally reducible to other kinds of explanation, as, for example, those common in physics or biology.

As in the case of equality, so here, I am not mainly concerned with historical theories but only refer to them as touchstones for a body of theory which we are all at least vaguely aware of from our political traditions. There are interesting differences among the classical theorists which I shall not allude to. And I am interpreting them freely, though, I think, not at all wrongly. In particular, the problem of the reducibility of such concepts as "action with knowledge" to purely a physicist's or a biologist's language is a long story, and I shall cut it short by appealing again to the requirement of adequacy over the whole cycle for which educational theory must (like political theory) be responsible. All of us who debate matters of educational theory and practice are trying to act with knowledge, and we describe children as acting that way as well; it is our aim for them. Since our children will one day be carrying on our same effort in education (on a higher plane we hope), we have no choice but to accept this irreducibility of intentional, personal language, not as a stark metaphysical necessity perhaps, but as a logical requirement of adequacy in our theorizing.

Men can be overwhelmed by superior physical force; they can be damaged or destroyed by disease; they can be constrained by physical limitations or by other men. But within such limitations there is a wide range of human behavior—of a kind which is emphatically human—involving perception, memory, knowledge, and choice. The existence of illusion, misremembering, ignorance and error in reasoning is part of such behavior, of course, and facts of this order may in one sense be explained in terms of physical or biological boundary conditions. But such categories of fact exist only by way of exception. An error is only equivocally the effect of physical causes; the explanation of an error requires that it be recognized as an error first, before an explanation is offered. Since a correct explanation will require that the error be correctly recognized; and *that* recognition, as well as the explanation, is an act of knowing. Thus all such privative concepts as error, illusion, etc., derive from corresponding affirmative ones and physical causes involved are not enough to explain such human behavior.

In the explanation of behavior in the normal range there is, indeed, a very essential reference to the phenomena of men's physical and social environment, but these phenomena are referred to *as* taken account of—perceived, recognized, enjoyed, compared, predicted, generalized about—and in that case these acts and their consequences in further action cannot be explained merely *by* the phenomena in question; the explanation is also in terms of how they are or are not taken account of and made use of.

Hobbes and Spinoza offer a general framework for this kind of explanation in the way the postulate is stated, connected with the idea of self-perpetuation. It is a "law of nature" analogous to Galileo's law of inertia that human beings will act to preserve and stabilize themselves. This is not something they *choose* to do, but is implicit in *every* act of choice. Learning and knowing depend not upon external impressions but upon an "endeavour outward" (Hobbes) or a "conatus" (Spinoza) which simply expresses the individual's nature, thus his self-determination or freedom.[11] Insofar as the individual organizes his experience in accordance with what he already knows, he extends his knowledge and his "power of acting" (Spinoza).

For both Hobbes and Spinoza emotion has a central function in this process; it monitors the gains and losses of this internal organization and power—a sort of feedback loop, as we would call it, which steadies the process. Thus, joy is not *what* men seek; it is the *evidence* of success in what they seek, as sorrow is the evidence of failure. "Affective education"—in a current mind-numbing jargon—is simply good education, education for self-direction and self-government.

Thus, freedom is something that men have by degrees; there is an innate core of freedom—a capacity for using knowledge in deliberate choice—which expands with experience and knowledge, so that it is not possible to draw a sharp distinction between self-preservation and self-development. In preserving their being men learn and, in learning, both the thing preserved and the means of preserving it are enhanced.

A contemporary expression of a very similar kind is to be found in the general theoretical framework of Piaget. This framework has, of course, a good deal more substantive psychological content built in and around it than one can find in the earlier thinkers (though I wouldn't be sure it is more penetrating than Spinoza's). But neither of the earlier writers knew how to be explicitly and empirically concerned with the full cycle of life; as is true of most thinkers of the past, they were fixated upon the presuppositions of adulthood. Piaget in this vital respect has broken fresh ground.

So in my reinterpretation of the postulate of freedom I shall make use of the logical pattern of the Piagetian terms *assimilation, accommodation,* and *equilibration,* using it as an example of the way in which a rather well-developed scientific theory can postulate and make essential use of an explanatory scheme not reducible to patterns of purely physical or biological causality. In the next section I shall indicate what I think is an important source of difficulty or incompleteness in one part of this theory as it has been put forward, but this is not to put it aside.

An important, implicit part of the idea of assimilation (suggested by the biological analogy) is that of a preexisting match between sensory input and the system of active processes which receives that input. Ultraviolet and yellow light will equally enter the eye and be scattered or absorbed as physical energy. But the sensitivity of the organism to these two "stimuli" is radically different. A few photons of the former may cause negligible changes in a cell or two, while a few of the latter may trigger the release of cellular energy throughout the body many orders of magnitude greater. From a purely energetic point of view the two photons are not much different; the difference lies in the optics and biochemistry of the receptor and the organization of the associated nervous system. From a neurophysiological point of view light frequencies near that of yellow light are "stimuli," others are not. And even within that range much else is excluded. In normal vision we do not see photons nor do we see retinal images made by them; what we are tuned to see are minute variations or modulations of the energy-input to our eyes, those, namely, which inform us of things around us: color, figure and ground, spatial relationship. Out of the virtual infinity of patterns which are in fact conveyed by the light, we *see* only those which are significant to us. The visual system involves a complex response-manifold within which specific physical inputs are "stimuli" and outside of which they are not. At far higher energy intensities there are of course more generalized biological and purely physical responses, at the limit of which the organism is destroyed. The decisive characteristic of neurophysiological response is the high-order amplification of selected (and energetically very minute) physical inputs. It is this fact which constitutes the stimulus, not as energy or momentum, but as thermodynamic information, as entropy change, and *this* constitution is entirely determined by the existence and nature of the response-manifold. But that is not all. The investigation of the stimulus-manifold, of the way we describe what a particular stimulus *is*, is entirely a matter of inference from the corresponding manifold of responses. We may know much about the environment of an organism without knowing what aspects of that environment will be responded to or, therefore, what constitutes "stimuli" within it. "Stimulus" is a neurophysiological concept at this level, not a concept of physics, and not yet, except by analogy, of psychology.

If we speak of learning in this neurophysiological sense, we may use any one of a variety of unconscious conditioning experiments as examples, including those of visceral, heartbeat, and breathing patterns. But clearly we cannot extend this scheme to other kinds of learning, such as learning the Pythagorean theorem or learning how to produce visceral conditioning. Learning in the educationally important sense is another jump in informational variety. It is in the range of these evolutionary capabilities that human culture, education, and individuality have their roots. The locus of education is, as its focus ought to be, in the concern for the way this accommodative evolution takes place.

It is in this context, I believe, that we can most fruitfully discuss another aspect of the postulate of freedom, the voluntaristic "negative" aspect which suggests not only that human behavior is not determined by *physical* boundary conditions, but that it is somehow unpredictably elective, erratic, and (to a suitably unprepared observer) "random." Indeed, the combination of high selectivity and high amplification gain in all response patterns of the brain, and especially in those characteristic of human learning, is calculated to defeat any pseudophysicist's explanation, and no physicist would find the effort interesting. We know enough about animal organisms to know we are dealing with systems precisely characterized by *this* kind of unpredictability (their survival depends upon it). We knew it all along, of course, but neurophysiology is needed to answer (like an ungrateful child) the mechanistic traditions that cradled it in its earlier history.

But it will not do to accept the strictly physical unpredictability of behavior as a *necessary* condition of freedom, without at the same time examining what kind of causality we put in its place as a viable alternative. Even in the case of simple conditioning we must learn how to *define* a stimulus before we can link it to a response. The relevant dimensions of informational inputs are not those of physics but a mapping of them into a manifold of responses. *Physically* different stimuli will evoke the same response on different occasions, and *physically* identical stimuli will evoke different responses. Behavioristic psychology recognizes this in a variety of ways (response set, intervening variables, and so forth). Thus, if we try to predict responses to stimuli we must first be able to *describe* the stimuli in relevant categories.

The jump from purely psychophysical learning phenomena to educationally significant learning is defined, in part, by the condition that in the latter case the definition of a "stimulus" is an act of the learner and not merely of the experimenter or teacher. The intentional meaning of *to learn how* or *to learn that* implies not only the de facto acting of a stimulus (as described by an investigator or teacher) but also a *taking* of the stimulus by the learner as an instance of a kind (correctly or not, for the purpose at hand) and a relating of it, so taken, to other categories. The verb *to learn* in such a context carries with it a truth-claim which is ineluctable, and this obvious fact escapes the net of theories of learning cast in associationistic or "S-R" language. One key to a positive theory of causality in the human domain is provided by this concept of recognition. The boundary line between assimilation of information which is unconscious (as in visceral conditioning, and so forth) and that which is conscious lies here. Recognition is the gateway.

Just as a neurophysiological stimulus is constituted as a stimulus by the response characteristics of a sense organ and of the whole organism, so at a conscious level a stimulus is constituted as such by some act of recognition. At its most primitive, recognition is the perception of difference and similarity, a preliminary mobilization of resources for meeting any new situation. The mapping is selective, so that differences and similarities perceived must be understood as standing out against a background of potential differences and similarities which go unrecognized. Recognition in turn directs recall, the search routine by which past experience is selectively brought to consciousness, to the locus of discrimination or choice. Recognition and recall may directly terminate a conscious phase of experience—in Dewey's language, may resolve a problematic situation. These processes may even become so habitual in standard situations that they lapse into the automatism of unconscious performance, into the mode of behavior which is in a gross quantitative sense our predominant way of being. In this sense we condition ourselves. Driving a car, riding a bicycle, typing, even solving equations can be described along a continuum. At one extreme is the fully conscious working out from an essentially problematic situation in which behavior is being defined and established. At the other extreme is the fluency of highly perfected response which has become literally unconscious—in which focused self-conscious discrimination has disappeared and in which our conscious capacities are occupied elsewhere if at all.

The postulate of freedom, of self-conscious agency, requires a nonphysical and nonbiological language and it cannot, therefore, be tested by purely physical or biological means of discrimination. But it does have negative implications of such a kind. We know that a pipewrench does not "think," nor does a typewriter, a telephone network, or an on-line computer console. If we take the nervous system or, better, the whole human organism as our subject matter, its operation as a physical system is in nowise excluded from study by the postulate of freedom. What is excluded is that this study should lead to explanations of human behavior which violate informational conditions—e.g., a pep pill which would "cause" me to write a good book, or an operant-conditioning regime that would "cause" me to understand some of the troubles of education.

If such an analysis of the postulate of freedom is at all correct, then it becomes possible to inject a certain theoretical discipline into recurrent controversies over the aims of education. Today there is a resurgence of criticism of the institutional habits of our schools on the ground that children are treated as things rather than as ends in themselves, that the school conceives the process of education as one of "transmitting" knowledge, "developing" skills, "training" children (or teachers!) by routines of instruction which in fact minimize opportunities for significant choice and self-direction. Children are not conceived as coagents in the process of education, but only as patients, recipients, and this general line of criticism sees such practices resulting in boredom, alienation, "failure." The questions thus raised lead to the next section, but one observation is possible here. Many of the critics who hold these views appear to operate with a simplistic notion of freedom, such that the implied cure for the troubles of education is simply a switch from the active-teacher–passive-child model.[12] It is the apparent moral presupposition of such a view that active planful intervention in children's affairs is per se a stultifying indignity. It treats "freedom" as an innate capacity or one which develops best when least hampered by adult direction. It thus cuts off the whole range of active human intercourse in which the transmission of culture can enhance children's freedom, their aptitude for significant choice. The view repudiated does not trust children's choices at all, whereas the critic's view sees no need to cultivate and help organize them.

Rationality

The postulate of freedom makes it explicit that the central sort of causality in educational theory is that of agency, of the human decision-maker, teacher, and learner, and adult and child. But "agency" as a disposition is a singularly blank one except as filled out, in theory, by reference to those special characteristics of human existence which can be attributed to it. In the philosophical traditions from the time of Plato and Aristotle the operative meaning of human agency has been associated with what I have called the postulate of rationality.

In the classics *reason* has two aspects. On the one hand it is a functional disposition or capacity; on the other hand it is an operational domain into which individuals enter but which is by its own nature objective and public. Private thinking may be more or less rational, but it may also be intuitive, idiosyncratic, wishful—irrational. But the valid communication of private thinking, its communication in such a form that others can accept it *as* valid, requires that it be mapped or translated into a form which is invariant to individual idiosyncrasy. The generalized adaptability of which I earlier spoke allows the creation of a public domain of thought and action, a domain invariant to the replacement of one individual agent by another. The development of rational capacity is in Piaget's language a kind of decentration which takes place along with the development of schemes of operations. Once thought is functioning within this scheme, it is per se rational. I think this is why the classical writers tended to restrict themselves to adulthood, to the "age of reason"; it was an implicit recognition of the developmental nature of the scheme. They did not study, as Piaget has tried to do, the way in which prerational thought at the same time prefigures the rational. In the conception of rationality which we now must seek, there must be certain invariants, not only between adults, but also along the life course of one individual growing up in association with others.

Piaget's conceptual trinity—assimilation, accommodation, equilibration—purports to do this, although of course only as filled out by empirical developmental evidence and only by means of subordinate concepts such as operation, coordination, decentration, and so forth. If there is a single central theme here which can be a candidate for our generalized concept of "rational," it is the tendency, manifest from early infancy, toward the organization of perception and behavior in terms of a hierarchy of invariant structures which is open at the same time to a reorganization of those structures as still higher levels of organization may require.

Seen from the point of view of the individual career, this unending process, with the stages and transitions it achieves, is "the life of reason." This does not mean that we are conscious of everything that happens in it. On the contrary, our ability to review and characterize what we have achieved or failed at is possible only from a point of view outside of that achievement or failure, and is part of a *further* integrative process not yet retrievable by us for review. The conscious agent is like a weaver who works at local pieces of the pattern without being able to see the pattern of the new weft except as the parts already finished may help him to define it. But without conscious agency and choice the whole process would cease.

Thus we come back to the concept of the human agent. Whether we think of the agent in traditional theological terms or as a center of coordinative activities in an open neurological system (or both), the "epistemic subject" is a necessity of thought in our framework, and as such does not have to be justified by outside interpretation. Our concern here is with function, not substance. We must see ourselves and others as agents, not because this mysterious essence is a tangible object of our awareness, for, if it were, it would be only one object among others and would not serve its function. We need the concept for a reason analogous to the need for coordinate systems in geometry. What I once organized and stored I may now retrieve for a new use provided I can now define the perspective, the viewpoint, from which I then worked but which was not *then* available to me for definition. In this sense there must be more retrieved than was stored. An example from Kant concerns the transition from a succession of perceptions to the perception of their succession. I hear each successive sound of a bell, but that fact does not imply that I perceive their succession. The first sound is fixed in my "circulating memory." The second does not merely "recall" the first, as though they might be confused. The recall brings a tag with it, so to say, and the second sound is modified as being second, as thus *related* to the first. Kant called this a synthesis in intuition, and it is in a sense a prototype of all higher syntheses, perpetual and conceptual. Along with the perception of succession in such individual perceptions there is also, of necessity, a recognition of the identity of the agent from one time to the next, who can retrieve now what *he* stored earlier.

When we talk about a child's ability to make use of resources which he has earlier assimilated and transformed, we are being concerned with precisely that sort of synthesis which Kant made the basis of his famous *Critiques*. But we are not taking it as something automatically given along with the definition of "the human mind"; we are taking it as a capacity still incomplete and evolving. Thus *we* seek a causative role in the process, and if we do not, we are not talking as teachers or educators. It is from this point of view that the framework of Piagetian theory, though developmental, is incomplete. Piaget does not profess to be constructing a theory of education; he leaves uncontrolled all those variables which educators must seek to define and find ways of holding within their hands. But he does, along with a neglected philosophical tradition, help us to define what some of those essential variables might be and, above all, what they are not.

In pursuing this line of discussion, and in trying to suggest what these essential variables might be, I shall first review some leading ideas of Kant, and then of John Dewey's maturest writing. From this

I shall try to suggest how we may begin to formulate some of the dimensions involved. This leads me to a critique of the developmentalist way of thought, which with its longitudinal perspective appears to ignore these modes of educational influence. The construction which begins to emerge from this critique is one which on the one hand implies a certain sort of diagnostic function by which a teacher tries to map a child's current patterns of involvement and levels of organization. It implies on the other hand the teacher's responsiveness, his aim to facilitate those sorts of assimilation, transformation, and synthesis which diagnosis indicates will match the child's current involvements and readiness—to make means available to the child which the latter does not yet quite know he needs. This of course has often been said. What is also familiar, in fact, though less often said, is that the core of this diagnosis is that "empathetic" adaptability of which I spoke earlier. A teacher builds a model of the child's performance within his own familiar ways of operating and thinking and stretches himself in the process. It is thus that he defines the child's strengths and weaknesses, the continuities and gaps. This means that his diagnostic description, though fully behavioral, is not "behavioristic." It is cast in the same language of agency and choice by which he communicates about his own thought and action.[13]

In the traditional array of "faculties," reason's appointed role was that of guiding and unifying the operation of the more special faculties—understanding, will, and feeling. Thus reason in this global sense was not restricted to "intellectual" matters. Its scope is indicated by the range of Kant's three *Critiques*: that of *Pure Reason*, in relation to knowledge of the natural world; that of *Practical Reason*, in relation to planning, decision-making, and morality; and that of *Judgment*, which could also be called the critique of man's aesthetic capacities. In the first *Critique*, the understanding is effective in relation to the concrete particulars of the phenomenal world as these are perceived and organized within the framework of the categories of knowledge. Reason by contrast stands above and guides the understanding; it is reflected in our concern with the *career* of knowledge, with the *ideals* of organization of knowledge, and with the *norms* which guide its pursuit.

In the second *Critique*, reason, by virtue of the role it plays, has a more commanding position. Moral choice, as Kant describes it, is a sort of adversary procedure out of which conduct is forged. This procedure, which forges out new patterns of conduct, takes place "before the bar of reason" with its categorical demands for consistency and finality in choice. But these demands are not coercive; reason is effective only through the respect it can command, and only in the sense in which respect *can* be commanded: through the enjoyment of that autonomy which reason alone can bestow upon the action of the will, which otherwise remains the captive of unexamined habit or impulse.

The role of reason in Kant's third *Critique* is less explicit and is developed less formalistically than in the first two works. From some modern points of view, though not in terms of historical influence, it is the most important of Kant's systematic writings. In both of its two parallel essays, one on aesthetics and the other on natural teleology, Kant is examining what he calls the *reflective* judgment, judgment under such circumstances that the validity of scientific inference or the finality of moral choice has no counterpart. In the domain of art Kant examines the faculties, as it were, *at play*, detached from theoretical or practical ends. This interplay of perception, imagination, and understanding, prized for its intrinsic affective content, enables Kant to study the operation of human analytic and synthetic capacities—so to say, the *style* of a rational being—without his usual concern to "justify." What is laid bare in the study of phenomena of aesthetic experience or of man's reflective effort to find aesthetic satisfaction in his relation to the world about him is characteristic of all experience; but elsewhere attention is distracted from this subjective aspect by preoccupation with objective content.

In what is in many ways his most important writing, *Art as Experience,* John Dewey covers or re-covers this very same ground, but from a different starting point and in a different style. Although he mentions the *Critique of Judgment* once—and then only to disparage Kant's "architectonic"—Dewey's aim and conclusion are essentially the same. Cognitive activity and decision-making, as these bring new order into our lives, give rise to recapitulation, expression, celebration in some concrete objective and socially available form; such expression is the very substance of art, whether called by that name or some other.

What is missing from Kant and Dewey both—and what is surely not easy to supply—is the developmental aspect, the theoretical formulation of which allows us to say that the conditions required by the cycle have been met. For Kant, reason appears full-grown as a universal and necessary capacity of the human mind. His method is predominantly that of the analysis of knowledge or morality as something given in adult experience, not as something in process. Dewey's method more nearly follows the course of experience. But in spite of many important insights along the way, Dewey's method is too purely reflective and too little derived from empirical observation to provide even the outline of a theory of the "life of reason" from the beginnings of learning. But when we examine the subject thus suggested, we find that our sources are very restricted. Wertheimer's pioneer work[14] has unfortunately remained pioneer for the most part, and what we have for the study of growing rational capacities in children is cast in the developmentalist mold. I believe this mold is inadequate, though not thereby useless, to the cause of educational theory.

A major fact of early education is its linkage, its interaction, with the postnatal stages of embryological development. Recognition of such linkage gives plausibility to a developmentalist view of education. The implicit metaphysics of this way of thinking is dominated by botanical or, rather, horticultural metaphors. Development is an unfolding from within, a cumulative realization of potentialities. There is no denial in this way of thought of external necessary conditions or of their "influence" on development. Children selectively assimilate the order of their environment, including the human culture. Such external materials of development are presumed to be there for the taking and if not, the child is deprived and his growth thwarted or stunted. The role of the teacher is to garden—to water, weed, spray, and fertilize, to cultivate. But in contrast with S-R theories the essential causality of the process is all internal. The rose may prosper or suffer because of the gardener's treatment, but it will be just that kind of rose, no matter what. So for education, the implied counsel is that of provision and remedy. Suitably provisioned, the process expresses an inner-directed schedule of developmental stages, each "laying the ground" for the next.

The legitimacy of such a descriptive metaphysics for education is relative to the range of questions we may seek to answer within it. In view of the manifestly inadequate provision for childhood in much of our society, the developmental viewpoint has implications we should preserve and insist upon. And where we can take for granted the prevalence of a sort of diffuse educational potential in a society —a material and human environment redundantly responsive to children's developing needs and abilities—this viewpoint is important by way of opposition to the nervous belief that everything learned or acquired must be "taught." For in such an environment children will predictably "grow up" without institutionalized planful intervention, without an educational technology trimmed to antecedently defined "behavioral objectives" of walking, talking, reading, carrying a glass of wine without spilling it, classifying, testing hypotheses, and so on. But when it is considered analytically as a mode of abstraction, the developmentalist scheme is inadequate to the deepest and most central concerns of education. It is inadequate because it buries under a metaphor just that level of interaction between "development" and "learning" without which our species would lack its most distinctive characteristics.[15]

What gets buried is the fact that learning is not only something which takes place within a framework which development provides, but that development is also something which takes place within a framework which learning provides. To make this reciprocity clear and emphatic, however, we must make explicit certain aspects of "learning" which schools have seldom recognized in practice and which educational theory has seldom insisted upon.

A great merit in the work of Piaget lies in the fact that he has directed his empirical research from the initial Kantian insight that learning is a selective process which depends not only upon the objective content available in any specific learning situation, but also upon the ensemble of resources *brought to* that situation by the learner. It is easy to suppose, in the interest of associationistic or behavioristic principles, that any such resources are simply the cumulative summation of past learning. Even on such an account, the center of gravity in any particular learning situation is, so to speak, on the inside. But as we can learn from a long philosophical tradition (in modern times most significantly from Hume and Kant), this explanation of our intellectual *modus operandi* is implausible in the extreme. The discrimination of similarity and difference is hardly an ability abstracted from similarities and differences which somehow forced themselves upon us before such discrimination was yet possible. The systematic organization of sensory experience in terms of space and time is not a mere abstraction *from* experiences which initially lacked that organization. Thus the succession of our perceptions does not add up to a perception *of* that succession nor do changes of locality as experienced automatically generate a grasp of the coexistence of localities in a comprehensive spatial framework. The recognition of causal relations or of genetic identity is likewise not "given" by empirical instances in which these characters are somehow forced upon us by our senses.

The major contribution of Kant to the discussion of these matters was not—as philosophers seem sometimes to believe—the introduction of the phrase "synthetic a priori," but an insight into the central role of hypothesis in learning and knowing, of the active or constructive nature of intellectual activity as contrasted with the passivity of the mind assumed in associationistic theories. It is on account of this constructive process through which the mind organizes its sensory information that Kant builds up his analysis of the mind-dependent order of space and time, the categories of the understanding based on the elements of Aristotelian logic, and the guiding role of reason. These are not taken from sensory experience but brought to it, a synthetic apparatus native to the mind.

But we, unlike Kant, must ask the genetic question. Does this *sort* of apparatus, regardless of the details of Kant's analysis, somehow appear full-blown in the mind of a child? Or is it there, latent, only to be *developed* by the cumulative passage of experience (but not altered by it)? Or is it the product of a more evolutionary process in which such intellectual powers evolve *as* devices, expedients borrowed or invented and reinforced on account of their demonstrated efficacy in ordering experience and extending it? The last named view is not Kant's, though passages can be found which would support it. I would like to develop this view at any rate as the culminating phase of the present paper.[16] Such a view requires no abandonment of the idea of native capacities. At any given moment of his career a child *already* manifests some such capacities in his behavior or, as we may put it, has a mind. Clearly also the subsequent evolution, although it must be deemed for each child unique at some level of scrutiny, will be characterized by strong family resemblances and at a certain remove of abstraction it is possible to talk about general "stages" of human development. From evidence gained by horizontal sampling across many individuals, it is possible to construct a composite longitudinal picture of the probable evolution of single individuals. Such use of the comparative method can prove very fruitful and *may* disclose patterns of development which will also be found universally in individual cases studied longitudinally. *May* disclose; on the other hand it is a familiar fact that the comparative method produces, through averaging, a sort of bland linearizing which *may* also, in the individual case, have a very slight correspondence with reality. What appears secondarily in such averaging, namely, fluctuation of pattern between individuals of the same age, or inconstancies and inconsistencies within single individuals at a given age—to both of which Piaget has given the label *décalages*—may be tell-tale signs of the essential individuality of development in a common world and cultural milieu.

But what is most important for the present argument is that, as it stands, the conceptual scheme of developmentalism is one that can only very partially answer to the demands of *educational* theory. For such a scheme aims to be able to tell us what children will be like independently of their detailed human (and educational) careers. To say this is not to imply that developmentalists think "environmental influences" are unimportant. It is simply to say that the effect of unexamined differences in children's individual careers is of necessity treated as a "residual variance" from an average pathway of development which reflects at the same time an average educational milieu. The criticism is thus not of the *beliefs* of investigators working in this way, but of their conceptualization of the problem and the means of investigation which they adopt to match that conceptualization, *as relevant to education.*

And there is, I think, another important qualification. The criticism that has just been made is, so far at least, identical with one made frequently by some educational psychologists in the United States who think of intellectual development as a mere "summation of learning" and thus susceptible of acceleration through subjecting children to little training regimes, and from whose viewpoint I wish to dissociate myself. Piaget makes a very nice joke of this possibility by referring to it as "la question Américaine." As a nation we are, it seems, addicted to accelerators. But in rejecting this view Piaget sometimes appears to reject learning as a *primum mobile* of intellectual development, thus appearing to contradict his own views of the processes of assimilation, accommodation, and equilibration.[17] This last triad does, after all, explicate very well one meaning of learning, though it is not that of some learning theorists. Learning of a developmentally significant kind (and, I would add, of an educationally significant kind) is not the sort of thing which can be reduced to little training routines, little time-tabled packages with their prespecified objectives and tests of attainment. That these are without significant developmental consequences is not hard to believe. What we are or ought to be concerned with in the theory and practice of education is the kind of educational milieu which *does* affect the growth of children as persons in all of their competencies; thus, it must not be an *a priori* conclusion that developmental dimensions are unresponsive to educational provisioning, either quantitatively or qualitatively. Yet in detaching development *conceptually* from dependence upon the kind of provisioning which a society makes for its children, or which particular adults make for particular children, and which devoted professional teachers seek to provide, we are in fact declaring the irrelevance of such efforts to any except minor variations on a theme set out ahead of time. The developmentalist framework simply does not answer to the concrete epistemological situation of a teacher, who not only can contribute to the richness of children's learning, but also can stabilize and support those intrinsically rare occasions, in the lives of children as of adults, in which the discovery of new order in experience can bring culmination, reward, and growth in new dimensions.

If the powers of the human mind (and its limitations) are in some sense congenital, they are also in a complementary sense the product of a cultural evolution which is faster than biological evolution but slower than individual maturation. This means that in a not negligible degree every human being has the potentiality to contribute in his own style of growth and learning to a social process which is as yet very far from frozen in finality. In this sense, then, the content of individual development not only recapitulates the stabilized achievements of others, but also in its variance and regressions from the pattern of those achievements—if you will, in its décalages—adds to them or alters them.[18]

But the most important step in the argument is not yet explicit. For all its potential value, Piaget's specific theory of stages lacks in the present view an essential dynamical aspect. It is already implied, I think, in the previous discussion of equality, individuality, and freedom: when we view an individual history up to some particular time (and this is the epistemological perspective of a teacher) and project this against any standardized pattern of developmental stages, we *may not* legitimately use this projection as a mode of explanation, but only as a basis for questioning, as a device for gaining perspective. But in such perspective we will not see very much which is relevant to the art of teaching unless it is linked to other sorts of judgment which take account of individual characteristics of personal style and motivation. From such a point of view the décalages of development are not fluctuations from a mean (which has somehow mysteriously become normative), but suggestions as to further provisioning of the environment, further communications and guidance to help a child direct his *own* learning in accordance with his *own* resources and dispositions. In short, it is at this point that we must again give theoretical support to an idea implicit in all personal affairs and transactions—the idea of autonomy or agency.

And this brings us back to the role of reason. When a child or adult is operating in intellectually familiar territory, using categories and operations already well practiced, his activity belongs under the heading which Kant labeled as the *understanding*. But when his questioning leads him beyond intellectually safe ground (as from a *personally* secure base of operations it easily may), he is in a situation which calls for new expedients of thought. What before was new empirical content in the context of old thought patterns becomes rather a need to try on, to fashion new expedients of thought in a context of experience not fitting familiar rubrics.

Such is the experience of a two-year-old friend of ours. After intense encounter with various musical instruments she first wanted to "find the music" inside the guitar—looking repeatedly inside to confirm, for us, the point of the question. Another day, she wanted to "see the music" inside of our phonograph. Consider also the question of an eight-year-old who had repeatedly harvested and planted spores from a mold to get new mold. He didn't want to know where *these* spores came from; he knew they came from molds. "But where do *spores* come from?" In both cases the questions outrun the resources available for answers, conceptually and empirically, so that some retreat to more modest (but related) investigations is in order. Yet in both cases a marker, an affective flag, has perhaps been placed beside a conceptual knot to be untied, and this knot will gather around it other later situations somehow alike, so that this first encounter (like the minute leader-stroke in lightning) will start a well-worn pathway in some future network of familiar relationships.

Such developments from the child mind to the adult mind, whether average in character or interestingly deviant, are neither the summation of many episodes of passive learning nor the fruit of some inner maturational process which owes nothing to conscious experience or self-conscious discrimination and choice. The two small illustrations were chosen to suggest the kind of situation in which a child's experience seems clearly to outreach his established intellectual capacities and cannot be dealt with either directly or by means of available transformations. Novelty is responded to, is vividly acknowledged, but accommodative learning is not yet able to provide a framework within which the novelty can be reduced to understanding. But this is the very situation which evokes what Kant calls the reflective judgment, which seeks to order and organize in the absence of assured determinative guidance. It calls forth that "play of the faculties" which may along the way evolve into a whole hierarchy of search procedures and even routines of inquiry by which we import new order into our lives.

It is this evolution (or the possibility of it) which meets the logical demand for the closure of the educational cycle—the evolution by which learning becomes a kind of career and evolves into the capacity to teach. It is the evolution for which I have chosen a traditional term—the life of reason. In encounters such as those suggested above, a teacher will not try irrelevantly to "explain," but instead will try to provide from many sources that which will enrich the empirical matrix of a child's thought or will suggest analogies and connections from previous experience which are, at that moment, unretrievable by the child himself. And although the outcome will never in principle be a foregone conclusion, respect for a teacher who has thus sometimes aided a child's growth is a source for that unique meaning of authority which Kant links both to persons as "ends-in-themselves" and, more abstractly, to the role of reason itself, which holds out in the face of novelty or disorientation the promise of higher levels of organization to be achieved.

To repeat, this account in no way implies that the processes of accommodative abstraction and learning are transparently visible to those who are the agents of these processes. On the contrary, the view of the participant is limited to that which he can at any moment bring to a focus in terms of his existing intellectual capacities. We can understand our own processes only, so to speak, in recapitulation, only from a point of view beyond those processes. And as teachers we understand the intellectual processes of children through an observant mapping of their behavior—a *reading* of their behavior—in terms of models of learning which we ourselves have built. (And which educational research might well both study as skillful teachers build them and then help clarify and formalize.) What we read is thus not imputed wholly to a child's "conscious self" but to the *child*, to the child as agent.

I have chosen these small examples deliberately from the sphere of natural and human phenomena as children encounter them to suggest that even in this domain the constructive, "poetic" process of choice—the experimentation with new ways of thinking and behaving—is the root of the dynamics of learning. In that sense the subject matter of Kant's second *Critique*, broadened beyond any exclusive reference to the specifically moral domain, is what is needed to complete a "developmental" theory of the mind. Choice in conduct is a search for ways of reorganizing conduct in the face of conflict, dissatisfaction, unbidden and forbidden impulses, new interests. Old habits of self-description and self-organization, already-made solutions, have been found wanting. In such situations the role of conjecture and improvisation, the role of other persons as authorities, is not different from what it is in the domain we mislabel as "purely" intellectual. And again the aim of finality, of coherent and self-consistent organization, marks what we mean by "the role of reason."

But, then, as we choose differently so we grow differently, and as we grow differently we come along different paths to frequent congruence and communication with others. (If this is correct, a

244   THE INFORMED VISION AND OTHER ESSAYS

genetic ethics should undergird Piaget's "genetic epistemology"—
the evolution of choice.) Conversely, for the lack of opportunity in
the presence of stifling coercion or from anxieties which drain creative energies, we remain undeveloped and primitive in our resources, at best compensating for what we have missed by other
developments which bring satisfaction and respect. Of such a kind,
I believe, are some of the "residual variances," the décalages, which
mark most human careers as measured against standard patterns of
attainment. These latter can define, no doubt, a common framework within which the residue of our growth can be mapped, at least
in part. But the dynamics of the process, the dynamics of learning
and choice, is more open-textured, more discontinuous and incomplete, more redundant and more surprising in its novelties, more
advanced and more regressive than horticultural analogies will
allow. No more standardized account is answerable, I believe, to the
perspectives of education.

REFERENCES

[1] Richard B. Braithwaite, *Scientific Explanation* (Cambridge: University Press,
1953), chaps. 3 and 4.

[2] I have worked out some of the logical details in *The Language of Nature* (San
Francisco: W. H. Freeman & Co., 1964), pp. 333-41.

[3] John von Neumann and Oskar Morgenstern, *The Theory of Games and Economic
Behavior* (Princeton: Princeton University Press, 1944).

[4] Thomas Hobbes, *Leviathan*, chap. 13; Rene Descartes, *Discourse on Method*, Part I.
From time to time the old beliefs of genetic determinism are brought out again. Niels
Bohr was once told of two identical twins separated early, one becoming a farm
worker and the other a university graduate. After thirty years they had the same IQ!
Bohr's characteristic response was: "Obviously, they must have been very different to
start with!" Of more serious concern is the periodic revival of claims concerning racial
inequality, usually authored by brains from my own genetic stock. I suggest that *we*
had better settle now for equality before there is an adverse change in the betting
odds.

Studies and arguments such as those advanced by Arthur R. Jensen in the *Harvard
Educational Review* (Winter 1968) share with the pure equalitarians the belief that
"nature" and "nurture" are additive variables, so that one can say "intelligence is X%
heredity and 100 − X% environment." Agricultural investigators have for a long time
understood, even in their much simpler field of study, that this is only a limiting case
and that *complementary* relations are more significant than additive ones. Cf. the
analysis by Richard C. Lewontin, *Bulletin of Atomic Scientists* (April 1970).

⁵ This redundancy is implied also by the fact, underlined in the writings of J. B. S. Haldane, that man has the widest variety in his gene pool of any animal except the dog. See "Human Evolution," in *Genetics, Paleontology and Evolution*, ed. Glenn L. Jepsen, Ernst Mayr, and George Gaylord Simpson (Princeton: Princeton University Press, 1949).

⁶ John von Neumann, "The General and Logical Theory of Automata," in *The World of Mathematics*, ed. James R. Newman (New York: Simon & Schuster, 1956), pp. 2070-98.

⁷ Cf. Descartes, *Discourse on Method, on Reason and Certainty.*

⁸ Many educational experiments sample children with statistical care, but the range of possible educational environments is sampled very poorly.

⁹ Again mathematicians will recognize that I am illustrating a theorem about vector inequalities. Perhaps it couldn't be done. And perhaps it couldn't be done because we're not clever enough. General postulates are not easy to prove or disprove, and that is what makes the choice of them so critical.

¹⁰ Although even after obvious gross inequities in early life, groups of children defined by ethnic and economic background still have extremely *uneven* profiles on conventional ability tests. See G. Fifer, "Social Class and Cultural Group Differences," *Proceedings of the 1964 Conference on Testing Problems* (Princeton: Educational Testing Service, 1965).

¹¹ Hobbes defines freedom in terms of the absence of external constraints upon this natural functioning of human beings. Spinoza criticizes Descartes for allowing a kind of irrational "freedom of will." The significant freedom in Spinoza's system is action which follows from adequate ideas. The power of the mind, he says, *is* knowledge. See his *Ethics*, Book II, prop. XLIX; but one must study the whole work. Sometimes this view of freedom, which Hegel also made his own, is stated paradoxically. By the measure of the adequacy of one's knowledge and insight, one's actions become free of accidental local causes. These do not account *for* one's action, they are taken *into* account. In a compressed formula one expresses this by saying "freedom is self-determination." But the formula is too condensed. Freedom is a special *kind* of self-determination, mediated by learning and choice. This is not an attempt to "escape" from the idea that human actions are explainable, but only to explain an important class of actions correctly. I have developed my own view more carefully in *The Language of Nature* (see note 2).

For those who wish to avoid the classics, a contemporary reexamination of these basic questions which avoids all those taboos called "anthropomorphism" is to be found in some of the literature of General Systems, particularly in the analysis of the concept of an "open" system which possesses a certain kind of stability in its interactions with a changing environment. See W. R. Ashby, "Principles of Self-Organizing Systems," in Heinz von Foerster, *Principles of Self Organization* (New York: Pergamon Press, 1962). The only "formula" which will predict the behavior of such a system is to process the same information it processes, in the same way. "I said, if I were a horse, where would I go? And I went, and there he was."

¹² For a careful initial discussion of what is involved here, see Anne M. Bussis and Edward A. Chittenden, *Analysis of an Approach to Open Education* (Princeton: Educational Testing Service, 1970).

[13] Here we can join issue, from the point of view of educational theory, with Martin D. S. Braine, "Piaget on Reasoning," in a recently republished monograph in *Cognitive Development in Children* (Chicago: University of Chicago Press, 1970), pp. 35-54. Braine criticizes Piaget's "epistemological confusion" in supposing that he is investigating "logical processes" going on in the child. As Braine says, if you think something you are independently familiar with is going on in someone else's mind, then your job is diagnostic, not purely descriptive. In the reformulation he offers of Piaget, this whole scheme of logical processes is taken out of the psychological domain and put back into that of subject matter, what we learn *about*. But this "epistemological confusion" of imputting an operational model to the child's thinking is *just* what a good teacher is constantly trying to do. A teacher is busy being a participant-observer of a child's learning and must therefore read behavior as indicative or diagnostic of what is "going on"; it is only through such a reading that he can summon up the resources which will match and assist the child's. Piaget's "confusion" is what makes him useful to us. Braine would make the same criticism, I think, of Kant.

[14] Wertheimer, *Productive Thinking*, enl. ed. (New York: Harper & Row, 1959).

[15] See Dewey's careful discussion in *Education and Experience* (New York: Macmillan Co., 1938).

[16] Piaget's answer is that experience is not only "sensory," but is also experience of the mind's own operational functioning *in relation* to the environment. Such self-representation derived from a growing operational competence is the *empirical* source of that logical and mathematical knowledge for which Kant could find no "empirical"—i.e., sensory—origin.

[17] For example, in his remarks on education in *Piaget Rediscovered: A Report on the Conference on Cognitive Studies* (Ithaca: Cornell University Press, 1964), pp. 113-17. On the other hand, more recently in *Science of Education and the Psychology of the Child*, trans. Derek Coltman (New York: Orion Press, 1970), Piaget shows a lucid, modest, and insightful recognition of the great distance between his own developmentalist schemes and the problems of education. One hopes that recent pedagogical schemes which apparently aim to "teach the stages" will be examined in the the light of this eminent psychologist's own strongly reasoned disclaimers. But I take heart in my criticism of the Piaget "stages" by a passage in which he reasserts the basic developmentalist axiom, the existence of a [logical] "boundary between the contribution of the mind's structural maturation and that of the child's individual experience" (p. 172).

[18] Compare Tony Kallet, "Away from Stages," *Mathematics Teaching*, Bulletin of the Association of Teachers of Mathematics (U.K.), 45, 1968. Republished in *Outlook* I (1970), Mountain View Center, University of Colorado, Boulder, Colo., 1971.